COMPUTER BOOK SERIES FROM IDG

WordPerfect 6 For Dummies

Cheat ...et

D0117507

General Information

Type **WP** at the DOS prompt to start WordPerfect:

```
WP
```

Then press the Enter key, and WordPerfect appears on your screen.

- ✔ Use the Insert key to switch between insert and typeover modes.
- ✔ Use the Backspace key to back up and erase.
- ✔ Use the Delete key to delete a character.
- ✔ Press the Enter key to start a new paragraph.
- ✔ Press the Tab key to indent or line up text.
- ✔ F1 is the help key (press the Esc key when you're done).

Press Shift-F7 means to hold down the Shift key and press the F7 key. Release both keys. The same rule applies to using the Alt and Ctrl keys: Press and hold the key and then press the second key. Release both keys.

Press the F7 key when you're ready to exit WordPerfect. Follow the instructions on the screen and save your document to disk. When you're asked `Exit WP?` press Y.

Com... ...nds

Command	Key(s)
Cancel	Esc
Copy Block	Ctrl-C
Cut Block	Ctrl-X
Exit	F7
File Manager	F5
Format Text	Shift-F8
Format Character	Ctrl-F8
Help	F1
Mark Block	Alt-F4
Open/Retrieve	Shift-F10
Paste	Ctrl-V
Print	Shift-F7
Quick Save	Ctrl-F12
Replace	Alt-F2
Save	F10
Search	F2
Spell Check	Ctrl-F2
Undo	Ctrl-Z

Document Filenames

A document must be saved to disk with a DOS filename. Here are the rules:

- ✔ The filename can be from one to eight characters long.
- ✔ The filename can contain letters and numbers in any combination.
- ✔ The filename cannot contain a space, a period, or any other symbol.
- ✔ Be brief and descriptive with your filenames.

Helpful Tips

- ✔ Let the computer do the work! Let WordPerfect format your pages and insert page numbers, headers, and footers. Don't ever do that stuff manually on the screen.
- ✔ Always save your documents to disk: press F10 to save.
- ✔ If a document has already been saved to disk, press Ctrl-F12 to update the document on disk.
- ✔ Press F5, Enter as an alternative to quitting to DOS and working with files.
- ✔ To start over with a clean slate, press F7, Y, N.
- ✔ If your document doesn't print, press Shift-F7, C and read the instructions on the screen.
- ✔ Never turn off or reset your computer when WordPerfect is on the screen. Always quit to DOS first.

... For Dummies: #1 Computer Book Series for Beginners

WordPerfect 6 For Dummies

Cheat Sheet

About the Keyboard Template

The *WordPerfect 6 For Dummies* keyboard template documents some of the most popular key combinations used in WordPerfect. Place the keyboard template over the top row of function keys on your keyboard and use it as a handy reference.

Note: Only the most common WordPerfect commands are on the template. In fact, the Merge key, F9, isn't documented on the template at all. After all, if you need help with merging, you'll probably be looking in the book (Chapter 17) anyway.

Oddball-Character Quick Reference

You can insert the oddball characters by pressing Ctrl-W and then selecting a character from the list displayed. Or you can type in the code numbers (listed next) into the dialog box. Press Enter and the character is inserted into your document.

Code	Character	Name
4,0	●	Dot
4,1	○	Hollow dot
4,2	■	Square
4,11	£	English Pound symbol
4,12	¥	Japanese Yen symbol
4,17	½	One-half
4,18	¼	One-quarter
4,19	¢	Cents
4,22	®	Registered symbol
4,23	©	Copyright symbol
4,41	™	Trademark symbol
5,7	☺	Happy face
5,26	☹	Mr. Grumpy
6,21	→	Right arrow
6,22	←	Left arrow
6,23	↑	Up arrow
6,24	↓	Down arrow

Getting Around in a Document

↑	Moves the toothpick cursor up one line of text.
↓	Moves the toothpick cursor down one line of text.
→	Moves the toothpick cursor right to the next character.
←	Moves the toothpick cursor left to the next character.
Ctrl-↑	Moves the toothpick cursor up one paragraph.
Ctrl-↓	Moves the toothpick cursor down one paragraph.
Ctrl-→	Moves the toothpick cursor right one word.
Ctrl-←	Moves the toothpick cursor left one word.
–	Moves the toothpick cursor to the top of the screen. If the toothpick cursor is already at the top of the screen, pressing the minus key moves you to the preceding screen.
+	Moves the toothpick cursor to the bottom of the screen. If the toothpick cursor is already at the bottom of the screen, pressing the plus key moves you to the next screen.
PgUp	Moves the toothpick cursor to the top of the preceding page. If you're on page 1, this key moves you to the top of that page.
PgDn	Moves the toothpick cursor to the top of the next page. If you're on the last page, this key moves you to the end of the document.
Home, ↑	Moves the toothpick cursor to the top of the screen (like the minus key).
Home, ↓	Moves the toothpick cursor to the bottom of the screen (like the plus key).
Home, →	Moves the toothpick cursor to the end of the current line (like the End key).
Home, ←	Moves the toothpick cursor to the start of the current line.
Home, Home, ↑	Moves the toothpick cursor to the top of the document.
Home, Home, ↓	Moves the toothpick cursor to the bottom of the document.

Say What You Think

Listen up, all you readers of IDG's ...For Dummies books! It's time to take advantage of the direct reader pipeline to the authors and editors of IDG Books.

We would like your input for future printings and editions of this title. Tell us what you liked about this book, how you think the book can be improved, and anything else you'd like to share. Did you like a particular chapter more than any other? And how about the chapters you didn't like? We want to know it all.

Please send your comments, questions, and suggestions to:

Reprint Coordinator
IDG Books Worldwide
3250 N. Post Road, Ste. 140
Indianapolis, IN 46226

Please be sure to include your name, address, and phone number.

Thanks for your input

WORDPERFECT 6 FOR DUMMIES™

by Dan Gookin,
author of best-selling
DOS For Dummies
and *WordPerfect For Dummies,*
and coauthor of *PCs For Dummies,*
Word For Windows For Dummies,
and the *Illustrated Computer*
Dictionary for Dummies

IDG Books Worldwide, Inc.
An International Data Group Company

San Mateo, California ✦ Indianapolis, Indiana ✦ Boston, Massachusetts

WordPerfect 6 For Dummies

Published by
IDG Books Worldwide, Inc.
An International Data Group Company
155 Bovet Road, Suite 310
San Mateo, CA 94402

Library of Congress Catalog Card No.: 93-78256

ISBN 1-878058-77-0

Printed in the United States of America

10 9 8 7 6 5 4 3

Distributed in the United States by IDG Books Worldwide, Inc.

Distributed in Canada by Macmillan of Canada, a Division of Canada Publishing Corporation; by Woodslane Pty. Ltd. in Australia and New Zealand; and by Computer Bookshops in the U.K. and Ireland.

For information on translations and availability in other countries, contact Marc Jeffrey Mikulich, Foreign Rights Manager, at IDG Books Worldwide. Fax: 415-358-1260.

For sales inquiries and special prices for bulk quantities, write to the address above or call IDG Books Worldwide at 415-312-0650.

 is a trademark of IDG Books Worldwide, Inc.

About the Author

Dan Gookin got started with computers back in the post slide rule age of computing: 1982. His first intention was to buy a computer to replace his aged and constantly breaking typewriter. Working as slave labor in a restaurant, however, Gookin was unable to afford the full "word processor" setup and settled on a computer that had a monitor, keyboard, and little else. Soon his writing career was underway with several submissions to (and lots of rejections from) fiction magazines.

The big break came in 1984 when he began writing about computers. Applying his flair for fiction with a self-taught knowledge of computers, Gookin was able to demystify the subject and explain technology in a relaxed and understandable voice. He even dared to add humor, which eventually won him a column in a local computer magazine.

Eventually Gookin's talents came to roost as he became a ghost writer at a computer book publishing house. That was followed by an editing position at a San Diego computer magazine, at which time he also regularly participated on a radio talk show about computers. In addition, Gookin kept writing books about computers, some of which became minor bestsellers.

In 1990, Gookin came to IDG Books with a book proposal. From that initial meeting unfolded an idea for an outrageous book: a long overdue and original idea for the computer book for the rest of us. What became *DOS For Dummies* blossomed into an international bestseller with hundreds and thousands of copies in print and many foreign translations.

Today, Gookin still considers himself a writer and computer "guru" whose job it is to remind everyone that computers are not to be taken too seriously. His approach to computers is light and humorous yet very informative. He knows that the complex beasts are important and can help people become productive and successful. Yet Gookin mixes his knowledge of computers with a unique, dry sense of humor that keeps everyone informed — and awake. His favorite quote is, "Computers are a notoriously dull subject, but that doesn't mean I have to write about them that way."

Gookin's most recent titles include *Word For Windows For Dummies* and the *Illustrated Computer Dictionary For Dummies*. He is also the author of the bestselling *DOS For Dummies,* 2nd Edition, and *WordPerfect For Dummies* and the coauthor of *PC For Dummies.* All told, he's written over 30 books on computers and contributes regularly to *DOS Resource Guide, InfoWorld,* and *PC Computing Magazine.* Gookin holds a degree in Communications from the University of California, San Diego, and currently lives with his wife and boys in the Pacific Northwest.

About IDG Books Worldwide

Welcome to the world of IDG Books Worldwide.

IDG Books Worldwide, Inc., is a division of International Data Group, the world's largest publisher of computer-related information and the leading global provider of information services on information technology. IDG publishes over 194 computer publications in 62 countries. Forty million people read one or more IDG publications each month.

If you use personal computers, IDG Books is committed to publishing quality books that meet your needs. We rely on our extensive network of publications, including such leading periodicals as *Macworld*, *InfoWorld*, *PC World*, *Computerworld*, *Publish*, *Network World*, and *SunWorld*, to help us make informed and timely decisions in creating useful computer books that meet your needs.

Every IDG book strives to bring extra value and skill-building instruction to the reader. Our books are written by experts, with the backing of IDG periodicals, and with careful thought devoted to issues such as audience, interior design, use of icons, and illustrations. Our editorial staff is a careful mix of high-tech journalists and experienced book people. Our close contact with the makers of computer products helps ensure accuracy and thorough coverage. Our heavy use of personal computers at every step in production means we can deliver books in the most timely manner.

We are delivering books of high quality at competitive prices on topics customers want. At IDG, we believe in quality, and we have been delivering quality for over 25 years. You'll find no better book on a subject than an IDG book.

John Kilcullen
President and C.E.O.
IDG Books Worldwide, Inc.

IDG Books Worldwide, Inc. is a division of International Data Group. The officers are Patrick J. McGovern, Founder and Board Chairman; Walter Boyd, President. International Data Group's publications include: **ARGENTINA's** Computerworld Argentina, InfoWorld Argentina; **ASIA's** Computerworld Hong Kong, PC World Hong Kong, Computerworld Southeast Asia, PC World Singapore, Computerworld Malaysia, PC World Malaysia; **AUSTRALIA's** Computerworld Australia, Australian PC World, Australian Macworld, Network World, Reseller, IDG Sources; **AUSTRIA's** Computerwelt Oesterreich, PC Test; **BRAZIL's** Computerworld, Mundo IBM, Mundo Unix, PC World, Publish; **BULGARIA's** Computerworld Bulgaria, Ediworld, PC & Mac World Bulgaria; **CANADA's** Direct Access, Graduate Computerworld, InfoCanada, Network World Canada; **CHILE's** Computerworld, Informatica; **COLUMBIA's** Computerworld Columbia; **CZECH REPUBLIC's** Computerworld, Elektronika, PC World; **DENMARK's** CAD/CAM WORLD, Communications World, Computerworld Danmark, LOTUS World, Macintosh Produktkatalog, Macworld Danmark, PC World Danmark, PC World Produktguide, Windows World; **EQUADOR's** PC World; **EGYPT's** Computerworld (CW) Middle East, PC World Middle East; **FINLAND's** MikroPC, Tietoviikko, Tietoverkko; **FRANCE's** Distributique, GOLDEN MAC, InfoPC, Languages & Systems, Le Guide du Monde Informatique, Le Monde Informatique, Telecoms & Reseaux; **GERMANY's** Computerwoche, Computerwoche Focus, Computerwoche Extra, Computerwoche Karriere, Information Management, Macwelt, Netzwelt, PC Welt, PC Woche, Publish, Unit; **HUNGARY's** Alaplap, Computerworld SZT, PC World, ; **INDIA's** Computers & Communications; **ISRAEL's** Computerworld Israel, PC World Israel; **ITALY's** Computerworld Italia, Lotus Magazine, Macworld Italia, Networking Italia, PC World Italia; **JAPAN's** Computerworld Japan, Macworld Japan, SunWorld Japan, Windows World; **KENYA's** East African Computer News; **KOREA's** Computerworld Korea, Macworld Korea, PC World Korea; **MEXICO's** Compu Edicion, Compu Manufactura, Computacion/Punto de Venta, Computerworld Mexico, MacWorld, Mundo Unix, PC World, Windows; **THE NETHERLAND'S** Computer! Totaal, LAN Magazine, MacWorld; **NEW ZEALAND's** Computer Listings, Computerworld New Zealand, New Zealand PC World; **NIGERIA's** PC World Africa; **NORWAY's** Computerworld Norge, C/World, Lotusworld Norge, Macworld Norge, Networld, PC World Ekspress, PC World Norge, PC World's Product Guide, Publish World, Student Data, Unix World, Windowsworld, IDG Direct Response; **PANAMA's** PC World; **PERU's** Computerworld Peru, PC World; **PEOPLES REPUBLIC OF CHINA's** China Computerworld, PC World China, Electronics International, China Network World; **IDG HIGH TECH BEIJING's** New Product World; **IDG SHENZHEN's** Computer News Digest; **PHILLIPPINES'** Computerworld, PC World; **POLAND's** Computerworld Poland, PC World/Komputer; **PORTUGAL's** Cerebro/PC World, Correio Informatico/Computerworld, MacIn; **ROMANIA's** PC World; **RUSSIA's** Computerworld-Moscow, Mir-PC, Sety; **SLOVENIA's** Monitor Magazine; **SOUTH AFRICA's** Computing S.A.; **SPAIN's** Amiga World, Computerworld Espana, Communicaciones World, Macworld Espana, NeXTWORLD, PC World Espana, Publish, Sunworld; **SWEDEN's** Attack, ComputerSweden, Corporate Computing, Lokala Natverk/LAN, Lotus World, MAC&PC, Macworld, Mikrodatorn, PC World, Publishing & Design (CAP), Datalngenjoren, Maxi Data, Windows World; **SWITZERLAND's** Computerworld Schweiz, Macworld Schweiz, PC & Workstation; **TAIWAN's** Computerworld Taiwan, Global Computer Express, PC World Taiwan; **THAILAND's** Thai Computerworld; **TURKEY's** Computerworld Monitor, Macworld Turkiye, PC World Turkiye; **UNITED KINGDOM's** Lotus Magazine, Macworld, Sunworld; **UNITED STATES'** AmigaWorld, Cable in the Classroom, CD Review, CIO, Computerworld, Desktop Video World, DOS Resource Guide, Electronic News, Federal Computer Week, Federal Integrator, GamePro, IDG Books, InfoWorld, InfoWorld Direct, Laser Event, Macworld, Multimedia World, Network World, NeXTWORLD, PC Games, PC Letter, PC World Publish, Sumeria, SunWorld, SWATPro, Video Event; **VENEZUELA's** Computerworld Venezuela, MicroComputerworld Venezuela; **VIETNAM's** PC World Vietnam

 The text in this book is printed on recycled paper.

Acknowledgments

The publisher would like to give special thanks to Patrick J. McGovern, without whom this book would not have been possible.

Credits

Vice President and Publisher
David Solomon

Acquisitions Editor
Janna Custer

Managing Editor
Mary Bednarek

Project Editor
Sandra Blackthorn

Editors
Mary Corder
Patricia A. Seiler
Diane Graves Steele
Darrin Strain

Technical Reviewer
Victor R. Garza

Editorial Assistant
Patricia R. Reynolds

Proofreader
Charles A. Hutchinson

Production Manager
Beth J. Baker

Production Coordinator
Cindy L. Phipps

Production Staff
Mary Briedenbach
Drew R. Moore

Indexer
Sharon Hilgenberg

Contents at a Glance

Cartoons at a Glance
By Rich Tennant

page 265

page 121

page 191

page xxii

page 233

page 288

page 7

page 330

page 58

page 297

Table of Contents

The 5th Wave

By Rich Tennant

DOYNK SOFTWARE

"It's been reported that we went a little crazy trying to bring this product to market on time..."

Introduction

∙∙

Welcome to *WordPerfect 6 For Dummies*, a book that's not afraid to say, "You don't need to know everything about WordPerfect to use it." Heck, you probably don't *want* to know everything about WordPerfect. You don't want to know all the command options, all the typographical mumbo-jumbo, or even all those special features that you know are in there but terrify you. No, all you want to know is the single answer to a tiny question. Then you can happily close the book and be on your way. If that's you, you've found your book.

This book informs and entertains. And it has a serious attitude problem. After all, I don't want to teach you to love WordPerfect. That's sick. Instead, be prepared to encounter some informative, down-to-earth explanations — in English — of how to get the job done by using WordPerfect. After all, you take your work seriously, but you definitely don't need to take WordPerfect seriously.

About This Book

This book is not meant to be read from cover to cover. If that were true, the covers would definitely need to be put closer together. Instead, this book is a reference. Each chapter covers a specific topic in WordPerfect. Within a chapter, you find self-contained sections, each of which describes how to do a WordPerfect task relating to the chapter's topic. Sample sections you encounter in this book include the following:

- ✔ Saving your stuff
- ✔ Cutting and pasting a block
- ✔ Making text italicized
- ✔ Doing a hanging indent
- ✔ Printing envelopes
- ✔ Cobbling together tables
- ✔ Where did my document go?

There are no keys to memorize, no secret codes, no tricks, no pop-up dioramas, and no wall charts. Instead, each section explains a topic as if it's the first thing you read in this book. Nothing is assumed, and everything is cross-referenced. Technical terms and topics, when they come up, are neatly shoved to the side where you can easily avoid reading them. The idea here isn't for you to learn anything. This book's philosophy is look it up, figure it out, and get back to work.

How to Use This Book

This book helps you when you're at a loss over what to do in WordPerfect. I think that this situation happens to everyone way too often. For example, if you press Ctrl-PgUp, WordPerfect displays a panel (or *dialog box*) asking for Macro Control. I have no idea what that means, nor do I want to know. What I do know, however, is that pressing the Esc key makes the annoying thing go away. That's the kind of knowledge you find in this book.

WordPerfect uses *key combinations,* several keys you can press together or in sequence to get the job done. This book shows you those key combinations in the following manner:

Shift-F7, C, Enter

This setup means that you should press and hold the Shift key and press the F7 key. Release both keys. Then press the C key. Then press the Enter key. But don't type the commas or any period that ends a sentence.

Whenever I describe a message or information that you see on the screen, I present it as follows:

```
This is a message on-screen
```

Any details about what you type are explained in the text. And, if you look down at your keyboard and find ten thumbs — or scissors and cutlery — instead of hands, consider reading Chapter 3, "Using the Keyboard Correctly," right now.

This book never refers you to the WordPerfect manual or — yech! — to the DOS manual. It does refer you to a companion book in this series, *DOS For Dummies,* 2nd Edition, published by IDG Books Worldwide. However, most of what you need DOS for can be accomplished in WordPerfect, so you can happily keep your DOS knowledge to a minimum.

What You're Not to Read

Special technical sections dot this book like mosquito bites. They offer annoyingly endless and technical explanations, descriptions of advanced topics, or alternative commands that you really don't need to know about. Each one of them is flagged with a special icon or enclosed in an electrified, barbed wire and poison ivy box (an idea I stole from the Terwilliker Piano Method books). Reading this stuff is optional.

Foolish Assumptions

Here are my assumptions about you: You use a computer. You use Word-Perfect — specifically, Version 6.0. Anything else involving the computer or DOS is handled by someone whom I call your personal guru. Rely on this person to help you through the rough patches; wave your guru over or call your guru on the phone. But always be sure to thank your guru. Remember that computer gurus enjoy junk food as nourishment and often accept it as payment. Keep a bowl of M&Ms or a sack of Doritos at the ready for when you need your guru's assistance.

You also should have a computer worthy of WordPerfect 6.0. That means you need color graphics, preferably of the VGA or SuperVGA variety. You also need a computer mouse. Although this program does work as advertised without a mouse, I highly suggest that you have one to benefit from the features WordPerfect 6.0 offers.

How This Book Is Organized

This book contains six major parts, each of which is divided into three or more chapters. The chapters themselves have been Ginsu-knifed into smaller, modular sections. You can pick up the book and read any section without necessarily knowing what has already been covered in the rest of the book. Start anywhere.

Here is a breakdown of the six parts and what you find in them:

Part I: Introducing WordPerfect (the Basic Stuff)

This is baby WordPerfect stuff — the bare essentials. Here you learn to giggle, teethe, crawl, walk, burp, and spit up. Then you can move up to the advanced topics of moving the cursor, editing text, searching and replacing, marking blocks, spell-checking, and printing. (A pacifier is optional for this part.)

Part II: Making Your Prose Look Less Ugly

Formatting is the art of beating your text into typographical submission. It's not the heady work of creating a document and getting the right words. No, it's "you will be italic" and "indent, you moron!" and "gimme a new page *here*." Often, formatting involves a lot of yelling. This part of the book contains chapters that show you how to format characters, lines, paragraphs, pages, and entire documents without raising your voice (too much).

Part III: Working with Documents

Document is a nice, professional-sounding word — much better than *that thing I did with WordPerfect. Document* is quicker to type. And you sound important if you say that you work on documents instead of admitting the truth that you sit and stare at the screen and play with the mouse. This part of the book tells you how to save and shuffle documents.

Part IV: WordPerfect's Bootiful Interface

Unlike its repulsive ancestors, WordPerfect 6.0 now has a friendly graphical screen, mice, dialog boxes, buttons, and all sorts of fancy gizmos that may make you yearn for the days of ugly colored text. Not! This part discusses how WordPerfect's graphical interface works and how you can coax it into making your document look purty.

Part V: Help Me, Mr. Wizard!

One school of thought is that every copy of WordPerfect should be sold with a baseball bat. I'm a firm believer in baseball-bat therapy for computers. But, before you go to such an extreme, consider the soothing words of advice provided in this part of the book.

Part VI: The Part of Tens

How about "The Ten Commandments of WordPerfect" — complete with Charlton Heston bringing them down from Mt. Orem. Or consider "Ten Features You Don't Use but Paid for Anyway." Or the handy "Ten Things Worth Remembering." This part is a gold mine of tens.

Icons Used in This Book

This icon alerts you to overly nerdy information and technical discussions of the topic at hand. The information is optional reading, but it may enhance your reputation at cocktail parties if you repeat it.

This icon flags useful, helpful tips or shortcuts.

This icon marks a friendly reminder to do something.

 This icon marks a friendly reminder not to do something.

 This icon flags information about using WordPerfect with a mouse (the computer kind — although if you like to work with the mammal variety, that's OK too).

 This icon flags a command you can access from the menu. (Because WordPerfect is heavily keyboard-bound, this icon often marks the easier way to do things.)

 This icon marks the occasional WordPerfect command that can be accessed from the standard Button Bar.

 This icon identifies the quick, no-commentary way to accomplish a WordPerfect task.

Where to Go from Here

You work with WordPerfect. You know what you hate about it. Why not start by looking up that subject in the table of contents and seeing what this book says about it? Alternatively, you can continue to use WordPerfect in the Sisyphean manner you're used to: Push that boulder to the top of the hill and, when it starts to roll back on you, whip out this book like a bazooka and blow the rock to smithereens. You'll be back at work and enjoying yourself in no time.

Bonus Tip!

If you're a former WordPerfect 5.1, 5.0, or even 4.2 user, then this book contains a Special Bonus Section just for you. Please turn to the back of the book to find "The Old Hands Guide." This section will help guide you through the new, fancy, graphical features of WordPerfect 6.0 and get you up to speed smoothly.

Part I

Introducing WordPerfect (the Basic Stuff)

In this part . . .

*W*riting came about because people just can't keep stuff in their heads. Primitive folks would tell great stories of the past — of heroes, of the hunt, of ferocious saber-toothed tigers, and of tipping over dozing mammoths. Yet, they would soon forget whether it was Ogg or Gronk who did what. So, to help them remember, they made marks on cave walls, which today would be called *graffiti*.

Over time, the cave markings evolved into writing on paper, which was easier to ball up and throw away when it didn't sound right. To make writing even easier, someone developed the typewriter and, eventually, the electric typewriter. Then, just as man was about to achieve his crowning glory in writing down and remembering stuff, they came up with the PC running WordPerfect word processing software. We forgot everything.

A computer running WordPerfect does to writing what tipping did to the noble mammoth: startled it and made it uncomfortable. Happily, using a word processor doesn't need to be like that. This part of the book attempts to explain it all to you in easily understood terms that will stay in your head. Welcome to the basic WordPerfect stuff.

Chapter 1
Word Processing 101

- -

In This Chapter

▶ Starting WordPerfect

▶ Reading the WordPerfect screen

▶ Entering text

▶ Editing a document on disk

▶ Getting help

▶ Understanding WordPerfect's imperfect commands

▶ Printing

▶ Saving your stuff

▶ Closing a document

▶ Moving on

▶ Exiting WordPerfect

- -

*T*his chapter offers an overview of how WordPerfect works, the way you probably use the program every day to get various word processing stuff done. *The Basics.* More specific stuff happens in later chapters and is cross-referenced here for your page-flipping enjoyment.

Starting WordPerfect

To begin using WordPerfect, you need to

1. **Prepare yourself mentally.**

   Do I really want to do this? You know, the typewriter has always been my friend. And WordPerfect? DOS? A computer? OK. I'll try. I'll be brave. (Take a swig of your favorite beverage here.)

2. **Turn on your computer, plus the monitor and anything else of importance (or that has busy blinking lights on it) around the computer.**

3. Contend with DOS or, if you're lucky, see a fancy menu system.

If you see a menu system, then select the WordPerfect option. You're done! If not, drearily move on to Step 4.

4. Start the WordPerfect program.

You've already started the computer. You've watched the miracle of DOS appear on the screen. Now you're probably staring at that horrid thing called the DOS prompt. Pain thyself no further! Type the following:

```
C:\> WP
```

That is, type **WP** for WordPerfect (or word processing, take your pick) and press Enter. That's it! No excess punctuation, no kowtowing, no utterances in Latin.

WordPerfect starts on the screen, displaying an opening banner. See the pretty screen. Big pen. Some possibly helpful information may be displayed, but it disappears too fast to be truly useful. Eventually, you see the initial *blank page,* which is discussed in the next section.

- ✔ Type **WP** to start WordPerfect. Don't type **WordPerfect** or **Oh, Lordy, What Am I Doing Here?** because it just won't work.

- ✔ If you know which document you want to edit, type its name after you type **WP.** For example, if you type **WP CHAP01** and press Enter, WordPerfect starts and automatically loads the document file CHAP01 for editing. Refer to "Editing a Document on Disk" later in this chapter for more information.

- ✔ If you see the dreaded error message Bad command or file name, then something is awry. Before loading your gun, refer to Chapter 24 and look for the section about what to do when you can't find WordPerfect.

- ✔ Your computer can be set up to automatically run WordPerfect. Think of the time such a setup can save! If you want the computer set up thusly, grab someone more knowledgeable than yourself — an individual I call a *computer guru.* Direct the guru to "make my computer always start in WordPerfect." If the guru is unable to do as you ask, frantically grab other people at random until you find someone bold enough to obey you.

- ✔ You can find additional information on starting the PC and contending with the DOS prompt in *DOS For Dummies,* 2nd Edition, published by IDG Books Worldwide. That book does for DOS what this book does for WordPerfect: makes it understandable.

Don't read this stuff!

The actual name of the WordPerfect program is WP.EXE. You only need to know the first part, the WP. The EXE means *executable,* and you pronounce it *ee-ecks-ee* (not *ecksee* or *ezzee* or *echcheey*).

When you type WP at the DOS prompt, DOS searches high and low through the hard drive for the program file named WP.EXE. It loads that file into memory and runs the WordPerfect software. To make all of this happen, all you have to do is type WP at the DOS prompt. You don't need to do anything else or buy anything else, and there are no messy dyes or powders.

The horrid truth is that WordPerfect is more than just the WP.EXE file. Often it's more like two or three dozen files, each of which contributes some small yet meaningful element of the WordPerfect program. All these files are stuffed into a special directory on your system.

Chapter 21 examines files and directories in detail — if you dare to look this information up.

Reading the WordPerfect Screen

After WordPerfect starts, you are faced with the electronic version of The Blank Page. This idea-crippling concept is the same one that induced writer's block in several generations of typewriter users. With WordPerfect, it's worse. Not only is the screen mostly blank, but no clues are offered about what to do next.

Figure 1-1 shows the typical, blank WordPerfect screen. (If your screen doesn't look like the one in the figure, refer to "Making your screen look like my screen" later in this chapter.)

Three things are worth noting on the blank WordPerfect screen (which really isn't that blank after all):

1. **The *menu bar* — the document's *crown of thorns.*** All the WordPerfect commands live on the menu bar, and it comes in really handy if you like using a mouse with your computer.

2. **A large empty white space.** Text you type and edit appears here.

3. **The *status bar* — the document's underwear.** On the left is a fractured bit of text that either gives the name of the document or lists the text font you've selected. On the right, some gibberish explains *where you are* in the document.

Whether you see the document's name or the text font on the left of the status bar depends on whether you have saved the document. (Saving is covered later in this chapter.)

Menu bar

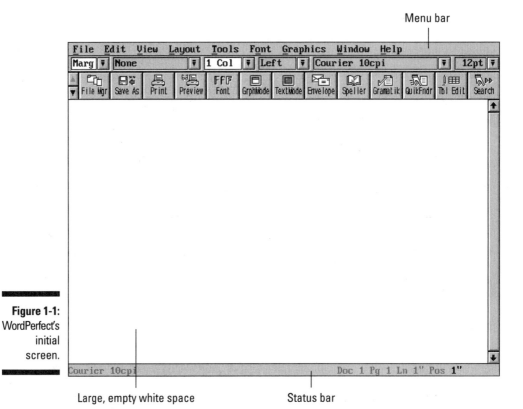

Figure 1-1:
WordPerfect's
initial
screen.

Large, empty white space   Status bar

If you see the document's name displayed, don't be taken aback if it looks strange. It's listed in DOS language — a DOS *pathname* (which explains all the colons, backslashes and other offal). The filename is the last part of the text you see.

If you see a text font, it probably is *Courier 10cpi,* which means *typewriter-looking text, big stupid size.* Chapter 8 goes into detail about this text font and others.

On the left of the status bar you always find four word fragments followed by numbers (like a tenth-grade algebra problem). Table 1-1 examines those fragments.

Table 1-1	Status Line Definitions
Word Fragment	**Description**
Doc 1	The number of the document you're writing or editing — Doc 1, Doc 2, Doc 3, on up to Doc Hollywood (Doc 9).
Pg *xx*	The number of the page you are on: 1 is the first page, 8 is the eighth page, and so on.
Ln *x.xx*"	The line you are on. Lines are measured in inches from the top of the page. Ln 4.89 means that you are on the line that's **4.89** inches from the top of the page.
Pos *x.xx*"	The distance from the left edge of the page. For example, Pos 3.19 means that you're 3.19 inches from the left edge of the page.

✔ My advice? Ignore all these weird numbers and concentrate instead on your writing. After all, only the truly disturbed whip out a ruler and measure a piece of paper in a typewriter as they go along. (The numbers come in handy later to tell you how much stuff you've written. Pretend that they don't exist for now.)

✔ If you don't see the menu at the top of your screen, refer to "Making your screen look like my screen," later in this chapter.

✔ The *cursor* is at the exact spot where the text appears when you type. It's a blinking vertical bar — like a blinking *I* or one of those bonus-life tooth-picks you pick up in a food-theme video game. You find the toothpick cursor somewhere in the large empty space on the screen. Characters you type appear to the left of where the cursor blinks, and then the cursor moves forward and waits for the next character.

✔ If you have a mouse installed, move it around on your desk or mouse pad, and you see WordPerfect's mouse pointer move on the screen. The pointer resembles a bent arrow, and it mimics the movements of the mouse on your desk.

✔ The screen isn't blank if you've directed WordPerfect to load a document for editing when it starts. Refer to "Editing a Document on Disk" later in this chapter for the details.

✔ When WordPerfect is busy, * Please wait * appears either at the bottom left corner of the screen or in a pop-up box over the middle of the screen. This message means *please wait.* It disappears when you no longer need to wait and can get busy typing again. Other messages may appear from time to time. Obey them.

The menu is here to stay

It took years of research and a beefy government grant to figure out that using menus is easier than remembering oddball function-key combinations. Yet when someone pointed out that restaurants use menus, and, of course, so does the Macintosh computer, the person in charge of the WordPerfect Department of Making Things Easier said, "See? I was right!" Yet they kept the function-key combinations just because so many WordPerfect users have broken fingers that they have a hard time using anything else.

You access the pull-down menus and their commands from the menu bar that appears on the top of the screen. On the menu bar are various words that represent the pull-down menus: File, Edit, View, Layout, and so on. You can access the menu a word represents in one of two ways:

- ✔ Use the mouse to click on the word.
- ✔ Press Alt plus the letter that is underlined in the word (Alt-F for File, Alt-E for Edit, and so on).

When you activate a menu, it covers up part of the document. On the menu are various menu items, which are actually WordPerfect commands that also are assigned to various and random function keys.

To select a menu item, click on it using the mouse. Or locate the underlined letter in the item and press that letter on the keyboard (no need to do the Alt-thing here). So to select the Open command from the File menu, press the O key because O is underlined.

Some menu items have triangles (▶) to their right side. These triangles indicate submenus, which appear glued to the sides of the main menus. When you click on a triangle menu, the secondary submenu appears, glued to the side of the main menu.

- ✔ Occasionally, the menu bar may wander off in search of alcohol. To bring it back, press Alt-=. (Press and hold Alt and press the equal sign.)
- ✔ If you pulled down a menu and need to make it go away, press Esc.
- ✔ To end your menu browsing, press the mouse's right button (the one you normally don't press when you want something to happen).

Making your screen look like my screen

Starting with Version 6.0, WordPerfect has a new graphical look. Or, if you have a high tolerance for pain or enjoy Leroy Nieman paintings, you can make WordPerfect 6.0 look like the older version, 5.1, which was just multicolored text on the screen and no graphics. The choice is yours; though, to keep your sanity I recommend using the graphical look, which is what I do, and I consider myself a relatively sane person. At times.

This book's figures and examples all assume that you're using WordPerfect in the graphics mode, as shown in the figures. If your screen doesn't look like the ones in this book, make it look like them by doing the following:

1. **Press Ctrl-F3, 3.**

   Press and hold Ctrl, and then press F3. Release both keys. The Screen dialog box pops up in the middle of the screen. Press 3 to select Graphics, and your screen then looks like the ones in this book.

   On my screen I also like to display the following items: the Ribbon, the Button Bar, and the Vertical Scroll Bar. You can activate these items from the View menu, as follows:

2. **Click on the word View with the mouse or press Alt-V.**

   The View menu appears, and you can use it to change WordPerfect's look (but, unfortunately, not its attitude).

3. **Select Ribbon from the View menu.**

   Use the mouse to click on Ribbon or press R if you're into the keyboard. The Ribbon appears on the screen. It's the thing just below the menu bar that says `Marg` on the left in Figure 1-1. The Ribbon is a handy place for changing the fonts and other fun stuff. It's good to have around.

4. **Activate the View menu again.**

   Click on View using the mouse or press Alt-V from the keyboard. (I prefer the keyboard, but I paid over $100 for my mouse and will try to get as much mileage from it as possible.)

   The same old View menu is displayed.

5. **Select Button Bar from the View menu.**

   Click on Button Bar with the mouse or press B. The Button Bar appears just below the Ribbon. The Button Bar is a handy place where you can use the mouse to quickly activate some of WordPerfect's more esoteric commands.

6. **Activate the View menu yet again.**

7. **Select the Vertical Scroll Bar item.**

   Click on Vertical Scroll Bar or press V. A scroll bar appears on the right side of the screen, enabling you to use the mouse to move to different parts of the document easily.

8. **Activate the View menu one last time.**

9. **Select Zoom.**

The Zoom menu item is actually a submenu, as indicated by the ▶ character. The submenu displayed when you select Zoom has several items that tell WordPerfect how *big* to display the document on the screen. The best option, in my opinion, is Margin Width, which enables you to see the entire page on the screen.

10. **Select Margin Width.**

Use the mouse or press M. You're done.

✔ Chapter 18 has more and exciting information about WordPerfect 6's new graphical interface.

✔ I use WordPerfect with the Ribbon, Button Bar, and Vertical Scroll Bar showing. Of all the gadgets you can have on the screen, I consider these to be the most handy. Examples later in this book show how each feature works.

Entering Text

To compose text in WordPerfect, use the keyboard — that typewriter-like thing sitting in front of the computer and below the monitor. Go ahead, type away. Let your fingers dance on the key tops! What you type appears on the screen, letter for letter — even derogatory stuff about the computer. (WordPerfect doesn't care what you write, but that doesn't mean it lacks feelings.)

New text is inserted to the left of the blinking cursor bar. For example, you can type the following:

Mother emphasized, "Don't say a thing about Grandma's mustache."

If you want to change *emphasized* to *reemphasized,* move the cursor to the start of *emphasized* and type **re.** Those two letters are inserted into the text. You don't have to delete anything, and all the text that follows falls neatly into place.

✔ The way you compose text on the screen is by typing. Every character key you press produces a character on the screen. This concept holds true for all letter, number, and symbol keys. The other keys, mostly the gray ones on the keyboard, do strange and wonderful things that the rest of this book tries hard to explain.

✔ If you make a mistake, press the Backspace key to back up and erase. This key may be named *Backspace* on the keyboard, or it may have a long, left-pointing arrow on it.

✔ Moving the cursor around on the screen is covered in Chapter 2.

- You use the Shift keys to produce capital letters.

- The Caps Lock key works like the shift lock key on a typewriter. After you press that key, everything you type appears in all capital letters.

- The Caps Lock light on the keyboard comes on when you're in All Caps mode. Also note that Pos on the bottom right of the screen becomes POS when Caps Lock is turned on.

- The number keys to the right of the keyboard make up the *numeric keypad*. To use those keys, you need to first press the Num Lock key on the keyboard. If you don't, the keys take on their arrow key functions. (Refer to the section on document navigation in Chapter 2.)

- The Num Lock light comes on when you press the Num Lock key to turn the numeric keypad on. Most PCs start with this feature activated; however, most users keep Num Lock off.

- Refer to Chapter 3 for some handy tips on typing and using the keyboard.

- No one needs to learn how to type in order to write. But the best writers are typists. My advice is to get a computer program that teaches you to type. Knowing how to type can make a painful experience like using WordPerfect a wee bit more enjoyable.

Typing away, la la la

Eons ago, a word processor was judged superior if it had the famous *word-wrap feature*. This feature eliminates the need to press Enter at the end of each line of text, which is a requirement when you're using a typewriter. WordPerfect and all other modern word processors have this feature. If you're unfamiliar with it, you should get used to putting it to work for you.

With WordPerfect, when the text gets precariously close to the right margin, the last word is picked up and placed at the start of the next line. You only need to press Enter when you want to end a paragraph.

- Press Enter to create a new paragraph. If you want to split one paragraph into two, move the cursor to the middle of the paragraph, where you want the second paragraph to start, and press Enter.

- Press Enter at the end of a paragraph, not at the end of every line.

- As you start typing — actually, after you press any key — the mouse pointer vanishes from the screen. To see it again, move the mouse on your desk. The disappearance of the pointer is a WordPerfect feature: by making the pointer disappear, WordPerfect makes the screen look less cluttered.

✔ Don't be afraid to use the keyboard! WordPerfect always offers ample warning before anything serious happens. You can use a handy Undo key, Ctrl-Z, to recover anything you accidentally delete, and an even handier Undelete key, which is called Esc (for escape) on the keyboard. Refer to Chapter 3 for details.

Crossing the line of death

Occasionally, you see a solid line stretching from one side of the screen to another — a black laser beam line of death, or the proverbial crack in the sidewalk your mother hopes you don't step on. What that thing marks is the end of one page and the beginning of another — a *page break*. The text you see above the line is on the preceding page; text below the line is on the next page.

✔ You cannot delete the line of death. It's like stepping on a roach. Instead, just ignore it. Think of it as a useful way of telling you where text stops on one page and starts on the next.

✔ You can see how the line works by looking at the scrambled statistics in the lower right corner of the screen. For example, when the cursor is above the line, you may see Pg 5 for page 5. When the cursor is below the line, you see Pg 6 for page 6.

✔ A double line of death (two lines of death on top of each other) marks a *hard page*. It symbolizes a definite "I want a new page now" command given by the person who created the document. Refer to Chapter 11 for more information.

Editing a Document on Disk

You use WordPerfect to create *documents*. The documents can be printed or saved to disk for later editing or printing. When a document has been saved to disk, it's considered a *file* on the disk (although you can still refer to it as a document).

Two methods are available for you to use when loading a document that is already on disk:

✔ Specify the document's filename after typing **WP** when you start WordPerfect from DOS.

✔ Open a document after WordPerfect has started.

The easiest way to load a document is to specify the document's filename after you type **WP** to start WordPerfect. For example, to automatically load LETTER.WP when you start WordPerfect, you type the following at the DOS prompt:

```
C:\> WP LETTER.WP
```

That is, you type **WP** to start WordPerfect, then a space, and then the name of the document file that you want to edit (**LETTER.WP,** in this case). Then press Enter. Notice that the command does not end with a period; you press the Enter key after typing the document name.

You also can load a document after you start the program by using the Open command. Follow these steps to load a document after WordPerfect is already running:

1. Press Shift-F10, the Open command key combination.

Press and hold down the Shift key and then press the key labeled F10 near the top of the keyboard (or along the side if you have an older keyboard). After you press Shift-F10, you see the Open Document dialog box in the middle of the screen, as shown in Figure 1-2.

2. Type the name of the document you want to load.

Make sure that everything is spelled correctly; WordPerfect is finicky about filename spelling. You can type the name in uppercase or lowercase; it's all the same to WordPerfect.

3. Press Enter.

The document is loaded and appears on the screen, ready for editing.

> ✔ Shift-F10 equals *Open?* The gang in the WordPerfect Department of Assigning Commands to Function Keys was working late that night.

> ✔ Ah-ha! Instead of using Shift-F10, you can select the Open command from the File menu. Use the mouse to click on File and then from the list that appears, click on Open.

> ✔ The term *editing* means *to read, correct, or add to the text already composed and saved to disk.* This task involves using the cursor-control keys, which are covered in Chapter 2. Also refer to Chapters 4, 5, and 6.

Figure 1-2:
The Open Document dialog box.

```
┌─────────────────────── Open Document ───────────────────────┐
│                                                              │
│   Filename: ┌──────────────────────────────────────────┐ ▼  │
│             └──────────────────────────────────────────┘    │
│            ┌─ Method (Shft+F10 to change) ──────┐  ⬉         │
│            │  ● Open into New Document           │           │
│            │  ○ Retrieve into Current Document   │           │
│            └────────────────────────────────────┘           │
│   │ File Manager... F5 │  │ QuickList... F6 │   │ OK │  │ Cancel │  │
└──────────────────────────────────────────────────────────────┘
```

✔ When you're done editing a document, you print it and save it back to disk — or do one and then the other. To learn how to print and save a document, see "Printing" and "Saving Your Stuff" later in this chapter.

✔ Documents must be saved to disk with a DOS filename. If you think stuffing something clever into a seven-character *vanity* license plate is tough, wait until you try to save that letter to Aunt Velma! DOS is very limiting with how files are named; refer to Chapter 16 for file-naming rules and regulations.

✔ If the document name you typed doesn't exist on disk, or if WordPerfect can't find it, you see an error message displayed in a pop-up dialog box:

```
File not found — BLECH
```

(BLECH would be replaced by the name of the file you wanted to retrieve.) Then WordPerfect redisplays the *retrieve* prompt. My advice: Try again and check your spelling. Or refer to Chapter 14, which explains how to locate a file and open it without using the Shift-F10 key command.

Getting Help

Obviously, working with a computer program that believes Shift-F10 is a handy mnemonic for *open* isn't going to be easy. This convention is akin to marking restroom doors with chromosome patterns rather than with silhouettes of men and women. Sometimes, perhaps often, you need help when using WordPerfect. For those times, you need to memorize only one key: F1.

The F1 key is the Help key. Press F1 and you enter WordPerfect's help system. There you can get information on all of WordPerfect's commands and discover how things are done.

The help system's first screen is shown in Figure 1-3. To make things happen, try one of these approaches:

Approach 1: Select Index to see a list of all the things WordPerfect does and for which help is available. To select Index, make sure that Index is highlighted (it appears in inverse text) and press Enter or double-click on Index with the mouse.

The next screen displays an alphabetic list of everything WordPerfect knows how to do. Use the cursor-control keys to pick through the list, highlighting various words. When you find one you're curious about, press Enter.

Approach 2: Try messing with the How do I? section, which displays a list of common things (or so they think) that you'll be doing in WordPerfect and tells how to do them. Press the → key until How do I? is highlighted and then press Enter. Or just double-click on How do I? with the mouse.

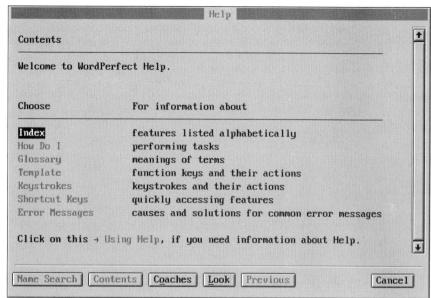

Figure 1-3:
WordPerfect's
main help
screen.

✔ Press Esc to exit help.

✔ WordPerfect's help isn't too helpful. Don't expect Dr. WordPerfect to pop out of the screen, put a calming hand on your shoulder, and point to the key you should press. This is WordPerfect — not a Disney cartoon.

✔ If you're ever stuck somewhere in WordPerfect, in the bowels of some menu or somewhere that's murky, just press F1. Helpful information on the topic at hand will be displayed.

Understanding WordPerfect's Imperfect Commands

To create a document, you use the typewriter keys. OK, understood.

To edit a document, you use the arrow or cursor-control keys, most of which are located just to the right of the typewriter keyboard area. This is all right; arrow keys we humans can deal with.

To do anything else in WordPerfect, you use the *function keys*. Welcome to the land of Kryptic Key Kombinations! Time to put on those white jackets with the long sleeves and don those Napoleon party hats!

WordPerfect assigns its commands to the most unusual array of key combinations in the known galaxy. (Although on planet Zoon, however, the Zoonian version of WordPerfect also employs two foot pedals and an elbow switch.) There are 48 WordPerfect commands assigned to 12 function keys plus 3 shift keys:

Function keys by themselves: F1 through F12

Shift key plus function keys: Shift-F1 through Shift-F12

Ctrl key plus function keys: Ctrl-F1 through Ctrl-F12

Alt key plus function keys: Alt-F1 through Alt-F12

To activate a command, you have to press the proper function key or function-key combination. For example, for Ctrl-F2, press and hold the Ctrl (Control) key and then press the F2 key. This action is the same one you use when you press Shift-F to get a capital F, but you're using the Ctrl and F2 keys instead. All the other key combinations work the same way.

✔ There is nothing wrong with the mathematics of how this works: *F1 through F12* plus *3 shift keys times 12 function keys* equals *48 key combinations.* The problem is, how do you remember which key does what?

✔ You don't have to tie your fingers in knots to use WordPerfect because it also has handy pull-down menus, as covered in the next section. The menus may be easier to use, but the function keys are quicker (providing you can hoist a basketball with one hand).

✔ I remember the various unmemorable function key commands by using what I call the *WordPerfect claw pattern.* I wax on and on about it in Chapter 3.

✔ WordPerfect's help system lists key combinations in the following manner:

```
Shift-F8,1,7
```

You press Shift-F8 (the key combination), then press 1, and then press 7. For heaven's sake, do not type in the commas! Also, if you need to press Enter, you see Enter listed like any other key. This book uses the same format.

Printing

After entering what you feel is the best piece of written work since Tolstoy, you decide that you want to print it. After all, dragging the computer around and showing everyone what your prose looks like on the screen just isn't practical.

To print a document in WordPerfect — the document you see on the screen (all of it) — do the following:

1. Make sure that the printer is on and ready to print.

2. Press Shift-F7.

You then see the Print dialog box, a busy place where printing and related activities happen. Don't bother with the details. Just blur your eyes at it and keep reading here.

3. Press 1 to direct WordPerfect to print the full document.

This option is normally highlighted, although I wouldn't trust WordPerfect to remember that, just as I wouldn't trust my 3-year-old nephew to walk across the white carpet with red Kool-Aid.

4. Press Enter.

The entire document that was on the screen is printed. Zip, zip, zip. The document comes out of the printer.

✓ Detailed information on printing is provided in Chapter 8. It includes information on making sure that the printer is ready to print.

✓ Shift-F7 brings up the Print dialog box. This key combination, or *claw pattern,* is a good one to memorize.

✓ You also can select the Print command from the File menu.

✓ To print only part of the document — a paragraph, page, or block — refer to Chapter 6.

Here are the quick steps for printing an entire document:

1. Make sure that the printer is on and ready to print. (OK, no shortcut here.)

2. Press Shift-F7, 1, Enter.

Saving Your Stuff

WordPerfect doesn't remember what you did the last time you used the computer. You have to tell it forcefully to *save your stuff.* The document on the screen has to be saved in a file on disk. To save it, you use WordPerfect's Save command.

To save a document to disk, follow these steps:

1. **Press the handy Save key, F10.**

   You see the Save Document dialog box, as shown in Figure 1-4.

   If, instead of seeing the Save Document dialog box, you see the Document Summary dialog box, then press the Esc key twice — enough to rid yourself of the Document Summary dialog box. (The Document Summary screen is optional when you save. I avoid it. To turn it off permanently, refer to the information box about the Document Summary dialog box later in this section.)

   If the document has been saved before, you see its name in the Filename box. It's the same name that you see all the time in the lower left corner of the screen. Move on to Step 3.

   If you don't see a name in the Filename box, then the document hasn't been saved to disk before. Your job now is to think of a name. Be clever; you have only eight characters (letters and numbers).

2. **Type the document's name.**

   Watch what you type! The techy box in this section on DOS filenames contains information to help you select a proper filename. If you make a mistake, use the Backspace key to back up and erase.

3. **Press Enter to save the file.**

   If you're editing an older, already saved document, you see a dialog box that asks whether you want to *replace* the file. Press Y for Yes. Then the file you've just edited in WordPerfect replaces the original file on disk. If you don't want to overwrite the original, then press N, go back to Step 2, and type a new name for the file. If you're saving a document for the first time, this message doesn't appear, and the document is saved to disk.

- ✔ F10 is the Save key. F10 equals save, F10 equals save. . . . Say it over and over until you're sure that you've memorized it.

- ✔ You can also save a document by selecting the Save command from the File menu.

Figure 1-4:
The Save
Document
dialog box.

Save Document 1

Filename: [   ]

Format: [WordPerfect 6.0   ] [▼]

[Setup... Shft+F1] [Code Page... F9]

[File List... F5] [QuickList... F6] [Password... F8] [OK] [Cancel]

✔ In the Button Bar, the second button from the left is labeled Save As. Clicking this button is the same as pressing F10 to save the document.

✔ If you enter a forbidden filename, WordPerfect screeches `Invalid filename` at you. Press Esc and try again (and read the techy box in this section).

Complicated — but important — information on DOS filenames

You need to name files according to DOS's file-naming rules. This task isn't as tough as memorizing stuff for a driver's license test, but it's darn close.

✔ A filename can be no more than eight characters long.

✔ It can include letters and numbers and can start with either a letter or a number.

✔ Filenames do not end with a period.

✔ Filenames can be followed by an optional three-character *extension*. The extension is separated from the main filename with a period.

✔ Common filename extensions for WordPerfect documents are WP and DOC.

Here are some sample filenames that are OK:

LETTER.DOC — A prim and proper filename, replete with optional period and three-character DOC extension. Mrs. Bradshaw, my third-grade computer science teacher, would be proud.

CHAP01.WP — Another OK filename, this time with the WP extension. Note how numbers and letters can be mixed — no oil and vinegar here!

01 — This is a fine, upstanding DOS filename. Numbers are okey-dokey, and the extension is optional.

LTR2MOM4 — No problems here.

STUFF.2DO — Just fine. The extension can contain numbers as well.

Here are some filenames you should avoid (with reasons why you should avoid them):

TO MOM — The filename contains a space. Heavens! Filenames cannot contain spaces.

BELLYBUTTON — This filename is too long and morally offensive to certain groups of people.

1+1 — Numbers are OK, but the + symbol is not; use only letters and numbers to name files.

I.LOVE.YOU — This is a weirdo filename because it contains two periods. The period is reserved for marking the filename extension only — nothing else.

CHOPSTIK.FOOD — The extension here is too long. Extensions can be only three characters maximum.

✔ Save documents to disk so you can work on them later! The documents can be reloaded into WordPerfect the next time you start. Refer to "Editing a Document on Disk" earlier in this chapter.

✔ After the document has been saved to disk, you see its name — actually its complicated DOS pathname with almond clusters — displayed in the lower left corner of the screen. This name is your clue that a file has been saved to disk.

✔ There is nothing wrong with replacing the older version of a file on disk. I do it all the time with everything I write: As the file is edited, I save it to disk, replacing the older version. That way, only the newest edition is saved, and my disk isn't littered with a bunch of old, not-yet-edited documents.

✔ There *is* something wrong with overwriting an unknown file on disk. For example, suppose that you decide to save a new letter document by using the filename LETTER, and you find that a file named LETTER already exists on disk. If you press Y to replace the existing file, the new file overwrites the old one. There is no way to get the original back, so use another, more clever name instead.

✔ Refer to Chapter 16 for more information on filenames and such.

Here is how you can quickly save a document you're working on — something you should do all the time. Press the following:

Ctrl-F12

Use this command often as you work on documents.

Don't avoid reading this if you want to avoid the Document Summary dialog box

I have no use for the Document Summary dialog box that comes up when you save a document in WordPerfect. Some large, bureaucratically anal corporations (and the government, of course) may need the information in this dialog box. But not a budding writer or anyone composing an epistle to a loved one. In those instances, this dialog box wastes time.

To switch off the Document Summary dialog box, press F10 as if you're going to save a document. The dialog box appears. Boo! Hiss! Press Shift-F1, 3. This action switches off this "feature." Press the F7 key twice to get back to the normal Save Document dialog box. There you can save your document or press the Esc key to continue editing. You'll never be bothered again by the Document Summary dialog box.

Closing a Document

If you're done working on a document, you can make it vanish from the screen. You make it disappear by *closing* it, which is similar to ripping a sheet of paper out of your typewriter — but without the satisfying sound of tearing paper.

To close a document, click on File on the menu bar. The File menu appears. Click on the word Close. The document window closes and vanishes from the screen. Zzzipp! (You have to say "Zzzipp!" yourself when you do this; WordPerfect is mute on the point.)

- ✔ If you try to close a document before it has been saved, WordPerfect pops up a warning dialog box. Select the Yes button and press Enter to save the document. If you want to continue editing, select the Cancel button and press Esc.

- ✔ No, WordPerfect has no function-key combination for this command, although WordPerfect is open to suggestions. Please try to have your suggestions not make sense.

- ✔ The Close menu item is found in the File menu.

- ✔ Why close a document? Because you're done working on it. Maybe you want to work on something else or quit WordPerfect after closing. The choice is up to you, and it's explained in the next section, "Moving On."

- ✔ If you're working on other documents, another one appears on the screen in place of the document you've just closed. Refer to Chapter 20 for information on working with more than one document at a time.

Moving On

After the document is closed, you have several options on what to do. (I won't mention the *take a break* or *play with the mouse pointer* options.) But within WordPerfect, you do have several options.

First, you can start work on a new document. How? Just start typing! WordPerfect gives you a blank screen at all times, even after you close a document.

Second, you can start work on another document on disk. Refer to "Editing a Document on Disk" earlier in this chapter.

Third, you can quit WordPerfect and do something else in DOS. Refer to the next section, "Exiting WordPerfect."

You don't have to quit WordPerfect when you just want to start working on a new document.

Exiting WordPerfect

It is the height of proper etiquette to know when to leave. This important information was personally related to me by the Queen of England in her response to my letter about Christmas party crashing. Oh, well. Leaving WordPerfect is accomplished by use of the Exit command. As you can guess by now, this command has a handy function key assigned to it: F7.

Pressing F7 doesn't quit WordPerfect right away. First, WordPerfect asks whether you want to save the document. This question is precautionary: No sense in quitting when you haven't saved your important words to disk.

A dialog box appears, asking whether you want to save the document. Press Y to save it, press N not to, or select Cancel if you've changed your mind and want to stay in WordPerfect.

I recommend always pressing Y to save the document. If you haven't yet saved your work, you are asked to enter a filename. If the document has been saved, you are asked whether you want to replace it. Press Y to replace the old document on disk. (Also, refer to "Saving Your Stuff" earlier in this chapter, for additional details.)

After the file is saved, you see another dialog box, asking whether you really want to exit WordPerfect. Press Y to quit WordPerfect and return to DOS.

✔ The F7 key is the Exit key. In addition to quitting WordPerfect, F7 also backs you out of various menus, and it returns you to the document. If you accidentally press F7, panic, and then press Esc to cancel.

✔ Using F7 is the proper way to exit WordPerfect. Do not, under any circumstances, reset or turn off your PC to quit WordPerfect. This behavior is utterly irresponsible, and you'll go to Computer Etiquette Jail for life if you're ever caught — and it's in Utah!

✔ If the document has already been saved to disk, but you've changed it since the last save, you see `Document has been modified` in the Exit dialog box. I recommend that you press Y and save the text if you want to keep your changes.

✔ When you're at the DOS prompt again and see that friendly C : \ >, you can start another program, safely shut off your computer, or give up, sell the computer, and start a new hobby like kayaking.

To quit WordPerfect, follow these steps:

1. Press F7.

2. Press Y to save the document.

3. Type in a name for the document if you haven't already done so.

4. Press Y to quit.

Chapter 2
Navigating the Document

In This Chapter

▶ Using the basic arrow keys

▶ Using Ctrl with the arrow keys

▶ Moving up and down one screenful of text

▶ Moving up and down by pages

▶ Moving to the end of the line

▶ Using the Home key

▶ Moving to the top of the document

▶ Moving to the end of the document

▶ Using the Go To command

▶ Navigating with the scroll bar

▶ Avoiding the useless horizontal scroll bar

▶ Getting unlost

*A*fter you have something *in there,* a document ready for you to work on, you need to get around that document. Getting around a document is like using a big city bus system, but it doesn't cost you $1.25 in loose change, and you don't have to sit next to anyone named Edna who hasn't bathed in a week. There are simple, but not quite obvious, ways to move around a document in WordPerfect. Having an easy way to get around comes in handy because the screen shows you only a small part of what you're working on.

Using the Basic Arrow Keys

The most common way to move around a document is to use the arrow keys on the keyboard. The arrow keys are rather nonspecific. A better term is the *cursor-control keys* because the keys move the little cursor/blinking toothpick on the screen. Moving the cursor is important for viewing different parts of the document as well as for locating text when you're editing.

The cursor-control keys are located in two spots on the keyboard: on the numeric keypad and between the keypad and the typewriter keys (see Figure 2-1). I know, it sounds redundant. But having two sets of cursor-control keys enables you to activate the numeric keypad and rapidly type in numbers while still having access to the duplicate cursor-control keys. Older PC keyboards lacked this luxury.

The four basic cursor-control keys are the up-arrow key, the down-arrow key, the left-arrow key, and the right-arrow key. They are found in an inverted T pattern next to the typewriter keys and on the 8, 4, 6, and 2 keys on the keypad:

↑   Moves the toothpick cursor up one line of text

↓   Moves the toothpick cursor down to the next line of text

→   Moves the toothpick cursor right, to the next character

←   Moves the toothpick cursor left, to the preceding character

✔ Both the cursor-control keys on the numeric keypad and the separate cursor-control keys work the same way; you can use either set. But note that the Num Lock feature needs to be off for the keypad cursor-control keys to work.

✔ You can move the toothpick cursor to any character on the screen by moving the mouse. When you move the mouse, the mouse pointer appears. Move the pointer to where you want the cursor to be and then click the mouse's left button. The toothpick cursor instantly moves to that spot.

✔ If the toothpick cursor is at the top line on the screen and you press the up-arrow key, the document scrolls downward on the screen, revealing the preceding line of text. The cursor moves up to that line.

✔ When the toothpick cursor is on the last line on the screen and you press the down-arrow key, the document scrolls upward to reveal the next line of text. The cursor moves down to that line.

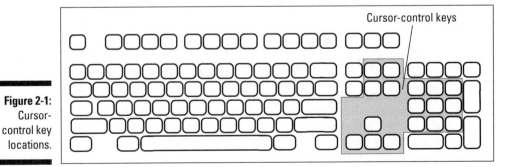

Figure 2-1:
Cursor-
control key
locations.

✔ Moving the cursor does not erase characters. The toothpick cursor hurdles over the characters leap-frog-like. Your words don't feel a thing.

✔ If you press the arrow keys and the cursor doesn't move, or if a menu appears instead, get frustrated. Then press Esc to cancel the menu mode and rejuvenate the blinking toothpick on the screen. You can then use the cursor-control keys as WordPerfect intended them to be used.

✔ As you move the cursor around on the screen, the position statistics in the lower right corner change to reflect the cursor's position on the page. The Pos value tells you how far the cursor is from the left edge of the page; Ln tells you how far the cursor is from the top of the page; and Pg tells you which page you're on.

✔ The toothpick cursor positions itself only between characters and the spaces that appear between words. You can't move the cursor to *outer space,* which is any place on the screen that is absent of text characters.

✔ Older PC keyboards have cursor-control keys only on the numeric keypad. To use them, you need to turn the Num Lock feature off by pressing the Num Lock key.

✔ Want to hop over eight characters at once? Press the Ctrl-R shortcut key (press and hold the Ctrl key and press R). The *R* stands for *repeat,* and Ctrl-R is the repeat shortcut key. Any key or command that you press after you press Ctrl-R is repeated, typically eight times. So Ctrl-R, → moves the cursor right eight places. The same trick works with the other three arrow keys.

Using Ctrl with the Arrow Keys

If you press and hold Ctrl (the Control key) and press an arrow key, the cursor jumps more than a single character:

Ctrl-↑   Moves the cursor up one paragraph

Ctrl-↓   Moves the cursor down to the next paragraph

Ctrl-→   Moves the cursor right one word

Ctrl-←   Moves the cursor left one word

✔ Press and hold the Ctrl key and then press an arrow key. Release both keys. You don't need to press hard; use the Ctrl key the way you use the Shift key to produce a capital letter.

✔ Ctrl-→ and Ctrl-← always move the cursor to the first letter of a word.

✔ Ctrl-↑ and Ctrl-↓ always move the cursor to the start of a paragraph.

Moving Up and Down One Screenful of Text

The screen shows you only one small part of the document — not a full page. To see the next or preceding screen, use the plus and minus keys on the numeric keypad:

- Moves the cursor to the top of the screen. If the cursor is already at the top of the screen, pressing the minus key moves the cursor to the preceding screen (the last few lines of the document).

+ Moves the cursor to the bottom of the screen. If the cursor is already on the last line of the screen, pressing the plus key shows you the next screen (the next few lines of the document).

✔ Only the plus and minus keys on the numeric keypad move the screen up or down. The plus and minus keys next to the Backspace key on the typewriter keyboard produce the + and – characters.

✔ You also can use the Home key to move to the top and bottom of the screen, as well as to the next and preceding screens. Refer to "Using the Home Key" later in this chapter.

Moving Up and Down by Pages

The keys labeled PgUp and PgDn are the Page Up and Page Down keys, respectively. These keys move you around in the document by pages, not by screens. Remember that a page has more lines than can be shown on the screen at one time. Here's what PgUp and PgDn do:

PgUp   Moves the cursor to the top of the preceding page. If the cursor is on page 1, this command moves it to the top of that page.

PgDn   Moves the cursor to the top of the next page. If the cursor is on the last page in the document, PgDn moves it to the last line on that page.

✔ If you want to see what's on the preceding screen, use the minus key on the numeric keypad. Similarly, if you want to see what the next few lines of text look like, use the plus key on the numeric keypad (see the preceding section).

✔ You can move to the bottom of the current page using the Go To command. Refer to "Using the Go To Command" later in this chapter.

✔ To move to the tippy top of a document, you use the Home key. Refer to "Using the Home Key" later in this chapter.

Moving to the End of the Line

Here's a quick one: To get to the end of a line of text, press the End key.

- ✔ You can move to the start of a line by using the Home key; see the next section.

- ✔ If you use the Ctrl key with the End key, you delete a line of text. Refer to Chapter 4 for more information about deleting text.

Using the Home Key

One of the handiest keys in WordPerfect is the do-nothing Home key. I say *do-nothing* because by itself the Home key does nothing. (Well, for me *home* invokes images of Mom baking cookies and her screaming at me because my stubbed toe is getting blood on the new carpet.) Yet, when used before pressing another navigation key, the Home key becomes the Big Key.

Here are the basic Home and arrow key sequences:

Home, ↑	Moves the cursor to the first line on the screen
Home, ↓	Moves the cursor to the last line on the screen
Home, ←	Moves the cursor to the start of the line
Home, →	Moves the cursor to the end of the line

Press the Home key once. Nothing happens. Then press the arrow key. Do not press and hold the Home key while you press the arrow key as you do with the Ctrl key.

- ✔ There's no key like Home.

- ✔ Home is a prefix key, the Big Key. You're telling WordPerfect, "Move *Big* in this direction."

- ✔ Home, → and the End key perform the same function (move the cursor to the end of the line).

- ✔ Home, ↑ and the minus key on the numeric keypad perform the same function (move the cursor to the top of the screen, or to the previous screen if it is already at the top of the screen).

- ✔ Home, ↓ and the plus key on the numeric keypad perform the same function (move the cursor to the bottom of the screen, or to the next screen if the cursor is already at the bottom of the screen).

Moving to the top of the document

Too many WordPerfect users press PgUp, PgUp, PgUp, and PgUp to get to the top of a document. This is akin to Captain Picard using a ladder to get to the surface of the planet when he could just beam down.

To beam to the top of a document, press these keys:

Home, Home, ↑

That is, you press the Home key twice and then press the up-arrow key. Using these keys zaps you to the very top of the document. No sweat.

Moving to the end of the document

To move to the very end of your document, press these keys:

Home, Home, ↓

That is, you press the Home key twice and then press the down-arrow key. This key sequence moves the cursor to the very end of the document.

You can use this command to see how big a document is: Press Home, Home, ↓ and then look at the number by the Pg hieroglyph at the bottom right corner of the screen. That number tells you how many pages are in the document.

Using the Go To Command

If you really want to fly around a document, then you need the handy Go To command. This command is truly wings for the cursor. To issue the Go To command, press the Ctrl and Home keys together:

Ctrl-Home

That is, press and hold the Ctrl key and press the Home key. Then release both keys. You can use this command to powerfully direct WordPerfect to move you all over the document by leaps and bounds. A dialog box appears over the heart of the screen, with the words Go to and a box for typing things in.

What can you type into the box? Try typing the following when you feel like zooming about a document:

↑ Just press the up-arrow key to zip to the top of the current page (not the screen, but the page — below the *black line of death*).

↓   Press the down-arrow key to zap to the bottom of the current page.

A number   You also can enter a page number to go to the top of that specific page. For example, press 1 and press Enter to go to the top of page 1. Or press Ctrl-Home, 5 and press Enter to see what's atop page 5.

✔ Press Esc if you change your mind and really don't want to go anywhere after you press Ctrl-Home.

✔ If you type a specific character at the Go to prompt, WordPerfect moves the cursor to the next occurrence of that character. But this is only a short-range command; WordPerfect may not find the character if it's too far away.

✔ Ctrl-Home, ↓ moves the cursor to the bottom of the current page. It is the only WordPerfect navigation command that moves you to the bottom of the current page.

Navigating with the Scroll Bar

If you love your mouse, you can use WordPerfect's graphical interface to help you traverse documents. What's needed is the Vertical Scroll Bar, which looks like a one-lane highway to the right of the document but works more like an elevator shaft (see Figure 2-2).

✔ To move the cursor up one line of text, click the mouse on the up-pointing arrow at the top of the scroll bar. (The cursor moves up, but the screen does not scroll.)

✔ To move the cursor down one line of text, click the mouse on the down-pointing arrow at the bottom of the scroll bar.

✔ In the middle of the scroll bar is an elevator button. If you compare the scroll bar's entire length to the length of the document, then the elevator button represents the part of the document that you see on the screen. (And the bigger the elevator button is, the more of the document you can see at once.)

✔ To see the previous screen of text, click on the scroll bar just above the elevator button.

✔ To see the next screen of text, click on the scroll bar just below the elevator button.

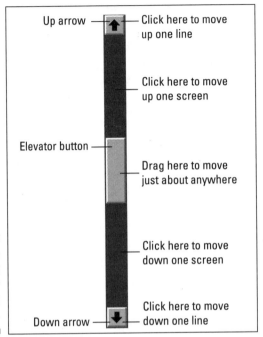

Up arrow — Click here to move up one line

Click here to move up one screen

Elevator button — Drag here to move just about anywhere

Click here to move down one screen

Click here to move down one line

Down arrow —

Figure 2-2:
The Vertical
Scroll Bar
lies in
waiting.

✔ To move to a specific position in the document, use the mouse to *drag* the elevator button up or down. The elevator button's position indicates which portion of the document you want to see.

✔ The scroll bar is not where Greek philosophers went to get drunk.

✔ If you want to make the Vertical Scroll Bar a permanent part of the WordPerfect screen, pull down the View menu and use the mouse to click on Vertical Scroll Bar. You also can press Alt-V, V.

Yup, it's kinda pointless to have the scroll bar around if you don't have a mouse. Better use the keyboard instead.

Avoiding the Useless Horizontal Scroll Bar

The Vertical Scroll Bar has merit. But WordPerfect also has a Horizontal Scroll Bar that appears on the bottom of the screen. You can use it to slide the document left and right, which is about the most useless thing I've ever heard of.

OK. Suppose that you want to view a document in Very Large mode. In that case, I can see having a Horizontal Scroll Bar. But rather than using the scroll bar, try using this tip:

The best way to view a document in WordPerfect is in the margin-to-margin mode. In that mode, you can always see all your text on the screen at the same time. To activate that mode, select the Zoom item from the View menu. A submenu appears. Select Margin Width and you'll be there.

Refer to Chapter 20 for more information on viewing your document.

Getting Unlost

Has this ever happened to you? You want to move the cursor down to the next screen, but you press PgDn rather than the plus key? Or how about that stray elbow that whacks a few cursor-control keys? You look up on the screen and discover that WordPerfect has moved itself elsewhere. Time to hunt for where you were. . . .

But wait! There's a handy trick for getting back to where you were:

Ctrl-Home, Ctrl-Home

Pressing Ctrl-Home (the Go To command) twice in a row resets the cursor to its previous position.

✔ Press and hold the Ctrl key and press the Home key. Release both keys. When the Go to dialog box appears, press the Ctrl key and press the Home key again. This key sequence moves the cursor back to its previous position.

✔ Pressing Ctrl-Home four times in a row moves you back to where you started.

✔ The Ctrl-Home, Ctrl-Home trick works great after Search and Search and Replace operations. It repositions the cursor to where it was when you started the search. This trick also works for most other commands that reposition the cursor.

Chapter 3
Using the Keyboard Correctly

In This Chapter

▶ Identifying keys on the keyboard

▶ Pressing and releasing keys

▶ Using the WordPerfect claw

▶ Knowing when to press Enter

▶ Knowing when to use the spacebar

▶ Using the Cancel key

▶ Using the Undo key

▶ Using the Undelete key

▶ Using Cut, Copy, and Paste

▶ Using the Help key

▶ Using the Repeat key

*S*ome people treat their computer keyboards as if land mines were under half the keys. But with the way things are in WordPerfect, the only way you can get anything done is by overusing the keyboard. The keys — many of them used in combination with each other — are how you make WordPerfect do its stuff.

If this chapter has a theme, it is *be bold!* WordPerfect doesn't do anything perilous unless you tell it to. Even then, it asks you a yes/no question before the dangerous something happens. You can press the handy Esc key to cancel just about anything. Think of the Esc key as a set of little high-density uranium thimbles to protect your fingers from those keyboard land mines.

Identifying Keys on the Keyboard

Welcome to Know Your Keyboard 101. Take a look at your keyboard and then take a look at Figure 3-1. Notice how the keyboard is divided into separate

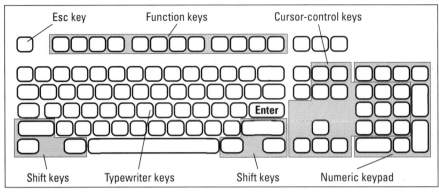

Figure 3-1:
Key locations
on an
Enhanced
Keyboard.
(The key
locations
vary on other
keyboards.)

areas, each of which has a special function. These areas are groups of keys that you use in WordPerfect — either alone or in combination with other keys:

Function keys: These keys, labeled F1 through F12, are along the top row of the keyboard. WordPerfect uses 'em all. You use those keys by themselves or in cahoots with the three different shift keys.

Typewriter keys: These keys are the standard alphanumeric keys that you find on any typewriter: A through Z, 1 through 0, plus symbols and other exotic characters.

Cursor-control keys: These are the arrow keys that move the cursor on the keyboard. Also lumped in are the Home, End, PgUp (Page Up), PgDn (Page Down), Insert, and Delete keys. Oh, and the big plus and minus keys on the keypad are counted as well.

Car keys: Don't leave them in the car. Nor should you have any exposed valuables lying about. Buy *The Club.*

Numeric keypad: These keys switch between being cursor-control keys and being numbers. Their split personality is evident on each key cap, which displays two symbols. The Num Lock key and its corresponding light are on if the numeric keypad is active. If the cursor-control keys are active, Num Lock is turned off.

Shift keys: These keys don't do anything by themselves. Instead, the Shift, Ctrl, and Alt keys are used in combination with other keys on the keyboard. In WordPerfect, all three keys are used with the 12 function keys to give WordPerfect its memorable command list.

Two individual keys worth noting are the Enter and Esc keys:

Enter: This key is marked with the word Enter and sometimes with a cryptic arrow-thing: ↵

You use the Enter key to end a paragraph of text.

Esc (Escape): The Esc key is the Cancel or *Oh no!* key in WordPerfect, but its location varies. Sometimes Esc is next to the Backspace key. Notice its location on your keyboard.

> ✔ Be thankful: A piano has 88 keys — black and white with no labels. It takes years to master these keys. A computer keyboard, by comparison, is easy to learn.

> ✔ Older PC keyboards have different layouts than the currently popular 101-key Enhanced Keyboard. Some older models have the function keys to the side of the keyboard, and some lack separate cursor-control keys. All keyboards work the same with WordPerfect, but this book assumes that you have the 101-key keyboard. (Go ahead and count 'em that baby really does have 101 keys.)

> ✔ Laptop keyboards are all goofed up. Primarily, they lack the numeric keypad. This is OK, but you'll miss the gray plus and minus keys that enable you to move up or down a screen at a time easily. As a good substitute, I recommend using the following keys instead:

Home, ↑ = keypad minus

Home, ↓ = keypad plus

Pressing and Releasing

Sorry to disappoint all you budding third-world dictators. The title of this section is "Pressing and Releasing," and it refers to entering various WordPerfect key combinations. It's not "Oppressing and Releasing," which sounds a bit liberal anyway.

WordPerfect uses key combinations to represent some commands. For example, if you press Shift-F7, you bring up the Print dialog box — which isn't really important right now. Instead, note that when I say, "Press Shift-F7," I mean "Press and hold the Shift key and then press the F7 key; then release both keys."

You use key combinations all the time. Always press and hold the first key and then press the second key. Press and release.

> ✔ You press and release key combinations just as you press Shift-F to get a capital F. It's the same thing, but with the odd Ctrl (Control) and Alt (Alternate) keys.

> ✔ Yeah, you really have to reach to get some of those function-key combinations. My advice? Use two hands. Or refer to the next section, "Using the WordPerfect Claw."

✔ You don't need to press hard. If you're having trouble working a command, pressing harder doesn't make the computer think, "Oh, lordy, she's pressing really hard now. I think she means it. Wake up, wake up!" A light touch is all that's required.

✔ Remember to release the keys. Press and hold the Shift key, press F7, and then release both keys. If you don't know which key to release first, release the second key and then release the shift key (Shift, Ctrl, or Alt).

✔ Some keys aren't used in conjunction with each other. For example, Home, ↑ moves the cursor to the top of the screen. But, because these keys are separated by a comma, you first press and release Home, and then you press the up-arrow key. If you need to press two keys together, the keys are shown in this book (and in the WordPerfect manual) with hyphens — Shift-F10, for example.

Using the WordPerfect Claw

Don't be ridiculous. No one memorizes WordPerfect commands. But WordPerfect users do remember various *claw patterns*. The claw patterns are the finger gymnastics you perform — the contortions you twist your fists into — in order to reach the various shift-function-key combinations.

For example, to press Alt-F1, I press the Alt key with the thumb on my left hand and press F1 with my middle finger. I use the same fingers for Alt-F4, but I arch them over the keyboard a bit. I press Shift-F10 with my left hand's pinky on the Shift key and my right hand's index finger on the F10 key.

As you use WordPerfect, you become familiar with your own personal claw patterns. After a while, you rely on them more than on the keyboard template or the Help key.

✔ It's OK to use two hands for your various claw patterns. Notice that the three shift keys are on both sides of the standard PC typewriter keyboard.

✔ Various WordPerfect users *claw* each other when they meet. For example, I hold up my hand in the Shift-F5 Date command pattern, and a fellow WordPerfect person tells me the current date.

✔ You don't need to memorize claw patterns if you use the menus. All WordPerfect commands are on the menus and are easily visible. Chapter 18 is the WordPerfect menu information fun booth.

Knowing When to Press Enter

On an electric typewriter, you press the Return key when you reach the end of a line. With a word processor, you need to press Enter only when you reach the end of a paragraph.

The reason you don't press Enter at the end of each line is that WordPerfect *word wraps* to the next line any words hanging over the right margin. Therefore, you need to press Enter only at the end of a paragraph, although having a short paragraph of just one line of text by itself is still OK.

- ✔ Some people end a paragraph by pressing Enter twice; others press Enter only once.

- ✔ If you want to indent the next paragraph, press the Tab key after pressing Enter. This feature works just like it does on a typewriter.

- ✔ If you want to double-space a paragraph, you need to use a special line-formatting command, which is covered in Chapter 10. You do not double-space lines with the Enter key.

- ✔ If you press the Enter key in the middle of an existing paragraph, WordPerfect inserts a new paragraph, moving the rest of the text to the start of the next line. Inserting the Enter key is just like inserting any other key into the text. The difference is that you insert an Enter character, which creates a new paragraph.

- ✔ You can delete the Enter character by using the Backspace or Delete key. Removing the Enter character joins two paragraphs together. If you press Enter more than once between paragraphs, deleting an Enter character cleans up any extra blank lines.

Knowing When to Use the Spacebar

A major error committed by many WordPerfect users is to mistakenly use the spacebar rather than the Tab key. Allow me to clear the air on this one:

- ✔ Use the spacebar to insert space characters such as you'd find between words or between sentences. You need to press the spacebar only once between each word or sentence, but some former touch typists (myself included) put two spaces between sentences. That's fine.

- ✔ To indent, line up columns of information, or organize what you see on the screen, you need to use the Tab key. The Tab key indents text to an exact position. When you print, everything is lined up nicely and neatly, which doesn't happen with space characters.

✔ If you're using Courier or another *monospaced* font, then spaces and tabs will line up, just as you see them on the screen. But most of the time you print in a fancier font. In that situation, nothing will line up if you use spaces where tabs should be; the document will look gross, and you'll shyly admit that you should have paid attention here.

✔ Use the Tab key to indent. Use the spacebar only to put spaces between words and paragraphs. I'm serious: Do not use the spacebar to indent or line up text. Your stuff will look tacky, tacky, tacky if you do.

✔ The Tab key and spacebar give different results because the tab character moves the cursor to a specific *tab stop.* The space character moves the cursor over a fraction of an inch. The results look the same on the screen, but they look different when you print the document because the space is much thinner than what you see on the screen.

✔ To set tab stops in WordPerfect, refer to Chapter 10.

Using the Cancel Key

The *Whoops! I wish hadn't done that* key in WordPerfect is Escape, which is labeled Esc on the keyboard. This key is powerful. When you press it, it stops whatever it was you did — blows off menus, zaps away dialog boxes, and forgives you for accidentally deleting any text.

Meaningless information about the Enter and Return keys

Enter or Return? Some keyboards label the Enter key *Return.* Most PCs use the word *Enter;* even so, some yahoos may call it the Return key. Why? (You really have to be hard up for trivia if you continue to read this stuff.)

The reason has to do with the computer's background. On a typewriter, the key is named Return. It comes from the preelectric days of typewriters, when you had to whack the carriage-return bar to move the paper over to the other margin so you could continue typing. From the computer's calculator background comes the use of the Enter key to enter a formula into the calculator. This is why some computers can't make up their mind whether it's the Enter or Return key. My keyboard says Enter on that key — in two places. So that's what I use in this book.

✔ Pressing Esc is the same as selecting a button with Cancel on it in a dialog box.

✔ Press Esc if you change your mind about using a menu command and want to get back to working on a document.

✔ Pressing the right mouse button (the one you don't usually click) has the same results as using the Cancel key — most of the time. If there's nothing to cancel, then pressing the right mouse button excites (I prefer the word *agitates*) the menu bar, highlighting File.

✔ Esc is also the Undelete key. It works in the Undelete mode when you're editing text and not attempting to use a WordPerfect command. Refer to "Using the Undelete Key" later in this chapter.

✔ Esc is the Cancel key in most DOS programs and in Windows. Get used to jabbing at it.

Using the Undo Key

Be bold! Why not? WordPerfect has a handy Undo key. Anything you do — *anything* — can be undone quickly with the handy Undo key, Ctrl-Z. Foul up a format? Undo it! Delete a massive swath of text? Undo it! Forget to file your income taxes? Hey, press Ctrl-Z all you want (but I doubt it will help you).

To undo something, first do something bad or something you didn't want to do. Then your next immediate step must be to use Ctrl-Z. Press and hold Ctrl and press Z. Release both keys. Whatever you did will be undone, saving you from certain embarrassment.

✔ You have to be quick with Ctrl-Z. Undo undoes only the last command you typed. If you edit more text, use another command, or exit WordPerfect, then Undo can't help you.

✔ You cannot undo printing or saving a file to disk; nor can you use Ctrl-Z to patch up a bad relationship or take back anything nasty you've said.

✔ To undelete text, you should really use the Undelete key, which is described in the next section.

✔ If you use Undo to restore deleted text, that text reappears in the document at the same spot it was deleted from. To restore the deleted text to another location, use the Undelete key.

✔ You also can select the Undo command from the Edit menu to undo any forbidden or heinous thing you've done.

✔ If the Undo key doesn't work, chances are some bozo has turned it off. (Maybe you, accidentally. No?) To turn it on, press Shift-F1, E, 4. When you press the 4 key, make sure that the box by the words `Allow Undo` has an X in it. If not, press 4 again. Press Enter twice to return to the document.

Using the Undelete Key

Better than the Undo key is the Undelete key. If you're like me, then you probably spend more time deleting text and changing your mind than you do making a formatting *faux pas*. And better than Undo, the Undelete key remembers the last three things you deleted, not just the last thing.

To undelete any text you've just accidentally zapped, press Esc, 1.

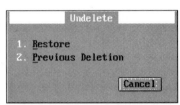

Figure 3-2:
The
Undelete
dialog box.

When you press Esc, you see a dialog box floating in the center of the screen, as shown in Figure 3-2. Also on the screen, you see the last text you deleted. The text is highlighted and stuck at the cursor's current position. To restore the text at that position, press 1.

Often, what you see highlighted is not the text you remembered deleting. If so, press 2. You then see the next-to-the-last thing you deleted. If that still isn't what you want, press 2 again to see the next-to-the-next-to-the-last thing you deleted. Unfortunately, that's as far back as the Undelete key remembers.

✔ The Esc key undeletes only text. Pressing Esc doesn't restore anything to a previous condition. Nor does it undo any formatting or font changes. You need the Undo key (Ctrl-Z) for those tasks.

✔ If you're viewing a menu or dialog box, then the Esc key works as the Cancel key. Only when you're editing text is it the Undelete key. In a way, this makes sense; if you're editing text and you delete something, pressing Esc to *cancel* is logical. Then again, the word *escape* always conjures up an image of WordPerfect's vanishing from my monitor and running away through one of the holes in the back of the computer.

✔ The Undelete key remembers only the last three chunks of text you deleted. Often, and to much chagrin, three chunks isn't enough. For example, you may find a lot of little bits of text and single characters — not that previous paragraph you mistakenly murdered. Undelete remembers each single character deletion as well as the big-chunk deletions. If the stuff you want can't be found, then it's lost forever. (Sniff, sniff.)

✔ You can also undelete text by selecting the Undelete command from the Edit menu.

Using the Kindergarten Keys: Cut, Copy, and Paste

Cutting, copying, and pasting text are covered in Chapter 6. However, three of the keys you use to perform those feats are covered here because by the time you get to Chapter 6, this stuff won't make any sense. The three keys are

Cut   Ctrl-X

Copy   Ctrl-C

Paste Ctrl-V

Now, Copy as Ctrl-C I can understand. *C* is Copy. But Cut is Ctrl-X? And Paste is Ctrl-V? Yeah. Looks like they put all the *English as your second language* new hires in the Keyboard Department at WordPerfect Corporation.

The truth is, these keys are quite common and appear in several programs to represent the Cut, Copy, and Paste commands. The logic here is that all three keys are together on the keyboard. Go head and look at your keyboard now. Or refer to Figure 3-3.

Figure 3-3:
How the kindergarten keys line up.

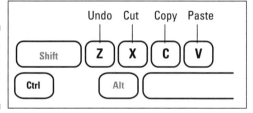

Using the Help Key

The handiest key on the keyboard is F1, the Help key. Here are some tips for using it in your fleeting moments of panic:

✔ When you're doing something, press F1 to display helpful information on options available for the something you're doing. If you're just editing text, F1 displays the help system, an overview of all the help WordPerfect has to offer.

✔ In the help system, you can double-click on any blue word with the mouse to get more information on that word. Or use the arrow keys to highlight the blue word and press Enter.

✔ Press F1 and select the blue word Template to see the detailed WordPerfect keyboard template. The template tells you which commands are associated with which function keys, plus various Shift, Ctrl, Alt, and Left-Foot Pedal combinations for each function key.

✔ Press F1 and select the blue word Index to see a complete list of WordPerfect's commands. Use the up-arrow or down-arrow key or PgUp and PgDn to peruse the list. Or press N to activate the Name Search command and then type the first few letters of the command you need help with. You'll be instantly beamed to that part of the list. Highlight the command that's puzzling you and press Enter to see what, if any, help WordPerfect has to offer.

✔ Press Esc (yes, the Cancel key) to exit the help system and return to the document.

Using the Repeat Key

Here's a weird one: WordPerfect has a special repeat key. You can use it to repeat a certain command or a specific character over and over. Need 40 hyphens? Let the repeat key do the work and stop woodpeckering your keyboard. Oh, this can be handy.

The repeat key is Ctrl-R. *R,* of course, stands for "Do this several times." After you press the Ctrl-R Repeat key, a dialog box is plastered on the screen. It looks like the one shown in Figure 3-4. Ignore the dialog box! Instead, press the key you want repeated. Here are examples:

Ctrl-R, →	This command moves the cursor right eight places.
Ctrl-R, Ctrl-←	This command moves the cursor left eight words.
Ctrl-R, PgUp	This command moves the cursor eight pages up in the document.
Ctrl-R, Delete	This command deletes the next eight characters.
Ctrl-R, Ctrl-End	This command deletes the next eight lines of text.
Ctrl-R, *	This command displays eight asterisks.

You can change the repeat value from 8 to any number from 1 up to several hundred if you like. You can change it on the fly or permanently. For on-the-fly changes, type the value when you see the dialog box and then type the cursor-control key, command, or letter you want repeated. Here are some examples:

Ctrl-R, 10, -   This command displays ten hyphens.

Ctrl-R, 5, Ctrl-Backspace   This command deletes the next five words.

Ctrl-R, 100, ↓   This command moves down 100 lines.

Press Ctrl-R, press a number, and press a command, cursor-control key, or letter. (Don't type in the comma above; the comma just marks where the number ends and the command, cursor-control key, or letter begins.)

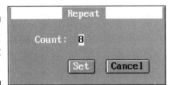

Figure 3-4:
The Repeat
dialog box.

To change the repeat value permanently, press Ctrl-R, type the new value, and then press Enter:

Ctrl-R, 10, Enter   This command changes the repeat key's repeat value to 10.

Ctrl-R, 40, Enter   This command changes the repeat value to 40.

Ctrl-R, 8, Enter   This command changes the repeat value back to 8.

✔ The Repeat key can be followed by all four arrow keys, the Ctrl-arrow keys, PgUp, PgDn, Delete, Delete word, Delete to end of line, Delete to end of page, and the Macro key. It also can be followed by any individual character.

✔ The Repeat key doesn't work with the Enter or Backspace key. And you can't use it to repeat a number key.

✔ Creating forms? Set the Repeat key to a large value — perhaps 40. Then use Ctrl-R and the underline character to create all the blanks for the *fill in the blanks* items.

✔ I use the Repeat key with the arrow keys to position the cursor in the middle of a large word.

Chapter 4
Deleting and Destroying Text

. . . .

In This Chapter

▶ Understanding insert and typeover modes

▶ Using the basic delete keys: Backspace and Delete

▶ Playing with the mystery delete grab bag

▶ Deleting a word

▶ Deleting to the end of the line

▶ Deleting to the end of the page

▶ Deleting odd shapes with blocks

▶ Undeleting

. . . .

*N*othing gives you such a satisfying feeling as blowing away text — especially if you're editing someone else's document. Of course, most of the destroying and deleting that goes on in WordPerfect is minor stuff: You delete that extra *e* in *potato,* slay a word here, and yank out a sentence there. It's much easier than using White Out on paper. Because you delete text on the screen, deletion occurs quickly and painlessly in the electronic ether. No mess, no white goop, and if you change your mind, WordPerfect has a nifty Undelete command to bring your text back to glowing phosphorescent perfection.

Understanding Insert and Typeover Modes

The Insert key on the keyboard controls WordPerfect's two methods of putting text on the screen. Normally, new text is inserted at the cursor position, just before the flashing toothpick. Any new text that you type appears at the cursor's position, pushing any existing text to the right and down as you type. This setup is called *insert mode.*

If you press the Insert key, you enter *typeover mode.* Typeover appears in the lower left of the screen. Any text you type in typeover mode overwrites any existing text.

If you press Insert again, `Typeover` disappears from the screen, and you're back in insert mode.

- ✔ The Insert key appears in two places on the 101-key Enhanced Keyboard: on the 0 key on the keypad (where you see *Ins*) and on a key that is just to the right of the Backspace key (where you see *Insert*). Both keys perform the same function.

- ✔ The new characters you type in insert mode appear right above the flashing cursor. Then the cursor moves to the right, awaiting the next character you type.

- ✔ `Typeover` in the lower left corner of the screen means that you are in typeover mode. Any new text you type will overwrite existing text. I point this out because a stray finger or elbow can press the Insert key and put you in the typeover mode when you don't want to be in it.

- ✔ Leaving WordPerfect in insert mode all the time is a safe bet. If you need to overwrite (replace) something, just type in the new text and then delete the old text.

- ✔ You can get back any text you've overwritten in typeover mode by using the Undelete key, Esc. See "Undeleting" at the end of this chapter.

Using the Basic Delete Keys: Backspace and Delete

You can use two keys on the keyboard to delete single characters of text:

- ✔ The Backspace key deletes the character to the left of the cursor.

- ✔ The Delete key deletes the character to the right of the cursor.

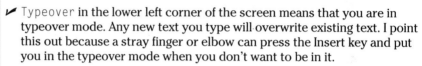

In the preceding text, the toothpick cursor is *flashing* before the *s* in *those*. (Trust me, it's flashing.) Pressing the Backspace key deletes the *o* in *those*; pressing the Delete key deletes the *s*.

- ✔ After you delete a character, any text after the character moves up to fill in the void.

- ✔ If you're in typeover mode, the Backspace key does not pull the rest of the text to the right. Instead, pressing Backspace replaces the character deleted with a space character and moves the cursor one notch to the left.

✔ Backspace works like the Backspace key on a typewriter. The difference is that when you press Backspace in WordPerfect, it backs up and erases. (The WordPerfect equivalent of the typewriter's Backspace key is the left-arrow key.)

✔ You can press and hold either Backspace or Delete to continuously *machine gun delete* characters. Release the key to stop your wanton destructive rampage.

Playing with the Mystery Delete Grab Bag

There's more to a WordPerfect document than what you see on the screen. Lots of hidden, secret codes are littered about the document. These codes change the font, center text, and bold, italicize, underline, and format the document. You don't see these codes on the screen, but you see their effects.

When you press the Delete or Backspace key, you may stumble over one of these codes. For example, you may be sitting there one day, making yourself happy by deleting text, when a dialog box pops up and asks the question

```
Delete [Bold On]?
```

The stuff in square brackets is the secret code you encountered while pressing the Backspace or Delete key. In this example, the code is the [Bold] code, which WordPerfect uses to mark the start of bold text in a document. In real life, you may see a variety of secret codes displayed, depending on how you formatted the document.

If you press Y in response to this question, you delete the secret code. Press N to leave it intact. My advice? Press N.

✔ Don't be surprised by the mystery codes in the document. You put them there as you create and format your text.

✔ If you dislike this feature, you can turn it off. Press Shift-F1, E, W. This action switches off the WordPerfect 5.1 Cursor Movement option (removing the little X in its box). When the X is gone, WordPerfect will no longer warn you when it deletes the secret codes. Press the F7 key twice to return to your document.

✔ To see the strange codes as they lie buried in your document, press Alt-F3. This action pops up a window at the bottom of your document that shows you all sorts of junk you can't see when you're editing. Press Alt-F3 again to make the ugliness go away.

Deleting Text

Backspace and Delete are OK for minor destruction. But for devastation on a larger scale, you need to rely on other, more powerful — almost nuclear — commands. With only a few quickie pecks at the keys, you can annihilate vast stretches of text — from whole words, to lines, to pages, to every written document in human history. (Actually, at the last minute they cut the Delete Every Written Document command out of the program.)

Deleting a word

WordPerfect enables you to gobble up entire words at a time by using one of two Delete Word commands:

Ctrl-Backspace   This is the traditional Delete Word command.

Ctrl-Delete   This is an alternative Delete Word command, popular in European countries.

To delete a word with Ctrl-Backspace, position the cursor at the first letter of the word or at any other letter in the word. Press Ctrl-Backspace and the word is gone! The cursor then sits at the start of the next word or at the end of the line (if you deleted the last word in a paragraph).

✔ Both of these key commands perform the same function. Most people use Ctrl-Backspace. Ctrl-Delete has another function when used with blocks; refer to Chapter 6.

✔ If the cursor is positioned on the space character between two words, Ctrl-Backspace deletes the word to the right.

Other ways (that you don't need to know about) to delete words

You have two additional ways to delete words in WordPerfect, both of which involve the handy Home key:

Home, Backspace   This command deletes from the cursor position to the start of the word.

Home, Delete   This command deletes from the cursor position to the end of the word.

These two commands are effective only when the toothpick cursor is hiding in the middle of a word.

✔ When the cursor is positioned in a sea of spaces, Ctrl-Backspace deletes the spaces up to the next word to the right.

✔ To delete several words at a time, use the Repeat key, Ctrl-R, before pressing Ctrl-Backspace. Refer to Chapter 3 for information on the Repeat key.

Deleting to the end of the line

WordPerfect does not have a command that deletes a line of text (at least, not a single command). Instead, it has a handy command that deletes from the cursor's position to the end of a line: Ctrl-End.

The Ctrl-End command deletes from where you are to the end of the line.

✔ This command does not delete to the end of a paragraph. If you have any additional text in the paragraph, it wraps up to the space after the cursor and replaces the deleted text.

✔ Ctrl-Home is the Go To command. Refer to the discussion of the Go To command in Chapter 3.

✔ Unfortunately, no command deletes from where you are to the beginning of the line. Think of how handy a command like that would be in the Post Office or at the bank.

✔ OK, to delete a complete line of text, first move the cursor to the start of the line with Home, ←. Then press Ctrl-End. The keystrokes are as follows:

Home, ←, Ctrl-End

These keystrokes delete a whole line of text.

Deleting to the end of the page

To delete all the text from the cursor's position to the end of the page, use the Delete to End of Page command: Ctrl-PgDn.

After you press Ctrl-PgDn (you can use either of the Page Down keys), a dialog box flies on the screen from nowhere and asks, `Delete remainder of page?` Press Y to delete text from the cursor's position to the end of the page; press Enter or N — and go "Whew!" — to avoid deleting the text.

✔ Of all the delete commands, I seem to stumble over this one the most often. Thankfully, any key but Y prevents the text from being deleted. And if you do accidentally delete text, you can use the Undelete key (Esc) to bring it back; refer to "Undeleting" at the end of this chapter.

> ✔ The *end of page* is defined as all the text from the cursor's position to just above the *line of death* across the screen that WordPerfect uses to identify the end of the page. If you don't have quite a full page, then Ctrl-PgDn deletes to the end of the document.

Deleting odd shapes with blocks

WordPerfect can delete characters, words, lines, and to the end of the page all by itself. To delete anything else, you need to mark the text to be axed as a *block* of text and then delete the block.

The 5th Wave   By Rich Tennant

Real WordPerfect Gurus

Real WordPerfect Gurus don't die; they simply "DELETE" themselves from society.

To delete a block of text, follow these steps:

1. **Mark the block**.

   Move the toothpick cursor to the start of the block, press Alt-F4 to start the block, and then use the arrow keys to move the cursor to the end of the block.

2. **Press the Delete key.**

   The block has been destroyed!

- ✔ You also can use the Backspace key to delete a block after you mark it.

- ✔ More information on marking blocks is found in Chapter 6.

- ✔ Marking a block with the mouse is easy: Just move the mouse pointer to the start of the block, press and hold the mouse button, and *drag* the mouse to the end of the block. Release the mouse button, and the block is marked.

- ✔ I don't recommend using the mouse to mark large blocks of text. This method can prove unwieldy and sluggishly slow. Use the keyboard instead or use the Select command in the Edit menu. Chapter 6 has all the details.

- ✔ Deleting blocks can be deadly! Remember the Undelete key if you make a mistake or quickly use the Undo command (Ctrl-Z) to get your block back.

- ✔ If you want to cut a block and move it elsewhere in the document, refer to the section in Chapter 6 on cutting and then pasting a block.

Undeleting

Deleting text can be traumatic — especially for the timid WordPerfect beginner. But editing is editing, and mistakes happen. If you want some of your freshly deleted text back, you can use the Undelete command, which you access through the handy Esc key. It usually works like this:

1. **Panic!**

   Oh, lordy! I just deleted cousin Jimmy from the will!

2. **Press the Esc key.**

   The text you just deleted appears at the cursor's position, highlighted (like a block). A dialog box, horning its way to the center of the screen, gives you two Undelete options: 1. Restore and 2. Previous Deletion.

3. **If you want to restore that text, press 1, for Restore (you also can press R).**

   Cousin Jimmy should be back in the money.

4. **If the highlighted text isn't what you want, press 2 (or P) for Previous Deletion.**

WordPerfect shows you the next-to-the-last thing you deleted. Press 1 (or R) to restore that text.

5. **If you still don't like what you see, press 2 (or P) again.**

WordPerfect shows you the next-to-the-next-to-the-last thing you deleted. Press 1 (or R) if you want WordPerfect to restore that text.

If you still don't see what you deleted, then it's long gone. The Undelete command remembers only the last three things that you deleted.

✔ The Undelete command works for anything you delete, no matter which delete command you used.

✔ The Undelete key is also the Cancel key. You use it to back out of menus, to cancel yes/no questions, and as a general panic key.

✔ The Undelete command does not reverse formatting or font changes. To undo those kinds of changes, use the Undo key, Ctrl-Z.

✔ After WordPerfect shows you the next-to-the-next-to-the-last thing you deleted, if you press 2 again, the program again shows you the last thing you deleted.

✔ The amount of text that the Undelete command remembers as one deletion is anything that you delete with any delete command up until the point when you type in new text, use a cursor-control key, or enter a WordPerfect command. Therefore, pressing Home, Backspace four times to delete four words is considered one chunk of deleted text by the Undelete key.

✔ You need to be quick with the Undelete key. It remembers only the last three things you deleted — everything from single characters to full pages and more.

Chapter 5
Searching and Replacing

*L*ittle Bo Peep has lost her sheep. Too bad she doesn't know about WordPerfect's Search and Replace commands. She could find the misplaced ruminants in a matter of microseconds. Not only that, but she could search and replace — maybe replace all the sheep with yellow Mazda Miatas. It's all really cinchy after you force the various purposes of the F2 key into your head. Sadly, only words are replaced. True, if WordPerfect could search and replace real things, there would be a lot fewer sheep in the world.

Finding Text

WordPerfect can locate any bit of text anywhere in a document. Well, not really. It can locate text above the cursor position or below the cursor position — one way or the other, but not both. One WordPerfect command looks for text down from the cursor position, and another command looks for text up from the cursor position. After all, Bo Peep can look in only one direction at any given time. Why should WordPerfect be any different?

Finding text down

The first, and most common, text-searching command in WordPerfect is the Search Down command, which finds text from the cursor's position to the end of the document. Here's how the Search Down key, F2, works:

1. **Think of some text you want to find.**

   For example, you decide to look for *sheep.*

2. **Press the F2 key.**

   The F2 key tells WordPerfect to *search from here to thither,* where *here* means *where the cursor is* and *thither* means *the end of the document.* After you press F2, you see the Search dialog box, which is shown in Figure 5-1.

3. **Type the text you want to find.**

   For example, type **sheep.** You can type the text in lowercase, mixed case, or uppercase. Whatever the case, WordPerfect always finds the match. (Read the technical information in the box about finding uppercase and lowercase text — if you dare.)

4. **Press F2 again to start the search.**

   If any text is found, it appears in the middle of the screen. The cursor is positioned right after the matching text. (If only Miss Peep could find her stray ovines this easily!)

   ✔ Type the text you want to find exactly as you think it appears in the document. Do not end the text with a period unless you want to find the period too.

   ✔ Oops! If you press Enter after you type the text, you need to press Enter a second time to start the search. (This is why the instructions recommend pressing F2 a second time to start the search.)

   ✔ If the text isn't found, you see Not found in the dialog box. Alas. You can try again or just accept the fact that the text doesn't exist and continue with your daily struggle.

   ✔ Tiny-handed people will appreciate that you also can access the Search command from the Edit menu. It appears as →Search.

```
┌─────────────────────────── Search ───────────────────────────┐
│                                                               │
│   Search For: │sheep_                                       │ │
│                                                               │
│   ☐ Backward Search          ☐ Find Whole Words Only          │
│   ☐ Case Sensitive Search    ☐ Extended Search (Hdrs, Ftrs, etc.)│
│                                                               │
│   [ Codes... F5 ] [ Specific Codes... Shft+F5 ]  [ Search F2 ] [ Cancel ]│
└───────────────────────────────────────────────────────────────┘
```

- ✔ The Search dialog box appears instantly when you click on the Search button in the Button Bar — the first button from the right on my screen.

- ✔ To find any additional occurrences of the text, press the F2 key twice: F2, F2. You press it twice because if you've previously searched for text, that text appears in the Search dialog box when you press F2. You can use the cursor-control keys to move around the text if you want to edit it.

- ✔ If WordPerfect can't find the text, consider using the Search Up command, which is discussed in the next section. Also check to make sure that you searched for the text in lowercase.

- ✔ To search the entire document, start at the top. Press the following keys to move to the top of the document:

  > Home, Home ↑

  These keystrokes position you at the tippy top of the document. From there, you can use the Search Down command, F2, to search through all the text.

- ✔ To return to where you started searching for text, use the Go To, Go To command. Press Ctrl-Home twice in a row: Ctrl-Home, Ctrl-Home.

- ✔ To cancel the Search Down command and return to the document, press the Cancel key, Esc.

- ✔ My sister, who is a veterinarian, tells me that most ruminants are ungulates. She says, "A ruminant is an animal with a four-part stomach, which contains a population of bacteria and protozoa capable of fermenting cellulose to utilizable nutrient substances." In other words, a sheep.

Annoyingly technical information on finding uppercase and lowercase text

WordPerfect finds any matching text in the document. But when you need to find text of a specific case, say *Sheep* versus *sheep* or *SHEEP,* then you need to tell WordPerfect to get picky. Just click in the little box by Case Sensitive Search in the Search dialog box. An *X* appears in the little box, and then WordPerfect only matches exactly what you type.

You can activate a Case Sensitive Search from the keyboard by pressing Enter after you type the search text and then pressing 2. (The number *2* appears next to Case Sensitive Search.)

Finding text up

Just like the reverse button on a VCR's remote, WordPerfect's Search command has a backward mode. The standard F2 Search Down command searches down, but the Shift-F2 Search Up command searches from the cursor's position to the top of the document. This command isn't as popular as the Search Down command, and yet both commands work the same way:

1. **Think of some text you want to find.**

   Think of something from a few pages back. For example, search for *ungulate* to look for a hoofed mammal.

2. **Press the Shift-F2 key.**

   Shift-F2 works just like F2, except it means *Search from here to hither*, where *hither* means *the start of the document.* After you press Shift-F2, you see the same Search dialog box that is shown in Figure 5-1. The difference is that the little box by Backward Search is checked, meaning that WordPerfect is now looking over its shoulder.

3. **Type in the text you want to find.**

   For example, type **ungulate** for a hoofed mammal.

4. **Press F2 to start the search.**

   Or press Shift-F2 if you like. Either way, the F2 key starts the search.

   If WordPerfect finds the text, it appears in the middle of the screen, with the cursor blinking at the end of the matching text.

   ✔ Note that you only need to press F2 to start the search, although Shift-F2 works as well. As with the Search Down command, avoid the temptation to start the search by pressing Enter.

   ✔ If WordPerfect can't find the text, you see Not found in a teeny dialog box.

   ✔ All other rules and regulations for finding text down apply to finding text up. Refer to the finding text down section for details.

   ✔ Most ungulates are herbivorous, and many are horned.

Finding the next matching text

If you want to continue looking for the same matching text after the initial find, press the F2 key twice:

   F2, F2

Or, if you're looking in the upward direction, press Shift-F2 and then F2:

   Shift-F2, F2

You don't need to press Shift-F2 a second time; F2 works fine and keeps the direction upward.

To find all the occurrences of a bit of text at once, perhaps to count the total number of *sheep* in the document, refer to "Using Replace to count your sheep" later in this chapter.

Finding secret codes and weird stuff

Laced throughout a document are secret codes and printing instructions. You don't see these codes on the screen, but they affect how the document looks and is printed. Basically, you can search for secret commands such as Bold, Underline, and Italics, and special characters, such as Enter and Tab, as you search for any other text.

To search for a secret code, you press the proper Search command: either F2 to search from the cursor's position to the end of the document or Shift-F2 to search from the cursor's position upward.

When the Search dialog box appears, you need to press F5 or click with the mouse on the Codes button. Another dialog box appears (see Figure 5-2), from which you can select secret codes to search for.

For example, suppose that you want to search for the next Tab character. To do so, press F5 at the dialog box you see in Figure 5-2 and look for Tab in the list. (You can press T to get there quickly.) When Tab is highlighted, press Enter or click on the Select button with the mouse. [Tab (all)] appears in the Search dialog box. [Tab (all)] is the way WordPerfect represents the Tab character.

Press F2 to search for the character or formatting command.

- ✔ Searching for codes isn't as necessary with WordPerfect 6.0 as it was with previous versions. You can see what's happening right on the screen, so the need to hunt for hidden codes is less. My advice is to use your eyeballs to look for things on the screen that you don't like and then use the formatting commands covered in Part II of this book to change them.

- ✔ The Search Codes dialog box contains way too many codes and secret commands, most of which are hopelessly cryptic. Table 5-1 lists the most common ones.

- ✔ The formatting commands have On and Off codes. When a word is marked in **bold,** it starts with a [Bold On] code and ends with a [Bold Off] code. All this secret stuff is hidden inside the document, but you can see it right on the screen.

- ✔ To search for the Enter key, such as you'd find at the end of a paragraph, you need to look for HRt, which means *hard return*.

Table 5-1	Common Codes and Secret Commands	
Key/Command	*Search Code*	*Symbol*
Bold text	Bold On	[Bold On]
	Bold Off	[Bold Off]
Enter	HRt	[HRt]
Hard page	HPg	[HPg]
Hyphen (-)	- Hyphen	[- Hyphen]
Italic text	Italc On	[Italc On]
	Italc Off	[Italc Off]
Page break	HRt-SPg	[HRt-SPg]
	SRt-SPg	[SRt-SPg]
Tab	Tab (all)	[Tab (all)]
Underline text	Und On	[Und On]
	Und Off	[Und Off]

✔ You also use the Shift-F5 key to look for secret codes. The difference is that you use Shift-F5 to look mainly for formatting codes. For example, to look for a line spacing code, you press Shift-F5 and then search for Ln Spacing in the list that appears. When you select Ln Spacing, yet another dialog box appears, asking you to enter the specific spacing command that you're searching for.

Finding random and variable text

The sour part about the Search command is that it's so darn precise. I'm an awful speller, so when I need to search for the word *performance,* first I need to look up how it's spelled, and then I can type it into the Search dialog box. Isn't this the time-consuming stuff that computers were supposed to help us avoid?

Why bother with this explanation when something good is on TV right now?

When WordPerfect wraps a line of text, it inserts what it calls a *soft return,* which is [SRt], in case you want to look for one using the Search command. The softness comes from WordPerfect's capability to juggle words in a paragraph so that the text continues to fit on the page after you edit it. The hard return [HRt] produced by the Enter key is a definite *I want a new paragraph* command.

To skirt around the precision issue, you can use one of the Search command's *wildcard* place holders. For example, to search for *performance* when you don't know whether it starts with *per* or *pre,* you tell WordPerfect to look for *p*formance.*

The asterisk (*) in *p*formance* stands for any possible letter combination. As long as the word starts with *P* and ends in *formance,* WordPerfect can find it. But you don't type the asterisk directly at the keyboard. Instead, you use the following steps from the Search dialog box to insert it:

1. **Start typing the text you want to look for, the part you know about, such as the *P* in *performance.***

2. **Press F5.**

   The Search Codes dialog box appears.

3. **Press the down-arrow key to highlight * (Many Chars) and then press Enter.**

   The [*] thing is inserted into the dialog box.

4. **Type the rest of the word or the text you want to look for.**

5. **Press F2 to start the search.**

   WordPerfect locates the first matching text it can find.

   ✔ This trick also works for complete sentences. For example, you can search for *Little Bo Peep has lost her [*],* and WordPerfect finds any matching sentence — no matter what the errant shepherdess lost.

   ✔ You need to press F5 and select * (Many Chars) from the list to make this trick work. Typing an asterisk or [*] into the dialog box directs WordPerfect to look for exactly those characters, which isn't what you want.

Using Super Find

Amazing things are hidden inside a WordPerfect document. You can search for the secret and hidden codes using the basic Search commands. But if you want to search through such things as headers, footers, footnotes, end notes, and the mysterious text boxes, you need to use the Super Find command. (Hum triumphant theme music here.)

Using Super Find is a cinch. You use the Super Find command the same way you use F2 and Shift-F2. The difference is that before you press either of those keys, you press the Home key. Yes, Home boosts the power of the normal Search commands. It's akin to having Captain Picard say, "Put sensors on maximum."

Here are the Super Find commands:

Home, F2   This is the super find down command.

Home, Shift-F2 This is the super find up command.

- ✔ The Super Find command works the same way that the regular Search commands work. The only difference is that text in the header, footer, footnotes, end notes, text boxes, captions — all the text, everything — is searched, in addition to the text in the document.

- ✔ You also can use Super Find with the Replace command, Alt-F2. Just press the Home key before you press Alt-F2 to have WordPerfect search and replace through headers, footers, and so on.

- ✔ To use the Super Find command to search through an entire document, press these keys:

Home, Home, ↑, Home, F2

The cursor moves to the top of the document, and then the search begins. If the text is in the document, WordPerfect finds it.

- ✔ Refer to "Finding text down" earlier in this chapter for details on how the Search command works.

Searching for and Replacing Text

Searching and replacing is the art of finding a bit of text and replacing it with something else. This happens all the time. For example, you can replace the word *goat* with *caprine* (yet another ungulate). WordPerfect does it in a snap, using the Alt-F2, Replace command.

1. **Position the cursor where you want to start searching for text.**

   The search always happens from the cursor's position *down* to the end of the document.

2. **Press Alt-F2, the Replace command.**

   You see the Search and Replace dialog box, which looks very much like the Search dialog box, but it has an extra box for entering text (see Figure 5-2).

3. **Into the Search For input box, type the text you want to find and replace with something else.**

4. **Press Enter.**

   Attention moves to the Replace With text box.

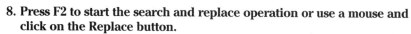

Figure 5-2:
The Search
and
Replace
dialog box.

```
                              Search and Replace
     Search For:    |_                                              |

     Replace With:  |<Nothing>                                      |

          [ ] Confirm Replacement        [ ] Find Whole Words Only
          [ ] Backward Search            [ ] Extended Search (Hdrs, Ftrs, etc.)
          [ ] Case Sensitive Search      [ ] Limit Number of Matches:

     [ Codes... F5 ]  [ Specific Codes... Shft+F5 ]    [ Replace F2 ]  [ Cancel ]
```

5. Type the text you want to use as a replacement.

For example, if you're replacing *goat* with *caprine,* you type **caprine** here.
Type it exactly the way you want it — no quotes, no period (unless you're
replacing with those characters).

6. Press Enter.

**7. Attention shifts to the many options in the dialog box, every one of
which now has a number by it.**

Don't get lost in the sea of options.

One option worth Xing in is Confirm Replacement, number 3. Press 3 to
put an X in that box if you want WordPerfect to ask you Yes or No every
time it's about to replace text in the document.

**8. Press F2 to start the search and replace operation or use a mouse and
click on the Replace button.**

☛ WordPerfect displays `Please wait` as it scans for text.

☛ If the mouse is glued to your hand, you can access the Replace command
from the Edit menu. It appears as →Replace.

☛ When you first see the Search and Replace dialog box, any previously
searched-for text appears in the Search For text box. Edit the text, if you
like, or type in new text. (You also can enter secret codes to search for;
refer to "Finding secret codes and weird stuff" earlier in this chapter.)

☛ If no text can be found for replacement, WordPerfect displays the Not
Found dialog box. Press Esc to return to the document for editing.

☛ If you direct WordPerfect to confirm each text replacement, then it stops
each time it finds the Search For text, highlights the text on the screen, and
displays the Confirm Replacement dialog box. Press N to keep the text as it
is; press Y to replace it.

☛ Press the Cancel key (Esc) to stop the search and replace operation at any time.

✔ Always type something in the Replace With text box. If you don't, WordPerfect systematically deletes each occurrence of the text that it finds, in a wanton round of wholesale slaughter. This process is called *searching and deleting,* and it's covered in a section in this chapter that has the same name.

✔ To return to your starting position — the place where the cursor was when you activated the Replace command — press Ctrl-Home twice:

> Ctrl-Home, Ctrl-Home

✔ When all the searching and replacing is done, you see a dialog box summarizing how many matches were found and how many of them were replaced. Both numbers will be the same unless you Xed the Confirm Replacement box and didn't replace some of the finds.

✔ Suppose that you goof and do a search and replace that doesn't quite work out. This happens to me once in about every six search and replace operations. The way out? Press the Undo key, Ctrl-Z, right after you search and replace.

✔ The Replace command works from the cursor's position to the end of the document. To replace all occurrences of text in a document, start at the top by pressing the following keys:

> Home, Home, ↑, Alt-F2

The double Home, up-arrow command moves the cursor to the top of the document. Then Alt-F2 starts the search and replace operation.

✔ To search and replace through the entire document, including headers, footers, footnotes, end notes, references, and so forth, press the Home key before you press the keys for the Replace command:

> Home, Alt-F2

Refer to "Using Super Find" earlier in this chapter for additional information.

Using Replace to count your sheep

If you just want to count the number of times that a word or phrase is used in a document, use the Replace command, Alt-F2, as described in the preceding section, but specify the same text for both Search For and Replace With. For example, do the following:

1. **Press Home, Home, ↑ to move to the top of the document.**

   Or just position the cursor where you want to start counting.

2. **Press Alt-F2.**

3. **Type the text that you want to find and count in the first box; press Enter.**

4. **Type the same text — exactly — into the second box.**

5. **Press F2.**

WordPerfect is rather dim here. It doesn't seem to mind that you're searching for and replacing text with the same text. In any case, when it's done, you see the Search and Replace Complete dialog box. The number by both Occurrence(s) Found and Replacement(s) Made tells you how many times the word or phrase appears in a document.

  ✔ Press Ctrl-Home, Ctrl-Home to return to your starting position after you count your pet word or phrase.

  ✔ To count all the words, sentences, and whatever in a document, use the Document Information command. Refer to Chapter 7.

Searching and replacing in a block

Although WordPerfect doesn't enable you to search through a block of marked text, you can search and replace inside a block. This feature is great if you just want to change some text in a paragraph, page, or some odd grouping of words. Follow these steps:

1. **Rope off the block of text that you want to search.**

   Move the cursor to the start of the block, press Alt-F4 to start marking the block, and then move the cursor to mark the end of the block.

   If you have a mouse, you can drag it over the text to select it. Refer to Chapter 6 for more information on selecting a block with the mouse.

2. **Press Alt-F2.**

   The Replace command only works with the text in the block; the rest of the document is safe from harm.

3. **Follow the steps listed in "Searching for and Replacing Text" earlier in this chapter to search and replace text.**

4. **Press F2 to start replacing text.**

   WordPerfect searches only the block of text you've marked.

  ✔ Use the Replace command on a block of text when you want to change text in only a small part of a document. The rest of the document will be unaffected by the Replace command.

  ✔ The text block is searched from the start to the end. When the last item has been found and replaced (or not), the block is unhighlighted.

  ✔ Detailed information on marking a block of text is offered in Chapter 6.

Searching and deleting

If you don't type anything in the Replace With text box, WordPerfect's Replace command systematically deletes all the matching text it finds. This is a scary thing, so be sure to X out the Confirm Replacement box. Otherwise, you could zap the document irrevocably.

Suppose that Bo Peep decides to become a truck driver and wants to get rid of her sheep. Here's how to delete the sheep from a WordPerfect document:

1. **Position the cursor at the beginning of the document or at the spot where text needs to be found and deleted.**

   (The Replace command always works from the cursor's position *down*.)

2. **Press Alt-F2, the Replace command.**

3. **Type the word, phrase, or text that you want to eliminate (*sheep*, in this case).**

4. **Press Enter.**

5. **In the next box, type nothing.**

   Or if something is in there already, press the Delete key to wipe it out.

6. **Press Enter.**

   Nothing appears in the box. That's OK. Nothing is just a place holder for, well, nothing.

7. **Check the Confirm Replacement box.**

   You don't have to confirm the replacements if you're dead-sure of yourself. Are you? If not, press 3 to put an X in the Confirm Replacement box.

8. **Press F2.**

   In moments, the text is gone. Bo Peep's sheep go pop, pop, popping away! If you've asked to confirm each find, then it takes a bit longer because you have to squint at the screen and then press the Y or N key on the keyboard.

   ✔ As with any search and replace operation, the text you replace — delete in this case — cannot be recovered by using F1, the Undelete key. You can change your mind — if you act now and hurry because operators are standing by — and press the Undo key, Ctrl-Z.

   ✔ As with any massive replacement operation, you may want to save the document to disk before you proceed. Press Ctrl-F12.

✔ If you haven't saved the document before, type a name for it. If you have saved it before, then pressing Ctrl-F12 saves it quickly without any bothersome typing on your part.

✔ Go ahead with the *search and destroy* operation. If you goof, reload the document by pressing F7, N, N.

✔ You press F7 to exit WordPerfect, N to not save the now-corrupted document, and N to stay in WordPerfect. Then use the Shift-F10 command to reload the document back into memory. Press the following keys:

Shift-F10, ↓, Enter

✔ Shift-F10 brings up the Open Document dialog box. You press the down-arrow key to see a list of the last few files you've saved to disk. The one you just closed is the first one listed. Press Enter to open it and try, try again.

Let's all wish Miss Bo Peep good luck in her new profession.

Chapter 6
Working with Text Blocks, Stumbling Blocks, and Mental Blocks

. . . .

In This Chapter

▶ Marking a block with the cursor-control keys

▶ Marking a block with the Search command

▶ Quick block-marking with the Select command

▶ Copying and pasting a block

▶ Cutting and pasting a block

▶ Pasting a previously cut or copied block

▶ Dragging a block around with the mouse

▶ Deleting a block

▶ Undeleting a block

▶ Formatting a block

▶ Spell-checking a block

▶ Searching and replacing in a block

▶ Printing a block

▶ Saving a block to disk

. . . .

A major advantage of a word processor over, say, a stone tablet is that you can work with blocks of text. Stone tablets, no way. You can break them up into blocks, but gluing them back together again is *tres gauche*. Hand such a thing with a report on it to your boss and she'll shake her head, muttering, "Tsk, tsk, tsk. This is tacky, Jenson."

A block in a word processor is a marvelous thing. You can rope off a section of text — any old odd section (a letter, word, line, paragraph, page, or rambling polygon) — and then treat the text as a unit, a *block*. You can copy the block, move it, delete it, format it, spell-check it, use it to keep the defensive line from getting to your quarterback, and on and on. Think of the joy: Years after childhood, WordPerfect has made it OK for us to play with blocks again.

Marking a Block

You can't do anything with a block of text until you *mark* it. Marking a block tells WordPerfect, "OK, my block starts here. No, *here!* Not over there. Here, where I'm looking, where the toothpick cursor is." Use the Start Block command, Alt-F4. That command *drops anchor,* marking the start of the block. You can then use the cursor-control keys to find the other end of the block. WordPerfect highlights the whole thing by using reverse text on the screen. After the block is marked, it's ready for you to do something with it.

Marking a block with the cursor-control keys

To mark a block of text by using the arrow keys on the keyboard, follow these handy steps:

1. **Move the toothpick cursor to the start of the block, before the first letter of the text you want in the block.**

   Be very specific. Tell the computer, "I want my block to start here," as you position the cursor.

2. **Press the Mark Block command, Alt-F4.**

   Press and hold the Alt key and press the F4 key. Release both keys. You see the following at the bottom left of the screen:

   ```
   Block on
   ```

   On the other side of the screen, on the bottom right, the numbers by the Pos indicator are shown in reverse text. Whether your right eye or your left eye is dominant, you should catch the clue that you're in block-marking mode.

   Block-marking mode is active until you give a block or formatting command or press Esc to cancel.

3. **Use the cursor keys to mark the block; position the cursor where you want the block to end.**

   Refer to Chapter 2 for various key combinations that you can use to move the cursor.

   As you mark the block, the text included inside the block is *highlighted,* or shown in reverse text on the screen (see Figure 6-1). That's OK. The text remains highlighted, and Block on continues to live at the bottom of the screen until you issue a block command.

4. When you've moved the cursor to the end of the block, you're ready to issue a block command.

You can copy the block, cut it and paste it elsewhere, format the block, print it, spell-check it, or do a dozen other interesting things that this chapter explains. Refer to the appropriate section later in this chapter for instructions on what to do with the block.

✔ Another way to start marking a block is by selecting the Block command from the Edit menu.

✔ If you don't like the menus but can't manage Alt-F4, then be happy in the knowledge that the F12 key performs the same function as Alt-F4. Pressing F12 requires only one finger and no claw pattern.

✔ Yes, until you type a block command, the block remains highlighted. This is OK; marking a block is an active thing.

✔ Before pressing Alt-F4, you need to position the cursor where you want the block to start.

✔ After you press Alt-F4, you can move the cursor up or down from the block's anchor point. Most people move the cursor down.

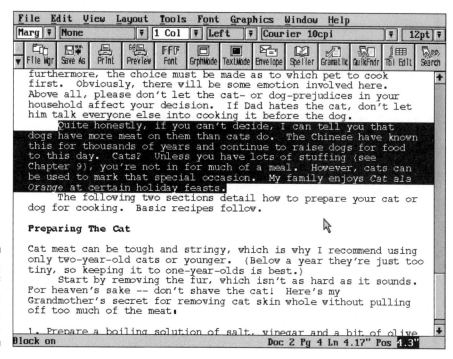

Figure 6-1:
A block of text is marked on the screen.

- Instead of using the cursor-control keys to mark a block, you can type a character. WordPerfect locates the next occurrence of that character and highlights all the text between it and the start of the block. You can repeat this action several times to make the block as large as you like.

- To cancel a block, press Esc. You also can press Alt-F4 again to turn off block-marking mode.

- To mark a paragraph, position the cursor to the start of the paragraph, press Alt-F4, and then press Enter. Because Enter marks the end of the paragraph, these keystrokes mark a paragraph block for you.

Marking a block with the mouse

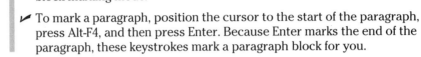

You also can use the mouse to mark a block of text on the screen. This method can be convenient whether you're a tepid or rabid mouse-o-phile.

To mark a block using the mouse, follow these steps:

1. **Position the mouse pointer at the start of the block.**

2. **Press and hold the mouse button.**

   (You will be *dragging* the mouse to the block's end, which highlights and selects the text as a block.)

3. **Drag the mouse pointer to the end of the block.**

4. **Release the mouse button.**

- You can use the cursor-control keys to continue marking the block or adjusting the block's end position. As long as the Block on message appears in the lower left corner of the screen, you're in block-marking mode. However . . .

- If you click the mouse on the document again, the block disappears. You can, if you want, press the Shift key and click the mouse to extend the selection.

- To quickly mark a word-sized chunk of text using the mouse, point the mouse at that word and double-click. To mark a sentence, triple-click. Clicking four times in a row marks an entire paragraph.

- WordPerfect scrolls the screen if you drag downward (toward yourself) with the mouse.

- I don't recommend using the mouse to mark a block larger than what you see on the screen. Scrolling with the mouse (by dragging it up or down) can be unwieldy.

Marking a block with the Search command

Marking a block can get sloppy with the cursor-control keys, and especially with the mouse. If you find yourself wasting a lot of time being precise about marking blocks, then consider using the Search command to locate the end of the block:

1. Position the cursor to the start of the block.

The cursor must be blinking right before the first character that you want to include in the block. Be precise.

2. Press Alt-F4.

This key combination turns on the `Block on` message at the lower left corner of the screen. You're in block-marking mode.

3. Press the F2 command.

The Search dialog box appears. Yes, you're still in block-marking mode, but now you can use the Search command to locate the end of the block.

4. Type in the text that you want to search for.

This text will mark the end of the block. *Do not press Enter.*

5. Press F2 to search for the matching text.

WordPerfect stretches the block highlighting down to the point in the text where the matching text occurs and includes the found text in the block.

6. When the cursor is at the end of the block, you're ready to use a block command.

Refer to the appropriate section later in this chapter for details. Note that until you type a block command, the block remains highlighted and `Block on` continues to blink.

✔ If no text is found when you use the Search command, the Not Found dialog box is displayed. Drat. Well, at least you're still in block-marking mode.

✔ To find the next occurrence of the matching text or to search for additional text to include in the block, you can press F2 again.

✔ There's no point in searching for individual characters with the Search command; WordPerfect does that automatically any time you press Alt-F4 to mark a block.

✔ You can still use the cursor-control keys to mark the block, either before or after you press F2 to find text. Blocking is a liberal thing. You're not limited to using only the cursor or Search-command method to mark a block.

✔ You can find more details about using the Search command in the discussion of the Search Down command in Chapter 5.

✔ You also can use the Search Up command, Shift-F2, to mark a block upward in the document. This feature is called *marking an Australian block.*

Quick block-marking with the Select command

If you need a sentence, paragraph, or page of text marked as a block, you can use the Select command in the Edit menu to mark it quickly without having to fuss with where the block starts or ends. The Select command is very accurate but not particularly handy.

1. **Position the cursor in the middle of the sentence, paragraph, or page you want to mark.**

2. **Now, you have to use the menus here, so don't complain to me: from the Edit menu, choose the Select command.**

   The Select command brings up a little sidekick menu with three options.

3. **Select Sentence, Paragraph, or Page to mark that much of the text as a block.**

✔ A sentence is not the same thing as a line of text. With the Quick cut or copy command, a sentence starts with a new line or after a period and ends with a period. All the spaces after the period and up to the start of the next sentence are included in the block.

✔ You can use the keyboard to select sentences, paragraphs, or pages quickly.

To select a sentence, press

> Alt-E, S, S

To select a paragraph, press

> Alt-E, S, P

To select a page, press

> Alt-E, S, A

Yes, that's *A* for *Page,* or *Paaage* as I like to say it.

Marking a block . . . again

So much of what you do in WordPerfect involves blocks. Often you need to do more than one thing to a block, which is frustrating because WordPerfect deliberately unmarks a block after you do something to it. The solution may be to go through the same painful block-marking steps again. Or you can try the handy Alt-F4-Go To command.

After you issue a block command, the block's highlighting disappears. Don't despair if you need to do more to the block and don't type any other key before you

1. Press Alt-F4.

This key combination reactivates block-marking mode.

2. Press Ctrl-Home, Ctrl-Home (the Go To command, twice).

The same block is highlighted again on the screen.

It's magic! This trick works best if you press Alt-F4, Ctrl-Home, Ctrl-Home right away. Do it immediately after you issue the first block command.

Doing Things with Blocks

I asked my six-year-old son, "What can you do with blocks?" And he said, "Anything. Build stuff. Make houses for your men." I asked him about cutting and pasting, and he looked at me and rolled his eyes. "Dad, you only cut and paste with scissors and glue. They teach us this stuff in kindergarten, you know." Obviously, the lad is a genius, and I've been using WordPerfect too long.

Regardless of what a six-year-old thinks, the rest of this chapter covers fun and interesting things you can do with blocks . . . in WordPerfect.

Copying and pasting a block

After a block is marked, you can copy the block and paste it into another part of the document. The original block remains untouched by this operation:

1. Mark the block.

Use the cursor to identify the start of the block. Press the Alt-F4 command to start the block. Use the cursor or Search command to locate the end of the block.

2. Press Ctrl-C, the Copy command.

Thwoop! The block's highlighting disappears, and the happy `Block on` message vanishes. This is OK. WordPerfect has read the block and stored it in memory. It won't forget the block, but now you need to find a location for the copy.

3. Move the cursor to the position where you want the block copied.

Don't worry if there isn't any room there; WordPerfect inserts the block into the text just as if you typed it there manually.

4. Press Ctrl-V, the Paste command key combination, to paste the block.

You now have two copies of the block in the document.

✔ Ctrl-C is the command for copying a block. *C* is for *Copy this block.*

✔ Ctrl-V is the command for pasting a block. *V* is for *Verily, I say unto you, paste the block here.*

✔ Additional information on marking a block is found in the first two sections of this chapter.

✔ After you paste the block, you may need to do a bit of editing to clean things up. Although WordPerfect makes room for the block, it doesn't add punctuation, move a period or quotation mark, or format the block. You may need to do those things manually.

✔ After you paste a block, you can paste it into the document a second time. Just position the cursor where you want to paste the block and press Ctrl-V, the Paste command key combination, again.

Here are the quick steps for copying a block in WordPerfect:

1. Mark the block.

2. Press Ctrl-C.

3. Move the cursor to the block's destination.

4. Press Ctrl-V.

Cutting and pasting a block

Cutting a block is like deleting it, but nothing is really gone. Instead, like an article you snip out of a newspaper, the cut block can be pasted into the document at another location. This feature is technically called a *move;* you move a block of text from one spot to another in the document. (Talk about writing moving text!)

Cutting a block of text works very similarly to copying a block. Follow these steps:

1. Mark the block of text that you want to move.

Locate the start of the block by using the cursor. Press Alt-F4. Use the cursor-control keys or the Search command to locate the block's end.

2. Press Ctrl-X, the command for cutting a block.

The highlighted block disappears!

That's OK. It has been stuffed into WordPerfect's electronic storage place, which is nestled deep in the computer's memory.

3. Move the cursor to the position where you want to paste the block.

Don't worry if there isn't any room for the block; WordPerfect makes room as it inserts the block.

4. Press Ctrl-V, the Paste command key combination, to paste the block at the cursor's location.

✔ Ctrl-X is the Cut, or Move, block command. *X* is for *Cutex thisex blockex.*

✔ Ctrl-V is the Paste block command. *V* is for *Vomit the block right here.*

✔ Additional information on marking a block is found earlier in this chapter.

✔ Cutting a block works just like copying a block, but when you cut a block, the original is deleted.

✔ Cutting a block is not the same as deleting a block. The Undelete command cannot recover a block that you've moved. To recover the block, you need to position the cursor and then paste the block by pressing Ctrl-V.

✔ The Undo key, Ctrl-Z, only undoes a block paste. It does not replace the block in its original position. To put it back where it came from, move the cursor back to the block's original location and press Ctrl-V to paste it there.

✔ You can use any cursor-control key commands when you're hunting for a place to paste the block. You also can edit text and do just about anything else. WordPerfect remembers the block until you quit WordPerfect. However, if you use the Ctrl-C or Ctrl-X commands to copy or cut another block, the first block is lost.

✔ The pasted block may not look the way you want it to look. Pasting is rough, and you always need to do a wee bit of editing to make the pasted block look just so.

✔ After a block has been cut and moved, you can paste it into the document a second time. See the next section for details.

Here are the quick steps for moving a block in WordPerfect:

1. Mark the block.

2. Press Ctrl-X.

3. Move the cursor to the block's destination.

4. Press Ctrl-V.

Pasting a previously cut or copied block

Whenever a block of text is cut or copied, WordPerfect remembers it. You can yank that block back into the document at any time — sort of like pasting text again after it has already been pasted. You use the Ctrl-V Paste command. (Don't ask me why; I assume that if the keyboard had a Blorf or Fragus shift key, WordPerfect would use it for the Paste key instead. You know, Shift-Blorf pastes a block of text. Forget it!)

To paste a previously cut block of text, follow these exciting steps:

1. **Position the cursor at the spot where you want the block of text to be pasted.**

   Always position the cursor first. The block will appear at the cursor's position, just as if you'd typed it there yourself.

2. **Press Ctrl-V, the Paste command.**

   Zap. The block is back on the screen.

   ✔ If you haven't used the other block commands to copy or cut anything, the Ctrl-V command will not paste anything. Duh.

   ✔ WordPerfect has a small brain. It remembers only the last block that is cut or copied. Anything that was cut or copied before the last block is gone, gone, gone.

   ✔ Here's yet another ungulate fact: Cows must eruct two liters of gas an hour, or they bloat and die. This requirement is due to the fermentation process that takes place in their rumens. (You'd be the same way if you could eat grass.)

Here are the quick steps for retrieving a previously copied or cut block in WordPerfect:

1. Position the cursor to where you want the block pasted.

2. Press Ctrl-V.

Dragging a block around with the mouse

"Here I come to save the day!"

After you highlight a block, you can use the mouse to move it somewhere else. You click on the block with the mouse, pressing and holding the button down. The mouse paws desperately at the block until it finally grabs it. Then you can drag the block to a new location and plop it down by releasing the mouse's button. Here are the action-packed steps:

1. **Mark a block using the mouse.**

   Use the mouse. After all, this is a mouse thing, and most of the time the mouse is lonely in WordPerfect. (Most mice refer to WordPerfect as the Function-Key Dungeon.)

2. **Position the mouse pointer somewhere over the block so that the pointer is pointing right at the block.**

3. **Press and hold the mouse's button.**

   This action is like a click, but it's really a drag. *Really* a drag.

   When you press and hold the mouse button down, two tiny rectangles appear at the end of the mouse pointer. These rectangles indicate that you're about to grab that block of text and drag it elsewhere. (I like to think that the pointer is the mouse successfully grabbing the text and putting it under its tiny armpit.)

4. **Move the mouse pointer to where you want the text to be moved.**

   Position the mouse pointer to an exact spot.

5. **Release the mouse button.**

   The text is cut from its original location and pasted into the spot where the mouse is pointing.

✔ Dragging text with the mouse is like cutting and pasting, but you do it with one movement.

✔ This feature is best used when you don't have too far to move the text. If you try to use the mouse to scroll the screen, you'll quickly lose your place, and the operation will be much more complex than necessary.

✔ The Undo key, Ctrl-Z, can undo any text moving that you attempt.

Deleting a block

Two ways are available for deleting a block — the complex way and the easy way. What say we do it the easy way, huh? Follow these steps:

1. **Mark the block.**

   Position the cursor at the start of the block. Press Alt-F4 to turn on block-marking mode. Position the cursor at the end of the block.

2. **Press Backspace.**

   The block is gone! No warning, no pleading, no regrets. Yes, WordPerfect probably hated the block as much as you did.

✔ You also can press Delete to delete the block.

✔ Additional information on marking a block is covered in the first part of this chapter.

✔ When you delete a block with the Delete or Backspace key, you can recover it with the Undelete key, Esc. This feature is what makes deleting a block different from cutting a block with Ctrl-X.

✔ Chapter 4 covers the vast subject of deleting and destroying text. Turn there to quench your destructive thirsts.

Undeleting a block

This task is simple. Suppose that you delete a block and — oops! — you didn't mean to. The handy Esc key comes to the rescue. Refer to the discussion of undeleting text in Chapter 4 for details.

Formatting a block

After you rope off a section of text as a block, you can format the text and characters as a single unit. Part II of this book covers formatting in detail. So instead of going over the details, I'll just list the various formatting things you can do to a block:

1. You can boldface the text, underline it, or make it italic by using the special Ctrl quick-key commands, Ctrl-B, Ctrl-U, or Ctrl-I.

The hard way to delete a block, if you care to read it

Deleting a block with the Backspace or Delete key seems simple, right? And would you expect WordPerfect to keep things simple? No! So WordPerfect provides an alternative, more complex, and devious way to delete a block. We're not talking straightforward information here:

1. Mark the block.

2. Press Ctrl-F4.

3. Shake your head and mutter to yourself, "Why didn't I just press the Backspace key?"

4. Press 3 for Delete.

The block is gone.

I included this method in response to the thousands of letters from big bureaucracies that insist that people are getting things done much too quickly with WordPerfect. I hope it helps.

2. You can change the text and make it look totally funky with the Font command, Ctrl-F8.

   The Font command enables you to alter the text's size and appearance.

3. You can change the position of the block by centering or right-justifying the text.

   Centering is done with the Shift-F6 command; Alt-F6 is the Flush Right command.

4. You can switch text in the block between uppercase and lowercase by using the Switch key, Shift-F3.

✔ To make these changes to a block of text, you first have to mark the block. Then you select the proper formatting command. The command affects only the text that is roped off in the block.

✔ Be aware that some of the function keys operate differently when a block is marked. I agree that this is weird, but WordPerfect gears its commands toward blocks when the Block on message is on the screen.

✔ Chapter 9 contains information on changing the text style (bold, underline, italic, and all that) and on shifting between uppercase and lowercase.

✔ Information on changing the position of a block — its *justification* — is covered in Chapter 10.

Spell-checking a block

If you want to spell-check a small or irregularly sized part of a document, you can block that section and then use WordPerfect's Spell command. This method is much quicker than going through the pains of using the full Spell command.

To see whether your spelling is up to snuff, follow these steps:

1. **Mark the block.**

   Move the cursor to the start of the block. Press Alt-F4 to begin the block-marking process. Move the cursor to the end of the block.

   The highlighted area marked by the block is the only part of the document that will be spell-checked.

2. **Press the Ctrl-F2 key, the Spell command.**

   WordPerfect compares all the words in the block with its internal dictionary. If a misspelled or unrecognized word is found, it is highlighted, and you are given a chance to correct or edit it.

   When the spell check is completed, WordPerfect displays a box that proclaims Spell check completed.

3. **Press Enter to continue working with the document.**

✔ Chapter 7 covers WordPerfect's spell checker in glorious detail. Refer to that chapter for additional information on changing or correcting your typos.

✔ For checking only a few words, activating the Spell command and pressing W to check one word at a time is quicker. For information on using this method, refer to the section in Chapter 7 on checking only one word.

General block information

For the idly curious, WordPerfect reports all sorts of rambling statistics about the block you've just roped off. Follow these bean-counting steps:

1. **Mark yer block.**

2. **Press Alt-F1, 4.**

   WordPerfect displays the Block Information dialog box. (Refer to Figure 7-5 in the next chapter to see what it looks like.)

3. **Gawk at the statistics.**

4. **Press Enter to return to editing the document.**

   Alas, the block will no longer be marked when you return. You need to mark it again if you want to do something else with it.

You can go ahead and get excited if this feature is one you've been craving.

Searching and replacing in a block

You cannot search for text in a marked block, but you can use WordPerfect's Replace command. When a block is on, Replace searches and replaces text only in the marked block. The rest of the document is unaffected.

A full description of the search and replace operation is offered in Chapter 5. I'm too lazy to rewrite all that stuff here.

Printing a block

WordPerfect's Print command enables you to print one page, several pages, or an entire document at once. If you want to print only a small section of text, you need to mark that section as a block and then print the block. Here's the secret formula:

1. **Make sure that your printer is on and ready to print.**

   Refer to Chapter 8 for additional information.

2. **Mark the block of text that you want to print.**

   Move the cursor to the start of the block, before the first character you want to print. Press Alt-F4 to turn on block-marking mode. Move the cursor to the end of the block.

3. **When the block is marked, press Shift-F7, the Print command.**

   You see the Print/Fax dialog box — an overwhelming place. Fortunately, WordPerfect has already set itself up to print the block, so there's nothing to mess with here.

4. **Press Enter to print the block.**

   In a few moments you see the *hard copy* sputtering out of the printer.

   ✔ When a block is highlighted, you can use the Print button on the Button Bar (third button from the left) to print it.

   ✔ Additional information on marking a block of text is found in the first section of this chapter.

   ✔ The block that you print appears on the page in exactly the same location and position it would occupy if you printed the whole document (which is why printing a block at the end of a document takes longer than printing a block at the beginning of a document). WordPerfect also prints any headers and footers.

   ✔ The full subject of printing is covered in Chapter 8. Refer to that chapter for information on printing options and setting up the printer.

Saving a block to disk

WordPerfect enables you to mark a block of text and then save that block to disk. The block isn't deleted from the document; its contents are just put into another WordPerfect document file on disk. This feature can be really handy for saving stuff you want to delete but may need later. Here's how you do it:

1. **Start by marking the block.**

   Move the cursor to the start of the block. Press Alt-F4 to activate the block-marking mode. Move the cursor to the end of the block.

2. **Press F10, the Save command.**

   A Save Block dialog box appears. It prompts you to think up a DOS filename under which to save the block.

3. Type in a filename.

Choose an acceptable filename: use only letters and numbers, and make it no more than eight characters long.

4. Press Enter.

A few grinds of the disk drive later, the block is saved to disk.

✔ Clicking the Save As button on the WordPerfect Button Bar saves a highlighted block to disk.

✔ The block is saved as a WordPerfect document file, complete with formatting information and such. It's not an ASCII file or text file (just in case you were wondering).

✔ A block is not deleted when you save it to disk.

✔ You need to enter a proper filename for a block you save to disk. Information on naming a file is in Chapter 16.

✔ If a file with the filename you've chosen already exists, you see a dialog box that asks whether you want to replace the file that is already on disk. Press N. If you press Y, you overwrite the file that is already on disk. You probably don't want to replace it.

✔ To load a block from disk into memory, use the Retrieve command, Shift-F10. This command is covered in Chapter 14.

You don't have to read this stuff on appending a block to a disk file

Sometimes you may want to write several blocks of stuff to the same file. You can't use the mark-block-F10 technique described in "Saving a block to disk" to do that. Each new file would overwrite the existing file, and you'd be stuck. However, you can use the Append command that is hidden in the Ctrl-F4 function key. This key is the Mess with Block command key that is normally used to cut, copy, and paste blocks. Abnormally, it's used to append one block to a WordPerfect file that is already on disk.

To append a block of text to an existing WordPerfect document file on disk, follow these steps:

1. Mark the block.

2. Press Ctrl-F4, the Mess with Block command.

3. In the dialog box, press 4 for Append.

4. In the next dialog box, type the name of the file that you want to append the block to.

5. Press Enter.

These steps stick the block at the end of a file on disk (which is what *append* means anyhow).

Chapter 7
Getting Along with the Electronic Mrs. Bradshaw

In This Chapter

▶ Checking your spelling

▶ Checking only one word

▶ Looking up a word in the dictionary

▶ Adding words to the dictionary

▶ Using the thesaurus

▶ Using Grammatik to ridicule your writing talent

▶ Examining pointless statistics

*E*veryone should have a third-grade teacher like Mrs. Bradshaw. The woman was a goddess in the annals of proper English grammar, pronunciation, and, of course, spelling. Nothing pleases an eight-year-old more than a smile from Mrs. Bradshaw. "Very good, Danny. There is no *e* at the end of *potato.*" The woman could probably correct the Queen.

What ever happened to Mrs. Bradshaw? The folks at WordPerfect somehow scooped the essence out of her brain, sliced it thin, and distributed it on the WordPerfect disks. Every copy of WordPerfect comes with a spell checker that's as efficient and knowledgeable as Mrs. Bradshaw (but without the little red check marks). Not only that, but her vast knowledge of English vocabulary and grammar has been included as well: WordPerfect's thesaurus and its grammar-checking program, Grammatik, offer improvements and suggestions quicker than Mrs. Bradshaw could disapprovingly frown over the misuse of the word *boner.*

Checking Your Spelling

One of the miracles of modern word processing is that the computer knows English spelling better than you do. Thank goodness. I really don't know how to spell. Not at all. The rules are obtuse and meaningless. There are too many exceptions. With WordPerfect, you don't need to worry about being accurate. Just be close, and the Spell command does the rest.

To check the spelling of words in a document, press Ctrl-F2, the Spell command key combination. Follow these steps:

1. **Press Ctrl-F2.**

   The Speller menu appears, floating in the middle of the screen. Figure 7-1 shows what it looks like.

2. **Select 3 (Document) to check the spelling of all the words in the document.**

   You don't need to be at the top of the document; WordPerfect automatically moves there to start testing the spelling of each word.

   If you want to check the spelling of words on a single page, select 2 (Page) from the dialog box.

   The screen splits in two. WordPerfect displays the document in the top part of the screen as it compares each word in the document against the words in its dictionary. The screen is shown in Figure 7-2.

   Any misspelled or unknown words appear highlighted (shown in reverse text) in the document. Alternative words, correctly spelled, appear in a box in the bottom part of the screen.

3. **Read the highlighted word in context at the top of the screen and then look for the properly spelled word in the bottom window.**

4. **Press the letter associated with the properly spelled word (A through Z).**

   If more choices are available, press the down-arrow key to see them.

Figure 7-1:
The Speller menu anxiously waits to find poorly spelled words in the document.

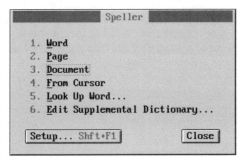

```
████████████      Speller      ████████████

   1. Word
   2. Page
   3. Document
   4. From Cursor
   5. Look Up Word...
   6. Edit Supplemental Dictionary...

  ┌─────────────────┐          ┌───────┐
  │ Setup... Shft+F1 │          │ Close │
  └─────────────────┘          └───────┘
```

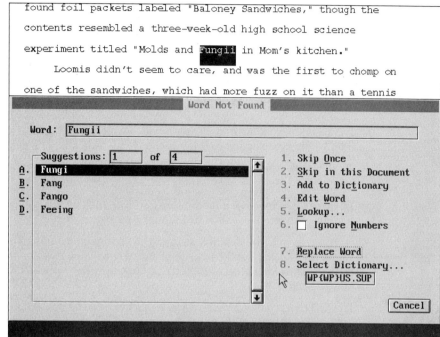

found foil packets labeled "Baloney Sandwiches," though the

contents resembled a three-week-old high school science

experiment titled "Molds and Fungii in Mom's kitchen."

    Loomis didn't seem to care, and was the first to chomp on

one of the sandwiches, which had more fuzz on it than a tennis

Word Not Found

Word: Fungii

Suggestions: 1 of 4

A. **Fungi**
B. Fang
C. Fango
D. Feeing

1. Skip Once
2. Skip in this Document
3. Add to Dictionary
4. Edit Word
5. Lookup...
6. ☐ Ignore Numbers

7. Replace Word
8. Select Dictionary...
  WP{WP}US.SUP

Cancel

Figure 7-2:
Spell-
checking a
document.

If the word is misspelled, but you don't mind, select 1 (Skip Once).

This action skips over the word and moves the program on to the next
misspelling.

**If you don't want to see that word flagged again, select 2 (Skip in this
Document).**

This action directs WordPerfect to ignore the word whenever it's found in
the rest of the document.

**If the word is spelled correctly and WordPerfect doesn't know it, select
3 (Add to Dictionary).**

This action adds the word to your personal dictionary, and WordPerfect
will never forget it.

**If you know how to quickly correct the spelling by yourself, select 4
(Edit Word).**

You can then edit the highlighted word on the screen. Use the left- and
right-arrow keys, and Backspace and Delete, to help you edit. Press Enter
when you're done editing (a message to this effect appears on the screen).

After replacing a misspelled word, WordPerfect hunts down the next
suspect word.

5. Repeat Steps 3 and 4 for every misspelled word.

WordPerfect continues in this manner until the end of the document. A dialog box announces `Spell Check Completed` when the spell check is completed.

This message must mean that the spell check is done. Or completed.

6. Press Enter and you're done.

✔ To check the spelling of only one word — which does come in handy — refer to the next section in this chapter, "Checking only one word."

✔ To check the spelling of a paragraph or an irregularly shaped block of text, refer to the discussion in Chapter 6 on spell-checking a block.

✔ To cancel the Spell command, press Esc. You may need to press Esc a second (or even third) time to get back to the document.

✔ From the menu, you can access the Spell command from the Tools menu. Select the Writing Tools menu item, and in the dialog box that is displayed, select 1 (Speller). Or press Alt-T, W, 1. Or simply press Ctrl-F2. Or just learn how to spell.

✔ To spell-check a document, you also can click on the Speller button on the Button Bar. It is the fifth button from the right. The picture on the button is an open book with one of Mrs. Bradshaw's red check marks over it.

✔ The WordPerfect dictionary is not a substitute for a real dictionary. Only in a real dictionary can you look up the meaning of a word to find out whether you're using the proper word in the proper context. No computer writer works with an electronic dictionary alone; usually a good, thick Webster's dictionary is sitting right within arm's length.

✔ WordPerfect assumes that any word with a number in it is misspelled. Select 6 (Ignore numbers) on the Spell menu if you get tired of having WordPerfect tell you that such words are misspelled; selecting 6 shuts off number checking. (I do this all the time, especially in this book where every function key is considered a misspelling by WordPerfect.)

✔ If you encounter a word that WordPerfect doesn't recognize but that is spelled correctly, select 3 (Add to Dictionary) to add the word to your personal dictionary. After you add a word to the dictionary, WordPerfect accepts it as spelled correctly from then on. The Add to Dictionary option differs from the Skip options (1 and 2), which only work until the spell check is complete. Refer to "Adding words to the dictionary" later in this chapter.

✔ If two identical words are found in a row, WordPerfect highlights them as a *double word.* Error, Error! The Double Word Found dialog box appears in the middle of the screen. You can use it to tell WordPerfect how to treat the duplicate word: select 1 or 2 to ignore the double word, 3 to delete the second word, 4 to edit the word, and 5 to disable the double-word checking feature (but it's a good idea to leave it on).

✔ My, but this is a long list of check marks.

✔ The Spell command also locates words with weird capitalization — for example, *BOner.* WordPerfect slaps the Irregular Case dialog box down in the middle of the screen. Select a word from the list that has letters which are the proper case, select 1 or 2 to ignore the weird word, select 4 to edit the word, or select 5 to disable the *weird word feature.* In the computer industry, where weird capitalization abounds, being able to disable this feature is a boon to productivity.

✔ The WordPerfect dictionary is good but definitely not as good as Mrs. Bradshaw. For one thing, it doesn't check words in context. For example, *your* and *you're* can be spelled correctly in WordPerfect's eye, but you may be using them improperly. The same thing goes for *its* and *it's.* For that kind of in-context checking, you need a *grammar checker,* such as Grammatik, which comes with WordPerfect. Refer to "Using Grammatik to Ridicule Your Writing Talent" near the end of this chapter.

✔ *Spell* here refers to creating words using the accepted pattern of letters. It has nothing to do with magic. Many people assume that a spell checker can instantly make their document better. Wrong! You need to read what you write and then edit, look, and read again. Pressing Ctrl-F2 doesn't fix things up. It just gets WordPerfect to find rotten words and offer some suggestions for replacements.

Here are the keys you press to spell-check a document:

Ctrl-F2, 3

Checking only one word

You don't have to spell-check an entire document when all you want to check is one word. Here is a great way to mentally deal with English spelling: Go ahead and spell the word the way you think it *should* be spelled. Then check only that word. WordPerfect looks up the accurate, wretched English spelling, and you're on your way. And the cool part is that you don't need to learn a thing!

To check the spelling of a single, suspect word, do the following:

1. Put the cursor somewhere on the word or just before it.

2. Press Ctrl-F2, the Spell command.

3. **Select 1 (Word) from the Speller dialog box.**

You want to proof only one word.

WordPerfect checks that word. If it's OK (and the way I spell, the odds are 50-50), the cursor jumps to the next word, and you see the Speller dialog box again (this happens too quickly to be useful). If the word is not OK, you see a half-screenful of possible alternative spellings and suggestions.

4. **Select a word from the suggested spellings and press the letter by that word.**

WordPerfect replaces the word that you supposed was correctly spelled with its proper and nonintuitive English spelling.

5. **If you're in the mood — or if you have a terrible parade of mangled and misspelled words — continue to select 1 to spell-check the next word.**

Press Esc to cancel the single-word spell-check feature.

✔ Refer to the first section of this chapter for additional information on working WordPerfect's Spell feature.

✔ Single-word checking is often a good way to immediately tackle a word you know is hopelessly wrong. Of course, my philosophy (or *filosofy*) is to spell any old which way and then run the spell checker for the whole document to catch everything at one time.

Looking up a word in the dictionary

A handy feature of the WordPerfect speller is its Look-up command. OK, it isn't *handy;* it's more curious. Calling something handy in WordPerfect is like saying that walking through heaps of rotting garbage wearing heavy boots is convenient.

The Look-up command enables you to find a word in the dictionary that you're thinking of but may not know how to spell. To use this command, follow these steps:

1. **Press Ctrl-F2 to bring up the Speller dialog box.**

2. **From the list in the dialog box, select 5 (Look Up Word).**

The screen splits in half. If the toothpick cursor was on or near a word on the screen, that word is highlighted, and WordPerfect places it in the Look Up Word dialog box that appears. This is OK, but it's not what you want.

3. **Type a word that you want to look up in the dictionary.**

If you don't know how the letters go, replace them with an asterisk (*). Or just type a similar word. Press Enter and WordPerfect looks the word up. Table 7-1 explains how everything works.

Table 7-1	Spell Checker Look-Up Examples
Example	*Explanation*
dan	When you enter this, WordPerfect displays *dan* plus all the words in the dictionary that look, sound, or are spelled similarly to *dan*. (It works with any name; try it with yours.)
bonnet	When you enter this, WordPerfect displays such interesting words as *bayonet, beaned, buoyant,* and *boned*.
rec*	When you enter this, WordPerfect displays all the words in the dictionary that start with *rec*.
*ing	When you enter this, WordPerfect displays all the words in the dictionary that end with *ing*. It comes in handy for budding poets.
s*itis	When you enter this, WordPerfect displays all the words in the dictionary that start with *s* and end with *itis* — lots of medical terms.

✔ Press Esc (the Cancel key) to return to the document.

✔ To look up another word, press the *Tab key and type the word. If you don't press Tab, WordPerfect assumes that you're picking a word from the list that is displayed (because they all have letters next to them). So, for heaven's sake, press Tab before typing another word!

✔ WordPerfect does not look up a specific word in a document; you have to type the word at the Word or word pattern prompt. I know, it sounds stupid. What do you expect?

✔ The word that is found can be pasted into your document. Yeah! Unfortunately, it can only replace the word that was highlighted when you first pressed Ctrl-F2. Boo! The look-up feature isn't really very useful — other than for just browsing through WordPerfect's dictionary.

Adding words to the dictionary

Some common words don't appear in WordPerfect's dictionary — Gookin, for example. Perhaps your last name is as unique as mine, or maybe your first name, city, business name, and so on, are all spelled correctly and yet unknown to WordPerfect. Therefore, each time you spell-check a document, the spell checker comes up with alternative suggestions for those words. Two options are available for avoiding this tautological conundrum.

The first, and most stupid, option is to select 2 (Skip in this Document) when the spell checker finds the word. Selecting 2 makes WordPerfect ignore that word during this spell-check run. But the next time you spell-check, you have to do the same thing. Dumb, dumb, dumb.

The second, and wise, option is to add said word to your *supplemental dictionary*. This dictionary is a list of words that WordPerfect skips every time you run the spell checker because you've told it that these words are all OK. Here's how to add words to the supplemental dictionary:

1. **Start the spell checker as you normally do.**

   Refer to the first section of this chapter for the persnickety details.

   Lo, you stumble on a word unbeknownst to WordPerfect and yet beknownst to you.

2. **The word is spelled just fine, so select 3 (Add to Dictionary) from the menu in the dialog box.**

   Selecting 3 stuffs the word into the supplemental dictionary, and you never have to mess with it again.

- After you add a word to the supplemental dictionary, WordPerfect knows and recognizes it as it does the words that come in the real dictionary — the one they made from Mrs. Bradshaw's brain.

- Be careful when you decide to add a word to the dictionary: Make sure that you don't select 3 when you really mean to select 2. Because . . .

- Removing a word from the dictionary is a pain. You may want to remove a word if you commit a flub and inadvertently put a seriously misspelled word into the dictionary. (I once added *fo* to the dictionary and had to spend three weeks in the WordPerfect penalty box — which is in Utah of all places!) To learn how to get a word out of the dictionary, you need to read the trivial drivel in the nearby technical information box.

- You can actually maintain several supplemental dictionaries on disk. To select or create a new dictionary, select 8 (Select Dictionary) after you press Ctrl-F2. Then type the dictionary's filename. If the file exists, WordPerfect uses it for the spell-check process. If the file doesn't exist already, WordPerfect creates it.

Using the thesaurus

If you think I'm smart enough to know how to use all the big words in this chapter correctly, you're grievously mistaken. Witness: *tautological conundrum.* That ain't me talkin'. That's WordPerfect's thesaurus in action. An amazing tool or astounding utensil or marvelous implement. You get the idea. The thesaurus helps you find *synonyms,* which are other words that have the same meaning but more weight or more precision.

Here's how to instantly become a master of big, clunky words in English:

1. **Hover the toothpick cursor in the middle of a simple word, say** *big*.

   (Adjectives are best for the thesaurus, but WordPerfect's statistical department tells me that the thesaurus contains more than 120,000 words.)

2. **Press the Writing Tools key, Alt-F1.**

   The dialog box that appears lists the Speller, the Thesaurus, Grammatik, pens, pencils, erasers, and other writing tools.

3. **Select 2 (Thesaurus).**

   Instantly, the bottom two-thirds of the screen converts into a three-column alternative word list. You can still see the original word, highlighted in context, at the top of the screen (see Figure 7-3).

   WordPerfect displays several alternatives for the word. The alternatives are grouped into categories.

4. **To replace the word in your document, highlight the new word that you want to use.**

5. **Press R (Replace) or click on the Replace button with the mouse.**

   After you select a word, WordPerfect returns you to the document. If you don't find an appropriate word, press Esc to cancel the thesaurus and return to the document.

No need to bother with this trivial drivel on the supplemental dictionary

If you flub and add the wrong word to the supplemental dictionary, all is not lost. You can edit the dictionary by using item number 6 (Edit Supplemental Dictionary) from the main Speller dialog box. In time of need, do the following:

1. Press Ctrl-F2, 6.

   You see a dialog box where you can select one of several supplemental dictionaries that you can use in WordPerfect. Unless you're seriously into this program, select the standard, *one we all use* dictionary file, WP{WP}US.SUP.

2. Use the cursor-control keys to highlight WP{WP}US.SUP from the list.

3. Press Enter.

   You see the Edit Supplemental Dictionary dialog box, where you can remove words in the supplemental dictionary that shouldn't have been put there in the first place.

I recommend glancing at the words in the supplemental dictionary once in a while, even when you're certain that it doesn't contain any incorrect words. Occasionally, a few do slip in, or you may find other words that shouldn't be there. In any case, checking every so often doesn't hurt.

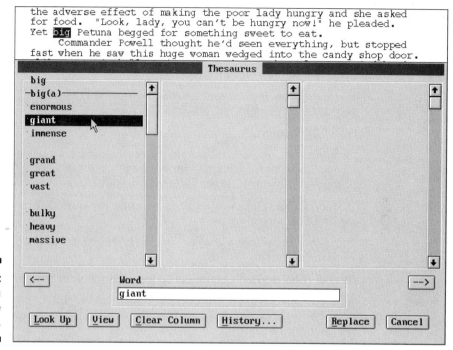

the adverse effect of making the poor lady hungry and she asked
for food. "Look, lady, you can't be hungry now!" he pleaded.
Yet big Petuna begged for something sweet to eat.
    Commander Powell thought he'd seen everything, but stopped
fast when he saw this huge woman wedged into the candy shop door.

Thesaurus

big

—big(a)—————

· enormous

 giant

· immense

· grand

· great

· vast

· bulky

· heavy

· massive

Word

giant

[←—] [—Look Up—] [—View—] [—Clear Column—] [—History...—] [—Replace—] [—Cancel—] [—→]

Figure 7-3:
Looking up a
word in the
thesaurus.

↙ A thesaurus is not a colossal, prehistoric beast.

↙ If one of the words is close, but not what you want — and the word has a
dot in front of it — highlight it and press Enter. WordPerfect displays
synonyms for that word in the next column. (If you find a word in that
column that you like, press R or click on the Replace button with the
mouse.) This feature works only for words that have a dot in front of them.

↙ If no synonyms are available for the word you selected, the thesaurus
displays a Word not found dialog box. Press Enter and then type a new,
similar word in the box at the bottom of the screen. Or just press Esc twice
to get back to the document.

↙ If the columns get junky, click on the Clear Column button to remove some
definitions.

↙ Use the down-arrow key to see some of the longer definitions displayed.

↙ Toward the bottom of the list are *antonyms,* which are words that have the
opposite meaning of the word that is highlighted in your document: fat-
skinny, round-square, smart-WordPerfect, and so on.

↙ Highlight the word that you want to use and press R to replace a word. If
you press Enter and the word has a dot next to it, instead of replacing the
word, WordPerfect shows you synonyms for that word.

✔ After inserting a new word, you may need to do a bit of editing; for example, you may add *ed* or *ing* to the word or replace *a* with *an*. Usually, a bit of editing is required whenever you replace one word with another.

Using Grammatik to Ridicule Your Writing Talent

Beyond spelling, most of us have trouble putting sentences together properly. Or is that *putting sentences properly together?* Or *properly putting sentences together?* Whatever. All the painful little rules of English can really bug you. But WordPerfect's Grammatik can really help you. Grammatik actually comes from the two words *grammar,* meaning *the rules by which we put our language together,* and *tick,* meaning *a blood-sucking bug.*

To see whether your writing is up to snuff, follow these steps:

1. **Press Alt-F1 to bring up the Writing Tools dialog box.**

   This dialog box is the same one that you use to run the thesaurus.

2. **Select 3 to activate Grammatik.**

   Grammatik is a text-mode program. If you've been working in graphics mode, everything shifts over to text mode. This is OK; Grammatik is concerned with how words are used and not with how they look.

3. **When the opening screen appears, press I to do an interactive check.**

   Grammatik picks its way through the document and pokes fun at your writing. See Figure 7-4 for an example of how Grammatik works.

   The top half of the screen shows the *error* as it appears in the text. The bottom half offers advice and suggestions for *improving* your writing.

4. **If you want to make a correction, press F3 to replace your text with what Grammatik suggests or press F9 to edit the text yourself (and press Esc when you're done).**

   If you want to tell Grammatik to spit up a rope, press F10 to look for the next error.

   When the check is done, WordPerfect returns you to the main screen.

5. **Press Q to quit Grammatik.**

   Any changes that you've made are saved in the document. Soon you're back in WordPerfect, disheartened but still able to write.

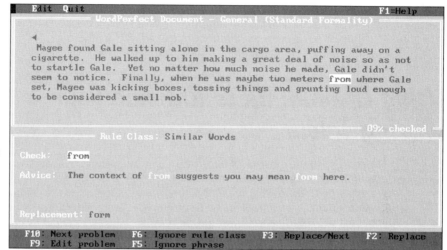

Edit Quit   F1=Help
═══════════ WordPerfect Document – General (Standard Formality) ═══════════

 ◄
   Magee found Gale sitting alone in the cargo area, puffing away on a
   cigarette. He walked up to him making a great deal of noise so as not
   to startle Gale. Yet no matter how much noise he made, Gale didn't
   seem to notice. Finally, when he was maybe two meters from where Gale
   set, Magee was kicking boxes, tossing things and grunting loud enough
   to be considered a small mob.

                                                            89% checked
═══════════════════════ Rule Class: Similar Words ═══════════════════════

Check: from

Advice: The context of from suggests you may mean form here.

Replacement: form

F10: Next problem   F6: Ignore rule class   F3: Replace/Next   F2: Replace
F9: Edit problem   F5: Ignore phrase

Figure 7-4:
Grammatik
makes an
inane
suggestion.

✔ It doesn't matter where you put the cursor; Grammatik always checks the entire document.

✔ To gauge your writing level, press T from Grammatik's main screen. The program displays statistics involving the readability of your text. Is it important? No. Does it matter? Probably not. Press Esc to return to the main screen.

✔ Like the speller, Grammatik isn't the final say-so in the way words go. It can offer you suggestions, but most of the best writers violate rules every day. (Please don't use that as an excuse, by the way.) So instead of getting frustrated, just take Grammatik's suggestions with a grain of salt, fix what you *know* needs to be fixed, and ignore the rest.

✔ The best information on English Grammar can be found in the handy *Strunk and White.* That's my code name for the book *Elements of Style* by Strunk and White. It's thin. It's cheap. It's the last word in writing English good. Or is that *writing good English?*

✔ Try to see how many revolting or offensive terms you can pack into a document. The speller may not know them, but Grammatik sure pops a button when it sees them.

Visiting the Department of Pointless Statistics

WordPerfect keeps tabs on everything that goes into the document — lots of little meaningless stuff like the number of words, sentences, pages, and so on and so forth. To see this information, follow these directions:

1. Press Alt-F1, the Writing Tools command.

2. From the menu, select option 4 (Document Information).

The Document Information dialog box appears, as shown in Figure 7-5. For longer documents, a Gathering Document Information dialog box may run a blue thermometer from left to right as WordPerfect scrutinizes the document.

3. Press Esc to return to the document.

✔ The Document Information dialog box is one of the best ways to find out how many pages long a document is. And because margins, font sizes, and spacing can affect the page count, you can use the *Characters* and *Words* statistics as well.

✔ The Document Information feature comes in handy for free-lance writers who are paid by the word or told to produce a document with a specific word length.

✔ To count the words on a page, in a paragraph, or in another specific portion of text, you first have to mark the text as a block. Then press Alt-F1, 4. Refer to the section on general block information in Chapter 6 for the gripping details.

✔ What's that smell?

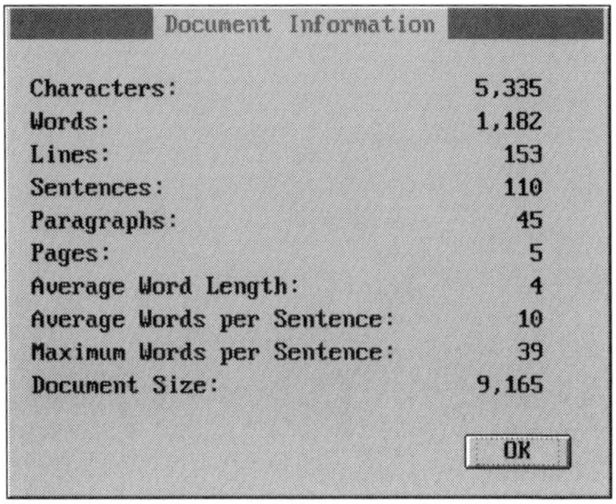

Figure 7-5:
Everything
you didn't
want to
know about
the
document.

Document Information	
Characters:	5,335
Words:	1,182
Lines:	153
Sentences:	110
Paragraphs:	45
Pages:	5
Average Word Length:	4
Average Words per Sentence:	10
Maximum Words per Sentence:	39
Document Size:	9,165

OK

Chapter 8
Send *This* to the Printer!

*T*wo guys are riding a bus. One of them, a WordPerfect dummy, says to the other, a typical, nondescript dummy, "I'm having trouble sending my document to the printer." And the nondescript dummy says, "Try Quicky-Printy, it's where Marge and I had our Christmas letter done last year." Baboom, boom.

The woes of using a computer are so subtle that, well, they drive you to create inane jokes. *Sending something to the printer* means nothing until you explain that a *printer* is a device connected to a computer, and it enables you to print things. Not to mention that if you're really good, the WordPerfect gods smile on you, and what you print may actually look somewhat like what you wanted.

Getting the Printer Ready

Before printing, you have to make sure that the printer is ready to print. You need to do more than just flip on the power switch.

Start by making sure that the printer is plugged in and properly connected to the computer. The cable that connects the computer and the printer should be firmly plugged in on both ends. (You only need to check the cable if you're having printer problems.)

The printer should have a decent ribbon. Old, frayed ribbons produce faint text and are actually bad for the printing mechanism. You'll have to pay more later in repair bills if you try to save a few bucks by using a ribbon longer than you should. Laser printers should have a good toner cartridge. If the laser printer's *toner low* light is on, replace the toner at once!

The printer needs paper. The paper can feed in from the back, come out of a paper tray, or be fed manually one sheet at a time. However the printer eats paper, make sure that you have it set up properly before you try to print.

Finally, the printer must be *on-line* or *selected* before you can print anything. Somewhere on the printer is a button labeled *on-line* or *select,* and the button should have a corresponding light. Press that button to turn on the option (and the light). Even though the printer is plugged in, its power switch is on, and it's doing its warm-up, stretching exercises, it won't print unless it's on-line or selected.

- ✔ Before you can print, you need to make sure that the printer is plugged into the wall, is plugged into the computer, is turned on, has a decent ribbon or good toner cartridge, has paper ready, and is on-line or selected. (Most printers turn themselves on in the on-line or selected mode.)

- ✔ Never plug a printer cable into either a printer or computer that is on and running. Always turn the printer and computer off whenever you plug anything into them. If you don't, you may damage the internal electronic components.

- ✔ Some special — OK, weird — printers are called *serial printers.* These printers plug into the computer's serial port rather than into the more logical printer port. I don't need to bore you with details about this stuff. However, if you have a serial printer (and I pity you if you do), you need to do some extra setting up before you can start printing. Refer to the printer manual or go out and buy *DOS For Dummies,* 2nd Edition, which is published by IDG Books Worldwide, and look in Chapter 9.

- ✔ If you're printing to a network printer — and it makes me shudder to think of it — then someone else is in charge of the printer. It should be set up and ready to print. If not, you can usually find someone to complain to.

- ✔ Chapter 23 contains additional information on setting up, or *installing,* the printer for use with WordPerfect. That chapter also contains troubleshooting information and a detailed anatomical guide to popular printers that tells you where to shoot the printer for either a quick death or a lingering, slow, and painful one.

Printing a Whole Document

If you think your work is worthy enough to be enshrined on paper, follow these steps for printing an entire document, head to toe:

1. Make sure that the printer is on-line and ready to print.

2. Press Shift-F7, the Print key combination.

You see the Print/Fax dialog box, which is the center for all sorts of printing havoc (see Figure 8-1).

3. Press 1 (Full Document).

The Full Document item is probably selected already. Pressing 1 just satisfies the general superstition about using WordPerfect — the pang that tells you every once in a while that something isn't going to work the way you expect it to.

4. Press Enter to start printing.

The printer warms up and starts to print. You return to the document as WordPerfect continues to print it. You can save that document to disk, start editing another document, create a new document, whip the mouse around in circles, or do whatever amuses you. WordPerfect continues to print in the background. You cannot exit WordPerfect, however, or printing stops.

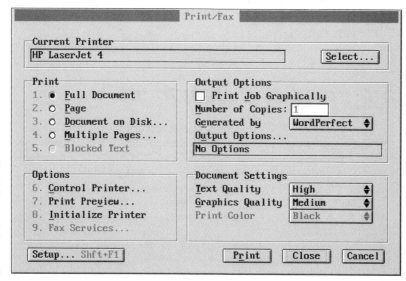

Figure 8-1:
The Print/
Fax dialog
box and its
armada of
options.

✔ You also can access the Print command from the File menu. It's labeled Print/Fax.

✔ If nothing prints, don't press Shift-F7, 1, Enter again. Probably something is awry, but WordPerfect's muffled voice hasn't alerted you to the problem. Read "Monitoring Printing" later in this chapter to see what message WordPerfect is trying to send you. Also, check to see whether the printer is on-line or selected.

✔ If you have a manual-feed printer, the printer itself begs for paper. It says, "*Beep!* Feed me!" You must stand by, line up paper, and shove it into the printer's gaping maw until the document is done printing. Refer to "Printing Envelopes" later in this chapter to figure this one out.

✔ Before you print, consider saving the document to disk and — if we're talking final draft here — doing a spell check. Refer to the section in Chapter 14 on saving a document to disk, as well as to the discussion of the spell checker in Chapter 7.

✔ If you try to quit WordPerfect while it's printing, you see a dialog box that says `Cancel print jobs?` Press N. Stay in WordPerfect until printing stops.

✔ You also can use the Print/Fax dialog box to send faxes directly from within WordPerfect. You need the proper fax hardware for the computer (no ordinary fax machine will do). Refer to Chapter 28 for more information on sending faxes.

To print an entire document, press these keys:

Shift-F7, 1, Enter

Printing Parts of a Document

Parts is parts. Most of the time, you use WordPerfect's Print command to print the whole document — the whole document and nothing but the document. But sometimes you want to print only a small sample of a document. Suppose, after all your hard work, that your boss (the jerk) wants to see only your conclusion. OK, just mark the conclusion as a block and print it. Or say your laser printer, like mine, occasionally prints two pages on top of each other. If so, you need to reprint only those two pages — not the whole document.

The following sections outline the procedures for printing minuscule to non-existent parts of a document.

Printing a specific page

Follow these steps to print only one page of a document:

1. Make sure that the printer is on and eager to print something.

2. Move the cursor so that it's sitting somewhere in the page you want to print.

Check the cryptic Pg counter in the lower right corner of the screen to make sure that you're on the page you want.

3. Press Shift-F7, the Print command.

The Print/Fax dialog box shows its sunshiny face. The item you want, Page, is number 2 in the list.

4. Press 2.

5. Press Enter to start printing.

You return to the document as that sole page is printed on your printer.

✔ To go to a specific page in a document, use the Go To command: Press Ctrl-Home and then press the page number. Press Enter and you're there.

✔ The page you print will have a header, a footer, all formatting, and so on — even a page number — just as if you had printed it as part of the complete document.

Here are the quick steps for printing a single page:

1. Move the cursor to the page you want to print.

2. Press Shift-F7, 2, Enter.

Printing a range of pages

WordPerfect enables you to print a single page, a range of pages, a group of pages, or all odd or even pages. To print a range or group of pages, follow these steps:

1. Make sure that the printer is on-line and ready to print.

2. Press Shift-F7, the Print command.

The Print/Fax dialog box comes up and says, "Hi." The item you want is number 4 on the list, Multiple Pages.

3. Press 4 (Multiple Pages).

The Print Multiple Pages dialog box appears on top of the Print/Fax dialog box.

4. Press 1 to highlight the Page/Label Range box.

5. Type the pages, the range of pages, or the secret codes for the pages you want to print.

Table 8-1 lists the kinds of entries that you can type in the Page/Label Range box.

6. Press Enter twice: Enter, Enter.

You see the Print/Fax dialog box again.

7. Press Enter to start printing.

The pages you specified — and only those pages — print.

✔ If you're printing the document on two sides of a sheet of paper, print the odd pages first. Then put the paper back into the printer upside down and print only the even pages.

✔ If you're printing odd and even pages, consider setting the *binding offset* to one inch: Press Shift-F8, 7, 9, 2, Enter (sounds like a phone number). Then press 1 for one inch. Press Enter to lock this setting in and then press F7 a few times to close the dialog boxes and return to the document.

Setting the binding offset to one inch provides an extra inch in the left margin for the odd-numbered pages and an extra inch in the right margin for the even-numbered pages. With this extra space, pages can be bound without losing any text in the gutter.

Follow these quick and easy steps for printing multiple pages:

1. Press Shift-F7, 4, 1.

2. Type the pages or range of pages that you want to print.

3. Press Enter, Enter, Enter.

Table 8-1	Acceptable Page-Range Entries
Entry	**Meaning**
x,y,z	Print pages X, Y, and Z where each number is a page number separated by commas.
x-y	Print pages X through Y. This entry specifies a range of pages to print. A hyphen separates the page numbers.
0	Print only the odd-numbered pages.
E	Print only the even-numbered pages.

Printing a block

When a block is marked on the screen and you press Shift-F7, WordPerfect asks whether you want to print the block. The Print/Fax dialog box appears, but item 5, Blocked Text, is automatically highlighted.

Check to make sure that the printer is on and ready to print and then press Enter to print just the block of text.

> ✔ The block prints on the page in the same position it would occupy if you printed the entire document. The page contains any headers, footers, page numbers, and so on, according to the document's format (which explains why it may take some time to print a block that's located at the end of a document).

> ✔ Chapter 6 explains everything you want to know about blocks (but have forgotten since childhood).

Printing a Document on Disk

Suppose that you've already edited a document and saved it to disk. You don't need to even load that document into WordPerfect to print it (assuming, of course, that it's *perfect*). To print a document that exists on disk, follow these steps:

1. **Press Shift-F7, the Print command.**

2. **Press 3 to select Document on Disk from the menu.**

   A Document on Disk dialog box pops in from the ether so that you can tell WordPerfect the name of the file that you want it to print.

3. **Type the DOS filename for the document.**

4. **Press Enter.**

   The Print Multiple Pages dialog box comes in from nowhere.

5. **Ignore the Print Multiple Pages dialog box and press Enter.**

6. **Press Enter again to start printing the document.**

   The document becomes a job in the WordPerfect printing machine. Zip, zip, zip. Soon it comes crawling out of the printer.

> ✔ This method is handy for printing common reports, resumes, and things on disk that don't need editing.

> ✔ If the file doesn't exist or you mistype the filename, you see an error message dialog box: File not found. Press Enter and try to reenter or edit the filename. Or just give up and press Esc.

✔ To locate a lost file on disk, refer to the discussion on finding lost files in Chapter 24. You also may want to check out Chapter 16, which explains how the handy F5 key works.

Follow these quick steps to print a document on disk:

1. Press Shift-F7, 3.

2. Type the DOS filename.

3. Press Enter, Enter, Enter.

Printing Several Documents at the Same Time

The best way to print several documents at one time is to use the F5 key, which is the File Manager command. You mark the files on disk that you want to print and then do a gang-print. This method is easier than loading each file into WordPerfect, printing it, clearing the file away, and then loading another file. (As I'm fond of saying, "Let the computer do the work.")

To print several files at one time, follow these steps:

1. **Make sure that the printer is on and ready to print.**

2. **Press F5 to bring up the Specify File Manager List dialog box.**

   In a text box, you see something similar to the following highlighted:

   ```
   C:\>WP6\LAUGH\BURP\GIGGLE\*.*
   ```

   What you see will vary, but, undoubtedly, it will be just as cryptic. It's a DOS *pathname*. (Quickly run screaming to Chapter 21 if you need help with pathnames.) WordPerfect is telling you, "Me find files in this directory."

3. **Most of the time, press Enter here.**

   However, if the files you want to print are in a different directory, type that directory name and then press Enter. (Again, scream off to Chapter 21 for more information.)

   The *File Manager* dialog box appears, nay, dominates the entire screen. Files are listed in the middle of the screen. Scan for the filenames of the documents that you want to print.

4. **Use the cursor-control keys to move the highlight bar to the name of a file you want to print.**

If the list of files is long, you can press PgDn to look for the next screenful of filenames.

5. Press the asterisk key (*) to mark a file or unmark a file if you've made a mistake.

An asterisk appears next to the file's name. The file is marked and ready for group action.

6. Repeat Steps 4 and 5 to mark the names of any additional files that you want to print.

7. Press 7 to select Print.

You see a dialog box that asks whether you want to print the marked files.

8. Press Y for Yes.

Then, of all things, you see the Print Multiple Pages dialog box. What a shock!

9. Press Enter.

WordPerfect thinks for a minute, and the disk drive churns away. Then the documents start to print.

10. Press Esc to exit the File Manager dialog box.

✔ Do not rename or delete any of the document files that you are printing. If you do, WordPerfect won't be able to find them, and all heck will break loose. You can rename or delete other files — just not the files you marked for printing.

✔ Additional information on using the F5 File Manager command is in Chapter 16.

Understanding the Miracle of Print Preview

As long as you're in graphics mode, WordPerfect gives you a good idea (not perfect, but close) of what a document will look like when it's printed. The Print Preview feature shows underlined, bold, and italicized text on the screen, plus any graphics, lines, tables, and other whatnots and whatsis. What's missing from the view are footnotes, headers, and footers, plus the overall Gestalt of the document. So to avoid making test prints of a document, which kills innocent trees and gives you bad, homeless-bunny nightmares, use the miraculous Print Preview feature.

To see what you're gonna get, do the following:

1. Press Shift-F7, the Print key combination.

The effervescent Print/Fax dialog box throws itself all over the screen. Happy, happy, happy. Joy, joy, joy. Of all this box has to offer, you want item number 7, Print Preview.

2. Press the 7 key.

The screen clears, and then a graphical depiction of the document appears.

3. Use the View menu to select one of several different ways of looking at the document.

If you choose 100%, you see the document at 100 percent, real-life size. The 200% View item shows the document in humongoid, twice-as-large-as-life size.

Full Page shows an overview of one page in the document; press PgDn or PgUp to see the next or preceding page. Choose Facing Pages to see two pages, left and right, side by side.

One of my personal faves is Thumbnails. When you select Thumbnails from the View menu, its hanger-on menu appears. If the document is long, try the 32 Page view. You see 32 little pages, each microdrawn to show what the document would look like if it were pasted, page for page, on a wall and you stood back 20 feet to look at it. Other page views show the micropages a little larger. Indeed, this is a cool feature.

4. Press F7 to return to the document for more editing.

✔ A quicker way to get to the Print Preview screen is to select the Print Preview menu item from the File menu.

✔ Nope, you cannot edit a document in the Print Preview screen. But you can confirm font and formatting changes.

✔ Refer to Chapter 20 for more information on viewing a document in the graphics mode.

✔ Here's something cool you can do: When you're viewing a document in teensy-tiny mode, drag the mouse over part of the text. A small graphical rectangle appears, which you can stretch like a rubber band as long as you hold down the mouse button. When you release the button, WordPerfect enlarges that rectangular portion of the text to King-Kong size on the screen. You can use this trick to scrutinize various parts of a document that are too microscopic to see otherwise.

Printing Envelopes

Yes, WordPerfect can print envelopes. It even has a Print Envelope command, but don't go looking for it anywhere in the Print/Fax dialog box. I mean, if you were expecting this program to make sense, you should have caught on by now.

The Print Envelope command is Alt-F12, although you also can find this command in the Layout menu. If you want to do an envelope instantly in the comfort of your favorite word processor, hey, you're on your own. To do the envelope in WordPerfect, follow these seven concise steps:

1. **Press Alt-F12.**

    You see the Envelope dialog box that is shown in Figure 8-2. You type the return address in one big white space and the destination address in another big white space.

2. **Press 4.**

    WordPerfect's attention moves to the return address part of the dialog box.

3. **Type your return address.**

    You know this address better than I do.

Envelope

1. **E**nvelope Size   Envelope (COM 10)   9.5" X 4.13"

2. ☐ **O**mit Return Address

3. ☐ **S**ave Return Address as Default

4. **Return Address**
```
Dan Gookin
IDG Books
155 Bovet Road
San Mateo, CA 94402
```

5. **Mailing Address**
```
Vice President Al Gore
Office of the Vice President
Old Executive Office Building
Washington, DC 20501
```

6. **POSTNET Bar Code:**

Setup... Shft+F1   **Print**   **Insert**   **Close**   **Cancel**

Figure 8-2:
The
Envelope
dialog box.

4. Press F7 when you're done typing the return address.

5. Press 5.

You boogie on down to the Mailing Address area, where you type the address of the person to whom you're writing the letter. Again, you know this address better than I do.

6. Press F7 when you're done typing the mailing address.

7. To print the envelope, press P.

The printer may beep or squawk at you, begging you to insert an envelope. You may need to experiment with this procedure a few times to determine which way the envelope goes.

Now if WordPerfect only had a stamp-licking function. . . .

✔ If you select the Insert button instead of Print (by pressing I or clicking the Insert button with the mouse), WordPerfect inserts the envelope into the document. Then the envelope prints whenever the rest of the document prints — a nifty trick for attaching envelopes to the end of letters you write.

✔ Because most letters start with the mailing address, WordPerfect scopes out that address and may — if you're lucky and it's a good day — automatically insert that address into the Mailing Address area right after you press Alt-F12. Cool.

✔ Envelopes go into a laser printer face up with the top part pointing to the left as you stand in front of the manual feeder. For a top-feeding dot-matrix printer, stick the envelope in upside down and facing away from you. Be sure to line up its left edge against the zero-inch mark (which should be somewhere unobvious and too tiny to see). Some printers have handy envelope feeders. Pray that yours is one of them.

✔ If WordPerfect displays a dialog box that claims that you must *define envelopes* before you print, you're in for it! You have to configure the printer to print on envelopes — even if you and the printer have printed on envelopes before. My advice is to call WordPerfect for technical support on this issue. The printer help number is in the WordPerfect manual.

Monitoring Printing

You can go off and do other things while WordPerfect is printing. For example, you can print a document, save it, and then start over with something new. WordPerfect continues to print. If you're printing a jillion documents, WordPerfect keeps track of them all and prints each of them, one after the other. You never need to sit and wait. Of course, you can't quit WordPerfect, so often you're left twiddling your thumbs.

Instead of burning excess calories by exercising your phalanges, you can become a passive participant in the printing process. It's like watching Congress on C-SPAN, but without the oratories, smiling, and back pats. Here's what you do:

1. Press Shift-F7, the Print command.

You see the Printer/Fax dialog box.

2. Press 6 (Control Printer).

You see an interesting dialog box that controls what WordPerfect calls *printer jobs* (see Figure 8-3). Printer jobs are all the documents you have lined up to print. If nothing is printing, this dialog box looks like church on Super Bowl Sunday.

You really can't do anything in the Control Printer dialog box except cancel a printing job, which is covered in the next section. But you can observe several interesting things about the documents that are being printed — and even discover why some documents aren't printing. You also can get an idea of how much more printing you have to do.

✔ Press F7 to exit the Printer Control dialog box and return to the document. Everything continues to print — even when you're not watching.

✔ Each file that WordPerfect prints is called a *job*. The jobs are numbered from 1 to 99, and then the numbering starts over again at 1. The numbers get higher the more you print and the longer you stay in WordPerfect.

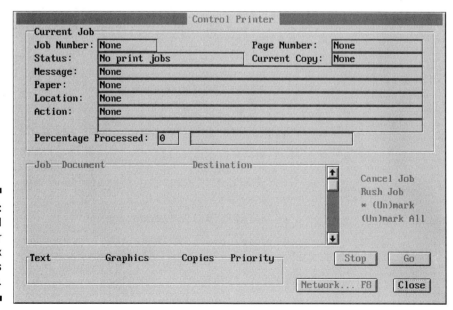

Figure 8-3:
The Control Printer dialog box monitors printing.

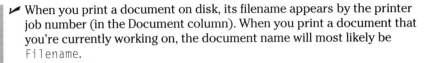

✔ When you print a document on disk, its filename appears by the printer job number (in the Document column). When you print a document that you're currently working on, the document name will most likely be `Filename`.

✔ If you quit WordPerfect before printing is done, all printing stops. A warning message is displayed, alerting you to this catastrophe. Press N.

✔ The Message and Action prompts near the top of the Control Printer menu often tell you what's going on and how to cure common problems. For example, if the printer isn't turned on and you're trying to print, you may see `Printer not accepting data` after the Message prompt. After the Action prompt, you see a suggested course of action: `Check cable, make sure printer is turned ON`. (In other words, turn on the printer.)

✔ The Control Printer dialog box is a great, busy screen that you can keep on the computer to convince the boss that you're really working hard. Consider putting a sticky note on the monitor: "Spooling; be right back." It's very effective.

Canceling a Print Job

Sometimes you tell the printer to print something and then change your mind. This happens all the time. (Rumor has it that Gutenberg originally wanted to print a hanging floral wall calendar.)

Or maybe the printer is slow, so you repeatedly pressed Shift-F7, 1, Enter too many times and you find yourself accidentally printing several dozen copies of the same document. Ugh.

Because WordPerfect prints in the background, pressing Esc doesn't cancel printing. Instead, follow these steps to cancel a print job:

1. **Press Shift-F7, the Print key. You see the Print/Fax dialog box.**

2. **Press 6 to wiggle yourself into the Control Printer dialog box.**

   You see a list of printer jobs on the screen. Look for the one that you want to cancel. If you're printing a lot of documents, then press the down-arrow key to list all the printing jobs. Most of the time, the job you want to cancel sits right on the top of the list.

3. **Highlight the name of the job you want to cancel.**

   Be observant! Pay attention to the names of the jobs. Filenames are listed, but the stuff you're working on right now will most likely appear as `Filename`.

4. Press 1, which selects the Cancel Job item from the menu on the right side of the dialog box.

A dialog box appears, asking whether you want to `Cancel highlighted print job?`

5. Press Y for Yes.

WordPerfect makes an attempt to stop printing. This effort is about as effective as a four-year-old's attempt to clean his or her room. While WordPerfect is trying to stop, you see a string of "I'm trying to stop, really" messages. Just be patient while WordPerfect clears its mind.

After the havoc has been wrought, you may see a `Press G to continue` message near the Action prompt. The job has been laid off.

6. Press G and then press F7 to exit from the Print menu and return to the document.

If you want to cancel more jobs, skip back up to Step 3 and cancel them as well.

✔ WordPerfect is not really done printing until you see the Status message `No print jobs.`

✔ Canceling a print job is not an immediate thing. After the Control Printer screen clears up and WordPerfect calms down, you may find that a few pages are still printing in the printer. Relax. Think of calm blue waters. Wait. Then pick up the pieces and start over.

Part II
Making Your Prose
Look Less Ugly

The 5th Wave   By Rich Tennant

In this part . . .

Formatting is what makes WordPerfect documents shine. It's what makes you boast when you show your printed labors to Microsoft Word users and they snivel, "Gosh, how'd you get it to print all on one page?" Few other things in life can make you swell with such pride.

Yet formatting isn't without its dark side. It involves many incantations and secret rituals, and it has a deep frustration factor. Some night you may wake up screaming, "Margins? Margins! Where the heck are my margins?" But then you'll realize that you've been having a nightmare and that this book, yea, this very part of the book, tells you exactly where to find your margins and how to make documents look oh so purty.

Chapter 9
Formatting Characters

*T*he most basic thing you can format in a document is the character. Characters include letters, words, text in paragraphs, and weird uncle Lloyd who trims the hair in his ears with a butane lighter. You can format characters to be bold, underlined, italicized, little, big, or in different fonts. WordPerfect gives you a lot of control, but there are pitfalls. For example, there is no one-key approach to formatting characters. But that's a disappointment you should be used to by now.

Changing the Way Text Looks

When you change the way a character looks, you apply an attribute to that character. This works like a beauty makeover. For example, Jacques would say, "*Voltaire!* You need some rouge on your *sheeks* and — *salle à manger* — where are your eyebrows? Let me help. A touch of *bleu* around *ze* eyes, see? There! *Et voilà,* the woman of the house is transformed into a *ting* of beauty. *Revenous à nos moutons!*"

Compared with a beauty makeover, applying attributes to characters is a little less dramatic, but it has the same effect. It makes text more attractive and can add meaning to your message. In WordPerfect, in addition to making text bold, underlining it, italicizing it, and changing its size, you can return text to *normal* and apply some less common attributes, such as shadow, strikeout, small caps, double underline, outline, and redline. Most of these attributes will have their place in your documents, and you're probably eager to start changing the boring old computer-looking text into text with zest and zing. Or should that be ZEST and *zing?*

Making text bold

| Bold |

To emphasize a word, you make it **bold.** Bold text is, well, bold. It's heavy. It carries a lot of weight, stands out on the page, speaks its mind at public meetings, wears a cowboy hat — you know the type.

To make text stand out, follow these steps:

1. Press Ctrl-B.

This key combination turns on the bold character format.

2. Type the word or characters that you want bold.

The text appears on the screen as bold text in graphics mode, darker and heavier than the other characters.

3. Press Ctrl-B again to turn off the bold character format.

This procedure takes care of formatting new text as bold. But if you have text already on the screen that you want to make bold, you need to block the text first. Follow these steps:

1. Mark the block of text that you want bold.

Move the cursor to the start of the block. Press Alt-F4 to turn on block-marking mode and move the cursor to the end of the block. The block appears highlighted on the screen.

2. Press Ctrl-B.

All text in the block appears bold, and the block highlighting disappears.

✔ You can use the F6 key, rather than Ctrl-B, to make text bold. Although F6 is one key less than Ctrl-B, nothing in my head's lexicon helps me remember that F6 has anything to do with bold text. On the other hand, the *B* in *Ctrl-B* stands for *Bold.* WordPerfect can almost be accused of making sense here.

✔ The Bold menu item in the Font menu also switches the bold character format on and off.

✔ You can mix and match character formats: text can be bold *and* underlined or bold, underlined, *and* italic. To use more than one format, you need to press the proper keys to turn on all the formats that you want to use before you type the text. Yes, you may have to type several WordPerfect character formatting commands before you type the text. It's a hassle, but everyone has to do it that way.

✔ To remove the bold character format from text, refer to "Making text normal" later in this chapter.

✔ If you're applying multiple character formats to the same block, you can quickly rehighlight the block with the Alt-F4, Ctrl-Home, Ctrl-Home block re-marking command.

✔ Refer to Chapter 6 for more information on marking blocks.

Making text underlined

Underline

Underlined text just isn't as popular as it used to be. Instead, people now use italicized text for subtle emphasis. Still, underlined text does have its place. I don't know where, or I'd come up with a cheesy example here.

To underline text, follow these steps:

1. Press Ctrl-U.

This key combination turns on the underline character format.

2. Type the text that you want underlined.

The text is underlined, right there on the screen. Everything is underlined, even the spaces between words.

3. Press Ctrl-U again to turn off underlining.

If you already have text on the screen that you want to be underlined, you need to mark the text as a block and then press Ctrl-U. Here are the steps to take:

1. Mark the block of text that you want to underline.

Position the cursor at the start of the block. Press Alt-F4 to activate the block-marking mode and move the cursor to the end of the block. The block appears highlighted on the screen.

2. Press Ctrl-U.

This action underlines the entire block — massive emphasis. The block highlighting disappears.

✔ You can use the F8 key, rather than Ctrl-U, to give text the underlined look. Ctrl-U makes more sense because *U* could be taken to mean *Underline*. F8 should just be said aloud in a Bingo hall to make everyone crazy.

✔ The Underline item in the Font menu also switches underlined text on and off.

✔ Chapter 6, king of the block chapters, contains more information about marking blocks.

Making text italicized

Italicized

Replacing underline as the preferred text-emphasis format is italics. I'm not embarrassed to use italics to emphasize, to highlight a title, or just because it looks so much better than shabby underlined text. It's light and wispy, poetic and free. Underlining is what the Department of Motor Vehicles does when it feels creative.

To italicize text, follow these steps:

1. Press Ctrl-I.

This key combination turns on the italic character format.

2. Type the text that you want italicized.

Magically, italic text appears on the screen. Everything is *slanting to the right* — just like the bridge crew on the Starship Enterprise when the Romulans fire a photon torpedo.

3. Press Ctrl-I again to deactivate italics.

If the text you want to italicize is already in the document, you have to mark it as a block and then change its character format. Follow these steps:

1. Mark the block of text that you want to italicize.

Move the toothpick cursor to the start of the block. Press Alt-F4 to switch on block-marking mode and move the cursor to the end of the block. The block appears highlighted on the screen.

2. Press Ctrl-I.

This deft move italicizes the entire block, slanting every letter to the right and making it look much better than primitive underlining makes it look.

✔ An alternative to using Ctrl-I is to select the Italics menu item from the Font menu.

✔ Refer to the discussion on marking a block in Chapter 6 for more information on marking blocks (as if you'd expect to find information on whittling blocks there).

Affecting text attributes

The most common character formats are bold, underline, and italics, which are described in the previous sections. WordPerfect has six other text formats that are not so common. You use the Ctrl-F8 key combination to apply these formats to characters or blocks of text. All the text formats are listed in Table 9-1, along with their key commands and examples of what they look like. As the table shows, using the Ctrl-F8 key combination is another way to apply bold, underline, and italics to text.

Table 9-1	Text Formats, Examples, and Commands	
Character Format	*Sample Text*	*Key Command*
Bold	Don't **bleed** on the rug!	Ctrl-F8, A, B
Underline	Don't <u>bleed</u> on the rug!	Ctrl-F8, A, U
Double Underline	Don't <u>bleed</u> on the rug!	Ctrl-F8, A, D
Italics	Don't *bleed* on the rug!	Ctrl-F8, A, I
Outline	Don't bleed on the rug!	Ctrl-F8, A, 5
Shadow	Don't bleed on the rug!	Ctrl-F8, A, A
Small Caps	Don't BLEED on the rug!	Ctrl-F8, A, C
Redline	Don't ~~bleed~~ on the rug!	Ctrl-F8, A, R
Strikeout	Don't ~~bleed~~ on the rug!	Ctrl-F8, A, S

To apply one of these weird text formats to characters as you type, start by pressing the key command as shown in Table 9-1. For example, to type a title in small caps, do the following:

1. **Move the cursor to where you want to begin typing.**

2. **Press Ctrl-F8, A, C.**

   In my head, I think, "*Ctrl-F8.* Somehow this means *Font* to WordPerfect. Then it's *A* for *Appearance* and *C* for *Caps.* Small caps = Font, Appearance, Caps." The more you do this, the more the letters may make some sense. Then again, don't count on it.

3. Type away, la, la, la.

4. When you're done, press Ctrl-F8, A, C again to turn off the attribute.

Use the preceding steps for any text that you want to change, substituting the appropriate formatting commands from Table 9-1 in Steps 2 and 4.

For changing the attributes on a block of text, follow these steps:

1. Mark the block.

Use the Alt-F4 command or any of the other handy block-marking tips that are covered in the better half of Chapter 6.

2. Pluck out a formatting command from Table 9-1 and press the keys for that command.

WordPerfect modifies the block with the attribute you select.

✔ All the text attributes that are splashed out for you in Table 9-1 are also in the Font menu. Pull down that menu to see them there in living gray and black.

✔ If you're into menus, you can use the Alt-O key combination to pull down the Font menu and then press each attribute's menu shortcut letter to quickly change text. This method is a wee bit faster than the Ctrl-F8 method (Yeah!), though the shortcut letters aren't the same (Boo!).

✔ Ctrl-F8 plus some letters is one of the few WordPerfect oddball command keys where using letters is better than using numbers. For some reason, Shift-F7, 1, Enter will always be *print the document* to me. But Ctrl-F8, A, C somehow works better for *F*ont, *A*ppearance, Small *C*aps.

✔ Don't expect your printer to be able to handle all these attributes. Small caps usually comes out OK. Strikeout works on most printers. But the redline attribute has a red line through it, which you can't get on most black-and-white printers (duh). And on my printer, I can print letters with the shadow attribute but not with the outline attribute.

✔ Removing character formats is covered in "Making text normal," which is just a few paragraphs later in this chapter.

Changing text size

| Fine Small Normal Large Very Large Extra Large |

Attributes — bold, italics, underline, and so on — are only half of the character formats. The other half deal with the text size. With text-size formatting commands, you can make text teensy-weensy or very large.

To change the size of text as you type, follow these steps:

1. Press Ctrl-F8, the Font key command.

You see the Font dialog box displayed, as shown in Figure 9-1. This dialog box has more options than a cow has flies. It's possibly the busiest place in all of WordPerfect. Take a deep breath.

2. Press 4.

This action on your part focuses WordPerfect's attention on the Relative Size area of the dialog box. (And I don't know about you, but I have some awfully hefty-sized relatives.)

Six different size options are available for text, with Normal used as a base. The smallest size is Fine and then comes Small. Bigger than Normal are Large, Very Large, and then Immense — I mean, Extra Large, or Sam's Club size.

3. Select the size format that you want by pressing the appropriate key, 1 through 6.

WordPerfect gives you a preview of the text size in the Resulting Font window at the bottom of the Font dialog box.

4. Press Enter to make the Font dialog box go back to where it came from.

5. Type the text that you want to be the selected size.

6. When you're done, press the right-arrow key to get out of that format.

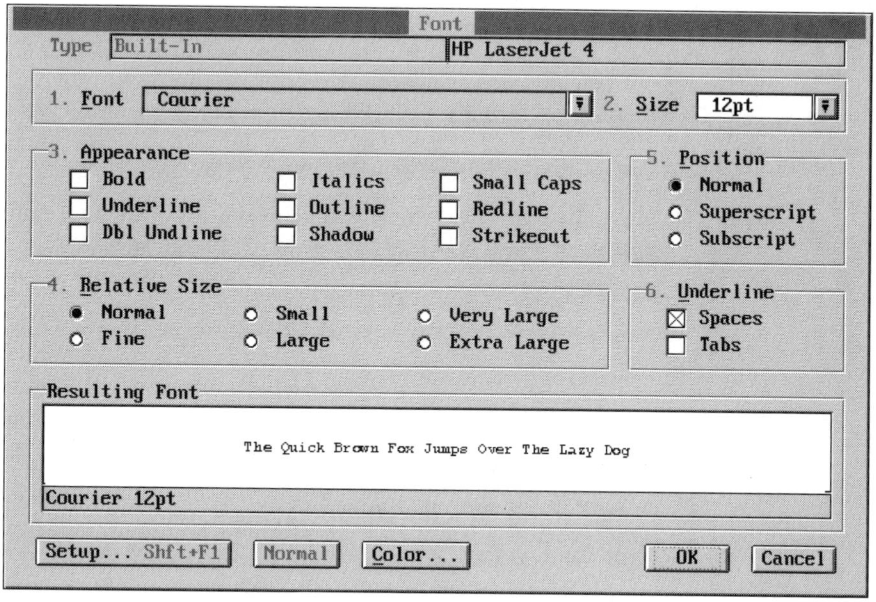

Figure 9-1:
The Font
dialog box.

The right-arrow thing is a shortcut. The WordPerfect Propriety Meisters want you either to go through Steps 1 – 4 again to turn off the text-size attribute or to select the Normal attribute. Now you know better, but you may have to press the right-arrow key and then backspace to start typing in the normal font again.

✔ If you want to apply a size format to text that is already on the screen, mark the text as a block before you go through Steps 1 – 4. No problemo.

✔ The text sizes appear on the Font menu in a special submenu area. From the Font menu, select the Size/Position item and then select the size that you want from the submenu that is displayed.

✔ The new text size shows up right on the screen. The biggest size is mammoth!

✔ Remember that you can press the right-arrow key to return the text to normal — or just select the Normal size from the Font dialog box.

✔ Is it just me, or should "The Quick Brown Fox Jumps Over The Lazy Dog" be replaced by "The Irate WordPerfect User Shows Up At Orem And Hacks Off Some Heads"?

✔ My son gets all his letters from Grandma in 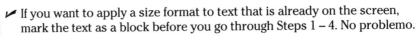 bigtype (which she learned how to do from this book).

Changing text position

Using an alternative text position refers to two things: superscript and subscript text. *Superscript* is text above the line — for example, the *10* in 2^{10}. *Subscript* is text below the line — for example, the *2* in H_2O. A *SuperSub* is a 10-inch long monstrosity at the local deli, which my wife forbids me to eat.

To produce either of these special effects, follow these steps:

1. **Move the cursor to where you want the superscript or subscript text to appear or mark text that you want to change as a block.**

2. **Press Ctrl-F8.**

   You see the Font dialog box, which is shown in Figure 9-1.

3. **Press 5.**

   WordPerfect's attention turns to the Position area of the dialog box.

4. **Press 2 to select Superscript or press 3 to select Subscript.**

5. **Press Enter to exit the dialog box.**

6. **Type the text that you want to be superscripted or subscripted.**

   If you marked a block before you took Steps 1 – 5, the text in the block will be either superscripted or subscripted after Step 5.

✔ To return to the normal text position, follow Steps 2 and 3, but press 1 (Normal) in Step 4 and then press Enter to exit the dialog box.

✔ Superscripted and subscripted text shows up on the screen just as it will be printed — above or below the other text.

✔ You also can change the superscript and subscript attributes from the Font menu. Select Size/Position and then select the appropriate position from the submenu that appears.

Making text normal

Sometimes you have so many character attributes going that you don't know what to press to get back to normal text. Welcome to Formatting Run Amok. Fortunately, WordPerfect has lent a tiny ear to your cries for help. You can use the Normal text-formatting command to shut off everything — all the size and attribute formats — and return the text to normal. Press the following key combination:

Ctrl-N

Just as *Ctrl-I* means *Italics* and *Ctrl-B* means *Bold, Ctrl-N* means *Normal.* Just start typing, and the text appears *normal* from that point on. Ahhh....

To make a whole block of text that you've already typed appear normal, do the following:

1. Mark the text as a block.

Position the cursor where you want the block to start, press Alt-F4, and use the cursor-control keys to mark the block. Or use the mouse to mark the block.

2. Press Ctrl-N.

All the text in the block appears normal — no attributes and no big text.

✔ The Fonts menu has a Normal menu item that does the same thing as the Ctrl-N key command.

✔ The Ctrl-N command does not affect superscripted or subscripted text. To make them normal, select the Normal item from the Fonts menu by pressing the following keys:

Ctrl-F8, 5, 1

Refer to the preceding section for more information on changing text position.

✔ What is *normal?* Normal is the current font — the typeface, size, and style that you've selected for a document. WordPerfect's Normal command just strips off any bold, big — or whatever — attributes that you have assigned to the text. (Refer to the very next section for a more detailed explanation of fonts.)

✔ Uncle Lloyd is not normal.

Changing the Font

Text can be bold, italicized, underlined, made big, made little, and on and on. But the text *font* — the basic characteristics of the text that you see when you print the document — is controlled by the printer, not by WordPerfect.

Your printer has certain *fonts* or *character sets* stuffed inside its brain. WordPerfect selects the basic character set, which usually looks like typewriter output (not too fancy), when it prints a document. You can change the character set, however, at any point in the document by selecting a different font that you think is more appropriate. (And I'm not going to tell you what's appropriate; you'll have to guess.)

Changing the typeface

Fonts consist of two elements: the typeface, which is how the font looks, and its size. To switch to a different font style, follow these steps:

1. **Press Ctrl-F8.**

   The Font dialog box comes up, as shown in Figure 9-1.

2. **Press 1.**

   This action selects the Font area, which drops down a list of fonts that the printer has or that you or your guru has added for use with WordPerfect.

3. **Use the arrow keys to select a font from the list.**

   The currently selected font has an asterisk by it.

   Some fonts have their own attributes: bold, italics, or bold and italics. These attributes are in addition to any character formats that you add in WordPerfect. For example, if you select the Times Roman Italic font, the text is italicized even though you don't see green or whatever on the screen.

   The Resulting Font box (that *Quick Brown Fox* thing) at the bottom of the Font dialog box previews all the fonts for you.

4. **Press Enter to select the new font.**

5. **Press Enter again to exit the Font dialog box and start using the new font.**

   Or press Esc (once or twice) to cancel the font change.

✔ Stick to character formats first (bold, italics, big, little) and then play with fonts later when you have time to goof off.

✔ The font that you select appears on the screen very closely resembling what will be printed. Occasionally, WordPerfect doesn't understand a font, and it may look different on the screen than it does when it's printed. Nothing man nor beast can do on Earth will change that, unfortunately.

✔ The Font menu has a Font menu item that leads you to the Font dialog box. (And I'm certain that the Redundant menu has a Redundant item that leads you to the Redundant dialog box.)

✔ The fifth button from the left in the Button Bar is the Font button. It has three big Fs on it For Font Finagling.

✔ A font is a character set. For example, Times Roman is a font. Helvetica is a font (one that has straighter lines than the Times Roman font does). This book is printed with the Cheltenham font for body text and Cascade Script font for section titles.

✔ You can use the Font command to change the font for a block of text. Just mark the block before you select the new font.

✔ To change the font for an entire document, move the cursor to the absolute tippy top of the document before you press Ctrl-F8, 1. To make it to the top quickly, use the triple Home Up command: Home, Home, Home, ↑.

Changing the typeface from the Ribbon

If you have WordPerfect's Ribbon displayed (just below the menu bar), you can quickly change the font from the Ribbon — provided that you have a mouse. To do so, follow these steps:

1. Use the mouse to click on the button for the Font drop-down list.

The button for the Font drop-down list is the second downward-pointing arrow button from the right on the Ribbon. The name of the current font (Courier, Times Roman, or whatever) is displayed in the box to the left of the arrow button.

2. Find the new font that you want from the list.

WordPerfect may take a moment to collect itself and summon all the font names to the screen. After that, use the mouse to scroll through the list by clicking on the up arrow or down arrow on the scroll bar for the list.

3. Double-click on the font name to select it.

Refer to Chapter 19 for more information on the Ribbon.

Changing the font size

The normal size for text is set by the size of the font that you're using. You select this size in the Font dialog box, to the right of where you pick the font (see Figure 9-1).

To select a new size for the font, follow these steps:

1. **Press Ctrl-F8.**

   Behold! The Font dialog box graces you with its presence.

2. **Press 2.**

   This action highlights the Size area of the dialog box, where you set the size of the font you're using.

   The normal size for most fonts is 12pt, where *pt* stands for *points*. Points measure the font's height. An inch is about 36 points, so a 12pt font is ⅓ of an inch high. An 18pt font size is big; an 8pt font size is small.

3. **Type the new point size for your text or press the down-arrow key and choose a size from the list that drops down.**

   For example, you can type 18 or you can press the ↓ key to display a list of point sizes and then move the highlight bar to the size that you want. The Resulting Font preview at the bottom of the screen shows you about how big the selection is.

4. **Press Enter to lock in the new font size.**

5. **Press Enter again to leave the Font dialog box.**

6. **Press Enter to select the new font.**

   ✔ As with changing the typeface, changing the font size affects the entire document from the cursor position to the end.

   ✔ Points measure the font's height — how tall it is on the page. The typical height is 12 points, about a third of an inch. The typewriter pica size is 12 points tall, and elite size is 10 points tall.

   ✔ You also can mark a block and then follow Steps 1 – 6 to change the font size for just that block.

   ✔ I recommend using the text-size attributes as described earlier in this chapter for changing text size. Messing with fonts means that your secret desire is to become a typesetter — and that's a bit much at this stage of the game.

   ✔ *Font* is one of those words that gets dumber and dumber the more you say it.

Changing the type size from the Ribbon

If you are displaying the WordPerfect Ribbon, you can take advantage of it to change the font size with the mouse. Here are the steps:

1. Use the mouse to click on the button for the Point Size drop-down list.

It's the first button from the right on the Ribbon. The current point size (such as *12pt* — or maybe *18pt* if you're writing to Grandma) is displayed.

2. Select a new size from the list.

To scroll through the list, click on the up arrow or down arrow on the scroll bar for the list. Remember that larger numbers mean bigger text.

3. Double-click on a font size to change the text size in the document.

✔ Refer to the preceding section for more information on font sizes.

✔ Chapter 19 contains more information on the Ribbon.

Converting Uppercase and Lowercase Letters

Uppercase and lowercase letters aren't considered part of a font, character attribute, or format. Anyway, WordPerfect has a fun feature that enables you to use all capital letters, all lowercase letters, or a mixture of uppercase and lowercase letters. This feature is the Switch Case command, and it can come in handy.

To switch text to all capital letters, follow these steps:

1. Mark the text that you want to convert as a block.

Position the cursor at the start of the block. Press Alt-F4 to switch on the block-marking mode and move the cursor to the end of the block. The block is highlighted on the screen.

Marking a block of text is a must for this command! Obviously, if you know before you type the text that you want it in all capital letters, using the Caps Lock key before you type it is easier than messing with an obtuse WordPerfect key combination.

2. Press the Switch key, Shift-F3.

You see the Convert Case dialog box that is shown in Figure 9-2. The dialog box has three options: U for uppercase (all capital letters), L for lowercase

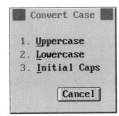

Figure 9-2:
The Convert
Case dialog
box.

(no capital letters), and I for initial caps (meaning that each word — except *and, of, on, in,* and the other words that are not capitalized in titles — starts with a capital letter).

3. **Press U, L, or I, depending on how you want the text in the block to look.**

   Ta-da. The text is converted.

   ✔ The Switch Case command key, Shift-F3, works only if a block is marked. Otherwise, this key sends you off into Document 2. If that happens, press Shift-F3 again to return to Document 1. (Also, refer to the section in Chapter 14 on working with two or more documents at one time.)

   ✔ The Undo command, Ctrl-Z, can handily undo any case-changing that you did with Ctrl-F3.

Inserting Oddball Characters

Look over your keyboard's keys. Yeah, there are the letters of the alphabet, plus numbers, and some weird symbols and such. WordPerfect can display all those characters just fine; you see them on the screen every day. But there are several dozen additional, interesting characters that you can display. Some you can see on the screen; others can only print. These are WordPerfect's *oddball characters.*

You insert oddball characters by using the Ctrl-W command, where *W* means *Weird.* Here is how you work the Ctrl-W command:

1. **Position the cursor where you want the oddball character to appear.**

2. **Press Ctrl-W.**

   You see the Weird Characters dialog box, otherwise known as the WordPerfect Characters dialog box, as shown in Figure 9-3. You can choose from several sets of characters, including Cyrillic (Russian) and Japanese characters. The characters are previewed at the bottom of the dialog box.

3. **Press Esc and then 2 to select a character set.**

   The character set list drops down. Use the arrow keys to highlight the name of a particular group of characters. (The Iconic Symbols character set is pretty fun to look at.)

4. **Press 3.**

   Attention moves to the Characters area of the dialog box.

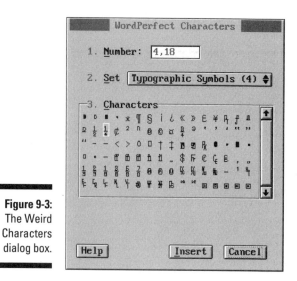

Figure 9-3:
The Weird
Characters
dialog box.

5. **Use the cursor-control keys to highlight a given character.**

   They're kind of tiny. Some of the sets have several hundred characters in them. Use the PgUp and PgDn keys to see all of them. (You don't want to miss out.)

6. **Press Enter to select a character.**

   The weird character is inserted into the document.

✔ Table 9-2 lists some popular characters. They're from either set 4, Typographic Symbols, or set 5, Iconic Symbols. The *Code* in the table is the set number, followed by the character number (the first character displayed in the box is character 1).

Table 9-2 Some Common and Useful Oddball Characters

Code	Symbol	Name
4,0	•	Dot
4,2	□	Square
4,17	½	One-half
4,18	¼	One-quarter
4,19	¢	Cents
4,23	©	Copyright symbol
4,41	™	Trademark symbol
5,26	☹	Mr. Grumpy

✔ If you like, you can type the numbers from Table 9-2, such as **5,26** for Mr. Grumpy, directly into the Number box when the WordPerfect Characters dialog box is on the screen. Just press 1 to activate the Number box, type the secret code number, and then press Enter.

✔ More symbols are listed in Appendix A.

No need to read this information if you're just passing by

The Ctrl-A key combination is called the *Compose command.* (Notice that it's *Compose,* not *compost.*) In addition to typing secret code numbers, you also can create special characters by welding two keyboard characters together. This can be fun.

For example, to create the plus-minus symbol, ±, do the following:

1. Press Ctrl-A. The Compose dialog box appears.

2. Type a plus and a minus, +-.

You don't have to press Enter. The plus-minus character automagically appears on the screen.

You can add accents above characters by typing the character and then the ', `, ~, ", or ^ key. For example, do the following:

1. Press Ctrl-A.

2. Type n~, the N key and then the tilde.

This action produces the ñ, en-ay, character, which is common in Spanish. Similarly, pressing Ctrl-A and then u and " produces ü, which makes an oo-ey sound in some languages.

Chapter 10
Formatting Sentences and Paragraphs

- -

In This Chapter

▶ Centering text

▶ Making text flush right

▶ Changing the justification

▶ Changing the line spacing

▶ Working with tabs

▶ Using alignment tabs

▶ Setting the margins

▶ Indenting a paragraph

▶ Double-indenting a paragraph

▶ Using the margin release

▶ Doing a hanging indent

▶ Undoing strange tab stuff

- -

After you format characters or text, the next biggest things that you can format in a document are sentences and paragraphs. This kind of formatting involves the position of the text on the page, the margins, lining things up with tabs or indents, and line spacing. You can do this stuff on the fly, but I recommend doing it just before you print the document (along with page formatting, which is covered in the next chapter). That way you can pull some of your hair out while you struggle with spelling and grammar and getting your ideas on paper. Then, when all of that is perfect and your blood pressure has dropped, you can pull out the rest of your hair while you struggle anew with WordPerfect's line and paragraph formatting. Ugh. Will it never end?

Centering Text

WordPerfect enables you to center either a single line of text or a block of text. Not too far left, not too far right — just exactly in the middle. Fair is fair.

If you want to center a single line of text, usually a title or heading, follow these steps:

1. Start on a new line, the line that you want to be centered.

If the line is already displayed on the screen, skip to the second set of directions, which follows this list.

2. Press the Center key combination, Shift-F6.

The cursor zips over to the center of the screen (or thereabouts).

3. Type the title or heading.

Try to limit what you type to one line of text. If you type more than a line, it becomes uncentered and you'll need to follow the second set of instructions.

4. Press Enter when you're done.

The line is centered.

If you want to center more than one line, perhaps a paragraph or more, type the text and then follow these steps:

1. Mark the text that you want to center as a block.

Move the cursor to the start of the block. Press Alt-F4, which activates block-marking mode, and then move the cursor to the end of the block. The block is highlighted on the screen.

2. Press the Center key command, Shift-F6.

The highlighting disappears, and the block is centered on the screen and centered left to right on the page when you print the document.

✔ The Center command, Shift-F6, centers only one line of text. For anything larger, you have to type in the text, mark it as a block, and then center it.

✔ If you press Shift-F6 and the title or heading turns out to be longer than a line, don't despair! Keep typing. When you're done, go back and mark the text as a block and then press Shift-F6 to center the block. (Follow the second set of instructions for centering text.)

✔ Chapter 6 has more information on marking blocks.

If you need to reapply character formatting to a block you've just centered, here's a quick way to rehighlight the block immediately after you center it:

1. **Don't move the cursor!**

2. **Press Alt-F4 to turn on block-marking mode.**

3. **Press Ctrl-Home, Ctrl-Home.**

   The block is rehighlighted, and you can assign a text attribute to it to make the characters bold, bigger, and so on. See the discussion on assigning attributes in Chapter 9.

   ✔ To uncenter a block, select left justification for it. (*Left justification* is fancy talk for the way the block looked before you centered it.) Refer to "Using the Ribbon to Change the Justification" later in this chapter.

Making Text Flush Right

Oh, I could really have a field day with the title of this section and my potty-mouth mentality. But I'm going to cut my editor some slack here. *Flush right* describes the way text is lined up on the screen. Normally, text is *flush left,* with each line starting even with the left margin. *Flush right* text is where each line starts even with the right margin. In other words, the text is slammed against the right side of the page — as if you'd picked up the paper and jerked it wildly until the text slid over.

You can flush right a single line of text or mark any size of text as a block and flush it right. If you want to flush right a single line, follow these steps:

1. **Position the cursor where you want to type a line flush right.**

   The cursor is on the same line but still at the left side of the screen. Don't use the spacebar or Tab key to move the cursor; the Flush Right command will move it in just a second.

   If the text that you want to flush right is already on the screen, skip to the set of instructions that follows this set.

2. **Press Alt-F6, the Flush Right key combination.**

   The cursor moves to the right side of the screen.

3. **Type the line of text.**

   The cursor jumps to the right side of the screen. The characters that you type push to the left, always staying flush with the right side of the document.

4. **Press Enter when you're done.**

To make more than one line of text flush right or to make text that you already have in a document flush right, you first need to mark the text as a block. Follow these steps:

1. **Mark the text that you want to flush right as a block.**

   It's best to use the Flush Right command on full paragraphs or sentences only. If you mark an odd section of text, then it's going to look just plain weird on the screen and even weirder in print.

   Mark the text by moving the cursor to the start of the block, pressing Alt-F4 to turn on block-marking mode, and then moving the cursor to the end of the block.

2. **Press Alt-F6, the Flush Right key combination.**

   The block is lined up on the right side of the page. (No sound effects, please.)

✔ The Flush Right command, Alt-F6, works best when you're typing only one line of text. For anything larger, enter the text first, mark it as a block, and press Alt-F6, as described in the second set of instructions.

✔ If the single line of text gets longer, just keep on typing. After you're done, go back, mark everything you want to flush right as a block, and then refer to the second set of instructions for flushing that block to the right.

TIP

Making the date flush right at the top of the document

A neat-o thing to flush right at the top of the document is the date. Most people start their letters that way. You can too. Just follow these handy steps:

1. Move to the top of the document, to the line where you want to put the date. It must be a blank line.

2. Press Alt-F6, the Flush Right key combination. The cursor zooms over to the right side of the page.

3. Press Shift-F5, 1. The current date is inserted into the document.

You can now continue to work on the document. The current date is proudly flushed right at the top of the page.

What Is the Justification?

Left Justification

Justification is a fancy term for all of this centering, flushing right, and the other ways to put text on the page. It's an old typesetter's term, rumored to be first used by Gutenberg himself. When he first saw page one of the Bible, all the words were flush right. Gutenberg, trying to contain his anger, said — with strain in his voice — "What is der justification fer dis?" And the smart-alecky typesetter said, "Right."

Center Justification

Right Justification

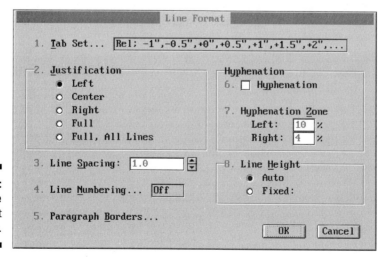

Full Justification

Pain was inflicted.

Today, *justification* refers to the way that text lines up on the page:

Left justification	All even on the left
Right justification	All even on the right
Full justification	All even all over
Center justification	Centered between the left and right
No justification	Football players' salaries

To change the justification in a document, follow these steps:

1. Move the cursor to the position in the document where you want the new justification format to take effect.

It's best if this place is at the beginning of a new paragraph or at the top of a page. Wherever you choose, the justification from that point down in the document is changed.

2. Press the Format key combination, Shift-F8.

You see the Format dialog box — not your final destination.

3. Press L for Line.

The nifty Line Format dialog box is displayed, as shown in Figure 10-1. Marvel at it for a moment.

Figure 10-1:
The Line
Format
dialog box.

Line Format

1. Tab Set... Rel; -1",-0.5",+0",+0.5",+1",+1.5",+2",...

2. Justification
   ● Left
   ○ Center
   ○ Right
   ○ Full
   ○ Full, All Lines

Hyphenation
6. ☐ Hyphenation

7. Hyphenation Zone
   Left: 10 %
   Right: 4 %

3. Line Spacing: 1.0

4. Line Numbering... Off

5. Paragraph Borders...

8. Line Height
   ● Auto
   ○ Fixed:

OK   Cancel

4. Press J for Justification.

Pressing J brings WordPerfect's focus to the Justification part of the dialog box, where there are five items. The first four items are of the most importance to you.

5. Press the key that is associated with the justification you want.

Press L for left justification.

Press C for center justification.

Press R for right justification.

Press F for full justification.

6. Press F7, the Exit key, twice: F7, F7.

You return to the document to enjoy your new justification.

✔ You also can get to the Line Format dialog box by selecting the Line item from the Layout menu.

✔ If you change the justification in this manner, the rest of the document is affected. The new justification takes over from the cursor's position to the end of the text or until another justification command is encountered.

✔ To change the justification later in the document, repeat these steps after you position the cursor where you want the new justification to start taking place.

✔ If a block is highlighted when you change the justification, then the new justification affects only that block.

✔ To change the justification for an entire document, first move to the very top of the document: press Home, Home, ↑. Then follow the steps for changing the justification.

✔ If you want the new justification to start on a new page, first issue the New Page command by pressing Ctrl-Enter. Then follow the steps for changing the justification.

✔ Typographers may use other terms for the various types of justification. They occasionally use the word *ragged* to describe how the text fits. For example, left justification is *ragged right,* and right justification is *ragged left.* A *rag top* is a convertible with a soft top, and a *rag bottom* is any child who is still in diapers.

To quickly change the justification in a document, press these keys:

For left justification:	Shift-F8, L, J, L, F7, F7
For center justification:	Shift-F8, L, J, C, F7, F7
For right justification:	Shift-F8, L, J, R, F7, F7
For full justification:	Shift-F8, L, J, F, F7, F7

Optional stuff on justification

Justification is a typographical term. Oh, now, don't everyone boo me at once. This term refers to the way text sits on a page. There are four types of justification:

Left   Left justification is the standard type of justification. Text is lined up on the left side of the page. Because we read left to right, this type of justification makes the text easier to read. Text on the right side of the page is uneven or *ragged*.

Center Text is centered. You can use the Center command, which is described in "Centering Text," earlier in this chapter, to center text.

Right   Right justification is the opposite of left justification. Text is lined up on the right side of the page; text on the left side of

the page is uneven or *ragged*. The Flush Right command, described earlier in the chapter, produces text that is right-justified.

Full   Full justification is where the left edge of the text is even and the right edge of the text is even. WordPerfect inserts spaces of varying sizes between the words in a line to make sure that both edges are even. Many newspapers and magazines use this type of justification.

Please don't memorize any of this stuff. Instead, look it up when you want to change the way text looks in an entire document or in just a few paragraphs. Then use the Format key combination, Shift-F8, as described in the friendlier part of the chapter.

Using the Ribbon to Change the Justification

The Ribbon is that thingy clinging to the underside of the menu bar — an optional doohickey that you can display and then use for quick font changes and new justification at the poke of a mouse.

An item in the middle of the Ribbon — the third item from the right, actually — displays and controls the justification in a document. It may say Left, meaning that the text that the toothpick cursor is hiding in is left-justified. Or it may say Right, Full, or Centered, depending on how wacky you've gotten with line formatting.

To change the justification from the Ribbon, follow these steps:

1. **Click the mouse on the little downward-pointing triangle to the right of the word** Left **(or whatever) on the Ribbon.**

   A list drops down with the four justifications: Left, Center, Right, and Full.

2. **Double-click on a new justification for the document: Click-click.**

   This action changes the justification from that point onward — just as if you had used the offensive keyboard commands described in the preceding section.

✔ If a block is marked on the screen and you change the justification by using the Ribbon, only the block is affected.

✔ Keep an eyeball on the Ribbon and the currently chosen justification. If you ever become overwhelmed by what you see on the screen, the Ribbon can provide a sane reminder of at least some of what's going on.

✔ Yes, you need a mouse to do this.

Changing the Line Spacing

On a typewriter, you change the line spacing with a double or triple whack of the carriage return. Sadly, although whacking your computer twice or thrice may help your attitude, it won't do diddly for the document's line spacing. Instead, you need to use WordPerfect's Line Spacing command, which is nestled with the other format commands that cling to the Shift-F8 key combination and the Line Format dialog box.

To change the line spacing, follow these steps:

1. **Move the cursor to the spot in the document where you want to change the line spacing.**

    For example, move to the top of the document to change the line spacing for the entire document or move to the beginning of a line or paragraph. (You can change the line spacing at any position in a document, but changing it at the start of a line is best.)

2. **Press the Format key, Shift-F8.**

    You see the Format dialog box.

3. **Press L for Line.**

    The Line Format dialog box appears (see Figure 10-1). Line Spacing is item number 3. The current line-spacing value is shown in the box by the words `Line Spacing`.

4. **Press S for Spacing.**

    The box by `Line Spacing` perks up and awaits your input.

5. **Type a new line-spacing value.**

    Press 1 for single spacing, press 1.5 for one-and-a-half spacing, press 2 for double spacing, press 2.5 for two-and-a-half spacing, and so on. Or you can click on the little up triangle or down triangle to increase or decrease the line-spacing values with the mouse.

6. **Press Enter to lock in the new line-spacing value.**

7. **Press the Exit key, F7, twice to return to the document: F7, F7.**

✔ The new line spacing shows up on the screen right away.

✔ Changing the line spacing at the start of a document, the start of a page, or the beginning of a paragraph is best. Changing the line spacing in the middle of a random bit of text looks ugly and weird.

✔ You can change the line spacing for a block of text by following the same seven steps. Start by marking the block and then press Shift-F8, L, S, and so on. After you press F7 twice, only that block has the new line spacing; the rest of the document is as spaced-out as it was before.

✔ To move to the tippy top of a document, press Home, Home, ↑. To move to the start of a line, press Home, Home, ←.

✔ If you want to change the line spacing a second time, move the cursor to the place in the document where you want to change the spacing and follow the steps for changing the line spacing again. You can have several different types of line spacing in a single document if you like.

✔ The Line Spacing command affects all the text in a document from the cursor's position to the end of the document — unless another Line Spacing format command exists to change it. A single document can contain several Line Spacing commands, if you like. But don't be a line-space glutton.

✔ To change the line spacing back to what it was before, move to the place in the document where you changed it. Then issue the Line Spacing commands again to make the line spacing whatever it was before you changed it.

Changing the line spacing has a terrific mnemonic: *L-S* for *Line Spacing.* Here are the shortcut keys:

1. Press Shift-F8, L, S.

2. Enter the new line-spacing value.

3. Press Enter, F7.

Playing with Tabs

To indent stuff in a document, you use the Tab key — never the spacebar. You press Tab to indent text or to move the toothpick cursor over to the next tab stop. Using Tab is so much better than using the spacebar because you can assign different values to the tab. (And Tab has only one calorie more than water.) Just as on the typewriter where you can make one tab scoot the carriage three inches, you can make WordPerfect take different-sized leaps across a line every time you press the Tab key.

The tab stops here

When you press the Tab key, WordPerfect moves the cursor over to the next tab stop. Normally, the tab stops are set every half inch. You can change this value to any interval, or you can customize individual tab stops if you like. But, I beg you, don't! Changing the tab stops is really a knotty thing to do. If you insist on changing them, follow these steps closely:

1. **Position the cursor in the document before the place where you want to change the tabs.**

   The new tab stops will be in effect only from that position to the end of the document (or until a spot where you change the tab stops again).

2. **Press the Format key, Shift-F8.**

   The Format dialog box appears.

3. **Press L (Line).**

   The Line Format dialog box comes up on the screen.

4. **Press T (Tab Set).**

   You see the Tab Set dialog box, which displays part of the document (see Figure 10-2).

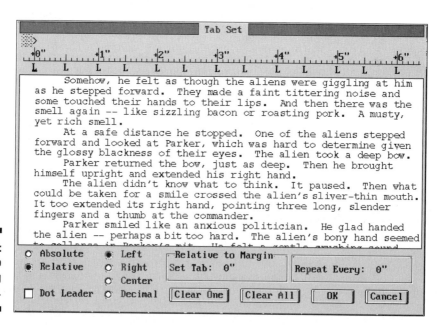

Figure 10-2:
The Tab
Set dialog
box.

At the top of the dialog box, you see a graphical representation of the tab stops that are already set. The numbers, +0, +1, and so on, show how many inches the tabs are set from the left margin. The tick marks and the Ls show you where the tabs are. Any changes that you make to the tabs are immediately shown in the window below the tab-stop bar, so you can actively see what effects your changes have on the document.

You use the controls on the bottom of the dialog box to mess with the tab stops.

5. Press A to delete all the tab stops.

The part of the document that is visible in the window collapses a bit because all the tab stops have just been sent to WordPerfect hell.

6. Use the left-arrow and right-arrow cursor-control keys and press L to place new tab stops on the tab-stop bar.

Press L where you want a tab. Continue to add tabs until all the tabs that you want are set. Press Esc when you're done.

If you want to set a tab every inch, press P to highlight the Repeat Every box. When you type a value, WordPerfect sets the tab stops to whatever interval you enter. For example, press 1 to set a tab stop every inch, press .5 to set a tab stop every half-inch, and so on.

7. Press F7, the Exit key, three times when you're done setting tabs.

This action returns you to the document.

✔ The Tab Set item in the Layout menu will instantly beam you to the Tab Set dialog box.

✔ After setting new tabs, you may have to scroll down a bit to get the new formatting to line up visually on the screen.

✔ You know, I really hate messing with tabs. Keeping them all at half-inch intervals — which WordPerfect does all by itself — works just fine for me.

✔ Each time that you reset the tab stops, they affect the rest of the document — up until the point where you set the tab stops again. A single document can have several tab stops in it.

✔ If you don't want to delete all the tab stops by pressing A, use the cursor to locate only the tab stops that you want to get rid of and then press Delete to remove them.

✔ When I'm working with many tabs, I usually press the Tab key only once before each new column of information. Then I follow the steps for resetting the tab stops so that the columns line up. Using one tab, rather than two or three, makes editing much easier. And moving the tab stops around makes the document look perfect-o.

✔ For tables of information, you really should use WordPerfect's Table command. Refer to Chapter 12 for information on setting up tables.

✔ The tab stops are measured from the right margin (see Figure 10-2). If you want to set *tab stops* relative to the left side of the page, press E to select Relative at the bottom of the Tab Set dialog box. Press B to select Absolute to have the *inch indicators* represent the distance from the left side of the page. Pressing E (Relative) lists the tab stops as measured from the left margin, which isn't always one inch — especially if you reset the margin.

A dreary explanation of the tab stop types, which you don't have to read

At the bottom of the Tab Set dialog box, you can choose from several different types of tabs.

The most common tab is L, the left tab. This tab works like the Tab key on a typewriter. Press Tab and the new text appears at the next tab stop. No mental hang-ups here.

The R tab is a right tab. Pressing Tab causes text to line up right-justified at that tab stop. The text is right-justified until you press Tab again or press Enter.

The C tab causes text to be centered on the tab stop. The text that you type is centered until you press the Tab key again or press Enter.

The D tab is a decimal tab that lines up numbers by their decimals. The number is right-justified before you press the period key and then left-justified afterward.

The dot-leader tab is used to produce a row of dots when you press Tab. You see this setup all the time in tables of contents:

Using Dot Leader Tabs.......150

After you set a dot-leader tab, pressing the Tab key produces the dots and lines up the numbers right-justified.

Alignment tabs

The alignment tab differs from normal tabs because you can use it to line up text at any tab stop — not just where you see an L or R or any of the other dorky settings from the overly complex Tab Set dialog box. Forget all that! Instead, do the following:

1. Press Ctrl-F6.

This key combination is the Tab Align command, and pressing it works just like pressing the Tab key: the cursor jumps to the next tab stop. You see the following displayed at the bottom of the screen:

```
Align char = .
```

This message tells you that WordPerfect lines up text based on the period character. (You can change the align character, as described in the nearby technical box.)

2. Type something.

The text pushes to the left. It continues to push to the left until you type a period — the align character. From that point on, the text moves right as it normally does.

3. Press Enter.

4. On the next line, press Ctrl-F6 and type something again, typing a period and then typing some more as you did in the preceding line.

See how the two lines align themselves on the period? That's the alignment tab. Oh, happy day.

✔ The Tab Align command enables you to line up text that may not be all the same length. It's best suited for lining up numbers or prices, which usually have a period in them.

Unnecessary information on changing the align character

You can change the align character if you like. Changing it enables you to line up other types of text, not just values. Follow these steps:

1. Press Shift-F8, C, D.

2. Type a new alignment character, perhaps a colon or a hyphen.

3. Press F7 to exit the menu and keep pressing F7 to close the various dialog boxes until you return to the document.

The character you typed in Step 2 is the character WordPerfect uses to align the text when you press Ctrl-F6.

Setting the Left and Right Margins

Every page has left and right margins, which serve as the *air* around the document — that inch of breathing space that sets the text off from the rest of the page. WordPerfect automatically sets margins one inch in from the right side and one inch in from the left side of the page. This setup is how most English teachers and book editors want things because they love to scribble in margins. But you can adjust both the left and right margins to suit any fussy professional.

To change the margins, follow these steps:

1. Move the cursor to the place in the text where you want the new margins to start.

The best place to set new margins is at the top of the document, the top of a page, or the start of a paragraph.

2. Press Shift-F8, the Format key.

You see the Format dialog box.

3. Press M for Margins.

The Margin Format dialog box appears, as depicted by renowned artist Fozwell Lumbago in Figure 10-3.

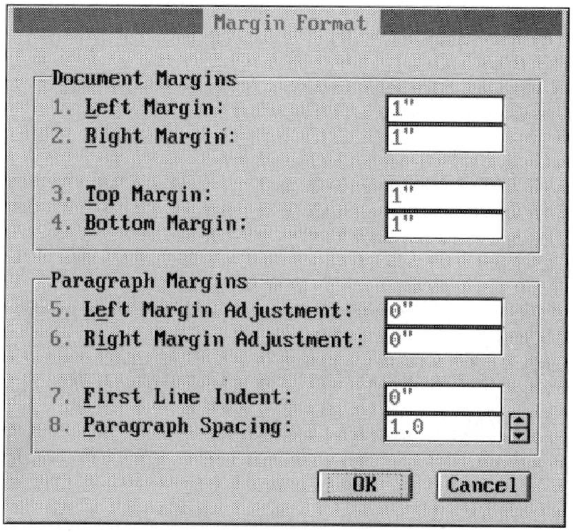

Figure 10-3:
The Margin
Format
dialog box.

```
┌─────────────────────── Margin Format ───────────────────────┐
│ ┌─Document Margins──────────────────────────────────────┐   │
│ │  1. Left Margin:                    [1"      ]         │   │
│ │  2. Right Margin:                   [1"      ]         │   │
│ │                                                        │   │
│ │  3. Top Margin:                     [1"      ]         │   │
│ │  4. Bottom Margin:                  [1"      ]         │   │
│ └────────────────────────────────────────────────────────┘   │
│ ┌─Paragraph Margins─────────────────────────────────────┐   │
│ │  5. Left Margin Adjustment:         [0"      ]         │   │
│ │  6. Right Margin Adjustment:        [0"      ]         │   │
│ │                                                        │   │
│ │  7. First Line Indent:              [0"      ]         │   │
│ │  8. Paragraph Spacing:              [1.0     ] [▲▼]    │   │
│ └────────────────────────────────────────────────────────┘   │
│                          [  OK  ]   [ Cancel ]                │
└──────────────────────────────────────────────────────────────┘
```

4. Press L to set the left margin.

Attention turns to the Left Margin input box.

5. Type an indent value for the left margin.

You set the margin relative to the edge of the page. For example, a value of 1 sets the left margin in one inch. A value of 2.5 sets the left margin in 2.5 inches. You don't have to type the inch symbol (").

If you don't want to change the left margin, don't type anything. WordPerfect does not reset the value when you press Enter, which you do in the next step.

6. Press Enter after setting the margin.

If you want to set the right margin, press R for Right and then repeat Steps 5 and 6. Likewise, press T or B to set the top or bottom margins on the page, repeating Steps 5 and 6 for each of those marginal settings. (For more information on setting the top and bottom margins, see Chapter 11.)

7. Press F7, the Exit key, to return to the document.

You may need to press F7 a second time to escape from the Format dialog box.

- ✔ A menu item named Margins lives in the Layout menu, and it will take you directly to the Margin Format dialog box if you're so inclined.

- ✔ You see some feedback on the screen regarding the new margin settings. The Pos indicator in the lower right corner of the screen starts at the value specified as the left margin. And if several margins exist in a single document, you see the text vary from wide to narrow on the screen.

- ✔ To move to the top of the document before you set the left and right margins, press Home, Home, ↑. To move to the left side of the page before setting the left and right margins, press Home, Home, ←.

- ✔ The margin change affects the document from the point where you change the margin to the end of the document. If you want to change the margins again, move to the place where you want new margins in the document and start with Step 1 of the preceding instructions. A single document can have several margin changes.

- ✔ Laser printers usually cannot print on the first half-inch of a piece of paper, (top, bottom, left, and right). This first half-inch is an absolute margin: although you can tell WordPerfect to set a margin of 0 inches right and 0 inches left, text still does not print in the first half-inch. Instead, specify a minimum of 0.5 inch for the left and right margins.

- ✔ If you want to print on three-hole paper, set the left margin to 2 or 2.5 inches. These settings provide enough room for the little holes, plus they offset the text nicely when you open up something in a three-ring notebook or binder.

- ✔ If your homework comes out to three pages and the teacher wants four, bring in the margins. Set the left and right margins to 1.5 inches each. Then change the line spacing to 1.5. Refer to "Changing the Line Spacing" earlier in this chapter. (You also can select a larger font; check the section in Chapter 9 on text size.)

Indenting a Paragraph

To offset a paragraph of text, you can indent it. I don't mean to just indent the first line, which you can do with the Tab key. Instead, you can indent the entire paragraph, lining up its left edge against a tab stop. Here's how:

1. **Move the cursor to the start of the paragraph.**

   The paragraph can already be on the screen, or you can be poised to type in a new paragraph.

2. **Press the Indent key, F4.**

3. **Type the paragraph, if you haven't already.**

   Otherwise, the new paragraph is indented to the next tab.

- ✔ F4 is the Indent key. It works like the Tab key but indents the entire paragraph's left margin to the same tab stop.

- ✔ To indent the paragraph to the next tab stop, press F4 again.

- ✔ To indent both the right and left sides of a paragraph, refer to the very next section. For another indenting trick, also check out "Doing a Hanging Indent" later in this chapter.

- ✔ If you're in a fair mood, refer to the section "The tab stops here" for information on setting tab stops.

Double-Indenting a Paragraph

Sometimes an indent on the left just isn't enough. Some days you need to suck a paragraph in twice: once on the left and once on the right — like I'd like to do to my love handles if I ever escape from my office and get out into the real world.

When do you need to double-indent a paragraph? Perhaps when you want to lift a quote from a paper written by someone else without being accused of plagiarism. I double-indent Abe Lincoln's material all the time. When I quote his stuff, I follow these steps:

1. **Move the cursor to the start of the paragraph.**

   If the paragraph hasn't been written yet, then move the cursor to where you want to write the new text.

2. **Press Shift-F4, the Double-Indent key.**

3. **Type the paragraph, if you haven't already.**

   Otherwise, the paragraph is indented to the next tab stop on the right and left margins.

- ✔ To suck up the paragraph even more, press Shift-F4 again.

- ✔ To indent only the left side of a paragraph, refer to the preceding section, "Indenting a Paragraph."

- ✔ Refer to "The tab stops here," earlier in the chapter, for information on setting tab stops — but only after a few swigs of Geritol.

Releasing the Margins

You're free, you're free! Run along. . . .

The margin release is a mystery. Remember that MAR REL key you'd stab during a lazy moment in typing class? What did it do? Why was it there? Would it fling the carriage across the room? The answer may never be known. WordPerfect has a Margin Release command, but you'd never know it. That's because the margin release in WordPerfect is really what's called a *back-tab*. Note that this feature isn't the same thing as a *back-stab*.

The back-tab key, a.k.a. the Margin Release key, is Shift-Tab.

Whereas the Tab key indents text one notch to the right, the back-tab (formerly called *margin release*) extends the text one notch to the left. I guess they call this feature a margin release because if you're at the left margin and press the back-tab, text sticks out into the margin, looking like a diving board in the middle of a cliff.

- ✔ The only true and practical use for the margin release is when you create a hanging indent. That excitement is bundled up in the next section.

- ✔ Hoo boy, nothing messes up text on the screen like a stray margin release. If you accidentally press Shift-Tab whilst in the middle of a paragraph, you notice that the text looks funny and reads weird. Unless you've turned into a New Age Poet, you probably pressed the Shift-Tab key combination accidentally. Keep pressing Backspace until you delete it or refer to the last section in this chapter, "Undoing Strange Tab Stuff."

Doing a Hanging Indent

A hanging indent has committed no felonious crime. Instead, it's a paragraph where the first line sticks out to the left and the rest of the paragraph is indented. To create such a beast, follow these steps:

1. **Move the cursor to the beginning of the paragraph that you want to hang and indent.**

   Alternatively, position the cursor where you want to type a new hanging-indent paragraph.

2. **Press the Indent key, F4.**

   The left side of the paragraph moves over to the first tab stop. (See "Indenting a Paragraph" earlier in this chapter.)

3. **Press Shift-Tab, the back-tab or Margin Release key combination.**

The first line of the paragraph moves back one tab stop. Ta-da! You have a hanging-indented paragraph.

✔ If you want to indent the paragraph even more, press F4 more than once. You also should press Shift-Tab an equal number of times if you want to even up the first line of the paragraph with the rest of the text.

✔ You need to slap a hanging indent onto each paragraph in the document individually. There is no Universal Hanging Indent formatting command in WeirdoPerfect.

Undoing Strange Tab Stuff

Indent tabs. Hanging indents. Margin releases. Nothing can mess up your text quicker. And trying to undo this stuff — if you are too slow with the Undo command (Ctrl-Z) — can be maddening. Here is the best help I can offer:

1. **Move to the first line of the paragraph you've indented or otherwise goofed up.**

You don't have to be at the beginning of the paragraph, just somewhere on the first line.

2. **Press Home, Home, Home, ←.**

You move to the start of the line — even though it may not look that way on the screen. You just have to trust me on this one.

3. **Press Delete.**

This action erases one of the tabs — indent, hanging, whatever. The text straightens itself up.

4. **Carefully repeat Step 3.**

Keep repeating Step 3 until you delete the first letter of the first word in the paragraph. Repeating Step 3 is essential because sometimes two or three weird Tab characters are in there. They must be destroyed to return the paragraph to normal.

5. **Retype the first letter of the first word in the paragraph.**

That should do it.

Chapter 11
Formatting Pages and Documents

· ·

In This Chapter

▶ Starting a new page

▶ Adjusting the top and bottom margins

▶ Setting the page size

▶ Centering a page, top to bottom

▶ Deciding where to stick the page number

▶ Adding a header

▶ Adding a footer

▶ Editing a header or footer

▶ Including footnotes and endnotes

· ·

*A*t last, the formatting three-ring circus has come to this. Formatting pages and documents isn't as common as formatting characters or even formatting paragraphs. This is major-league stuff that affects the entire document, and it can really be handy: adding headers and footers, page numbers — even footnotes. This is the stuff of which professional-looking documents are made. This chapter explains it all so carefully that even amateurs like you and me can fool them, too.

Starting a New Page

A new page is a hard page, although no general difficulty is involved. The term *hard page* means "Give me a page right now! I want the next line I type to be at the top of the page!" WordPerfect dutifully obeys, provided that you know the Hard Page command.

Two ways are available for you to start a new page in WordPerfect:

1. Keep pressing Enter until you see the black laser beam line of death — a solid line that stretches from one side of the screen to the other and denotes the start of a new page.

   Needless to say, this method is tacky and wrong.

2. Press Ctrl-Enter, the Hard Page key combination.

   That action inserts a dual line of death — two laser beams that are like yellow lines down the highway — denoting the start of a new page. This is the preferred way to start a new page.

✔ A hard-page break works just like a regular page break, but you control where the break occurs in the document. Move the cursor to where you want the hard-page break to be and press Ctrl-Enter.

✔ Pressing Ctrl-Enter inserts a hard-page character in the document. That character stays there, always creating a hard page no matter how much you edit the text on previous pages. The first approach to creating a page break doesn't take into account any editing that you may do on the text.

✔ You can delete a hard-page break with the Backspace or Delete key. If you do so accidentally, just press Ctrl-Enter again or use Esc to undelete.

Adjusting the Top and Bottom Margins

WordPerfect likes a one-inch margin all around the page: top, bottom, left, and right. Adjusting these margins was covered in Chapter 10. If you want to adjust the top and bottom margins to something other than one inch, follow the steps outlined there, but press T or B for the top or bottom margins.

✔ To move the cursor to the very top of a document before resetting the top and bottom margins, press Home, Home, Home, ↑. To move the cursor to the top of a page, press PgUp, PgDn. Keep an eye on the page numbers in the lower right corner of the screen to make sure that you're on the proper page.

✔ The top and bottom margins are relative to the edge of the paper. A one-inch margin means that the text starts one inch from the paper's edge.

✔ The Ln indicator in the lower right corner of the screen reflects the new value for the top margin each time you start a new page. Other than that, there is no visual feedback when you change the top and bottom margins (although if you move up and down too far, you notice that the pages get shorter on the screen).

✔ If you want to center text up and down on a page, refer to "Centering a Page, Top to Bottom" later in this chapter.

Setting the Page Size

Most printing takes place on a standard 8½ x 11-inch sheet of paper. But WordPerfect enables you to change the paper size to anything you want — from an envelope to some weird-sized sheet of paper. The weirdness I'll leave up to you, and printing envelopes is covered in Chapter 8. The following steps describe how you change the paper size to a wide, 11 x 8½-inch sheet of paper:

1. **Position the cursor at the top of the document or at the top of a page where you want to start using the new paper size.**

2. **Press the Format key combination, Shift-F8.**

   You see the Format dialog box.

3. **Press P (Page).**

   The Page Format dialog box appears. Stare at it long enough, and you'll turn to stone.

   The item you're interested in is number 4 (Paper Size/Type).

4. **Press 4.**

   You see the Paper Size/Type dialog box, which is shown in Figure 11-1. A scrolling list in the Paper Name box displays the different paper sizes that are available for the printer. Letter (Portrait) is probably highlighted. You want Letter (Landscape), which is the same type of paper turned on its side. (WordPerfect will print on it sideways. No sense in turning the printer on its side.)

5. **Use the up-arrow or down-arrow key to highlight Letter (Landscape).**

   Or if your the adventurous type, you can select another paper size from the list. I wouldn't.

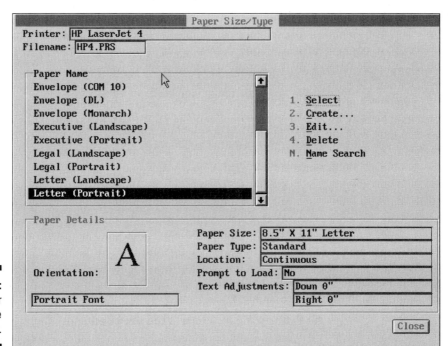

Figure 11-1:
The Paper
Size/Type
dialog box.

6. **Press Enter to lock in the selection.**

7. **Press F7 twice to return to the document.**

✔ The wide paper format, 11 x 8½, is called the *landscape mode* by WordPerfect's Department of Naming Things. The standard 8½ x 11-inch paper is called *portrait mode.* Think of a picture of a person and then of a landscape to help commit these ideas to memory. Or just call them *up-and-down* and *wide modes,* like I do.

✔ Use the same method to select legal size paper if that's what you want to print on. (I guess printing on normal-sized paper is illegal.) The Legal (Portrait) paper size option in the Paper Size/Type dialog box is the one you want to use in Step 5.

✔ Use the wide format when printing lists and items for which normal paper is too narrow. It also makes the people who look at your handiwork exclaim, "How did you do that?"

✔ To move to the tippy top of the document, press Home, Home, Home, ↑. To move to the top of a page, press PgUp, PgDn and then check to make sure that you're on the page you want. You need to issue the Page Size command at the start of a page.

Centering a Page, Top to Bottom

To put text in the center of a page, you need to do two things: Center the text between the left and right margins and center the text between the top and bottom margins. Centering the text between the left and right margins is covered in Chapter 10. To center text top to bottom, follow these steps:

1. **Move to the top of the page you want centered.**

   Press Home, Home, Home, ↑ to move to the top of the first page or press PgUp, PgDn to move to the top of the current page. Check to make sure that you're on the page that you want.

2. **Press the Format key, Shift-F8.**

   You see the Format dialog box.

3. **Press P (Page).**

   You see the Page Format dialog box.

   You want item 2 (Center Current Page).

4. **Press 2.**

5. **Press Enter to lock in the selection.**

6. **Press the Exit key, F7, to return to the document.**

✔ No visual feedback on the screen shows you that the page is centered. Instead, the page looks like one dwarfed page. Refer to the discussion on Print Preview in Chapter 8 to find out how to get a sneak peak at the centered page.

✔ The Center Page command works on only one page at a time. To center more than one page, select option 3, Center Pages. That option centers text (up and down) on all the pages from the cursor's position to the end of the document. Major formatting!

✔ The Center Page command centers all text on the page, top to bottom. It's a good idea to keep as little text on the page as possible — a title, description, and so forth. End the text with a Hard Page command (refer to "Starting a New Page" earlier in this chapter).

Deciding Where to Stick the Page Number

If the document is more than one page long, you probably want to number its pages. WordPerfect can perform this task for you automatically, so stop putting those forced page numbers in the document and follow these steps:

1. Move to the tippy top of the document.

Press Home, Home, Home, ↑. You want to move to the tippy top because the Page Numbering command affects all the pages in the document only if it starts at the top of the first page.

2. Press the reliable Format key, Shift-F8.

The Format dialog box is displayed.

3. Press P (Page Format).

Not done yet.

4. Press N (Page Numbering).

You see the interesting Page Numbering dialog box.

Still not done.

5. Press P (Position).

At last, the Page Number Position dialog box is displayed (see Figure 11-2). The dialog box shows three page layouts. The first is for every page, and the other two show page-number positions for odd and even pages.

6. Press the number that corresponds with the position on the page at which you want the page numbers to appear.

For example, press 6 to have page numbers appear at the bottom center of each page.

7. Press Enter to lock in your choice.

```
╔═══════════════════ Page Number Position ═══════════════════╗
║ Page Number Position                          ┌Page┐        ║
║   1. ○  Top Left                 Every        │1 2 3│       ║
║   2. ○  Top Center               Page         │     │       ║
║   3. ○  Top Right                             │5 6 7│       ║
║   4. ○  Alternating, Top                      └────┘        ║
║   5. ○  Bottom Left                           ┌Page┐ ┌Page┐ ║
║   6. ○  Bottom Center            Alternating  │ 4  │ │ 4  │ ║
║   7. ○  Bottom Right             Pages        │Even│ │Odd │ ║
║   8. ○  Alternating, Bottom                   │ 8  │ │ 8  │ ║
║   9. ◉  None                                  └────┘ └────┘ ║
║                                                            ║
║   A. Font/Attributes/Color...                              ║
║                                                            ║
║                                        [  OK  ] [ Cancel ] ║
╚════════════════════════════════════════════════════════════╝
```

Figure 11-2:
The Page
Number
Position
dialog box.

8. Press the Exit key, F7, to return to the document.

You may need to press F7 several times to make every dialog box disappear and to get back to text editing mode.

✔ You don't see the page numbers on the screen. To see them, use the Print Preview command, as covered in Chapter 8.

✔ You also can create page numbers by sticking the page number into a header or footer. Refer to "Adding a header" or "Adding a footer" later in this chapter. If you do end up putting the page number in a header or footer, you do not need to use the Page Numbering command.

Here are the quickie keys for putting a page number at the bottom center of every page in the document:

1. Press Home, Home, Home, ↑.

2. Press Shift-F8, P, N, P, 6, Enter.

3. Press F7 a few times.

Putting Hats and Shoes on a Document

You're almost ready to send the document to that big party the printer is having. But, because you don't want your baby to look underdressed (or unprofessional), you really should dapper it up a bit. Give the document a header to use as a hat and a footer to use as shoes for each of its pages. Your document will truly look dandy.

Adding a header

A *header* is not a quickly poured beer. Instead, it's text running along the top of every page in a document. For example, at the top of each page in this book is the part name or chapter name. Those are headers. You can stick headers on your work, complete with a title, your name, the date, the page number, dirty limericks — you name it.

 A header is a document-long thing. The header appears in the document from the spot where you created it to the end of the document. Therefore, to have the same header in an entire document, you need to start at the beginning, the first page. Follow these steps:

1. **Move the cursor to the top of the document or to the top of the first page where you want the header to appear.**

   Press Home, Home, Home, ↑ to move to the top of the document. Then press PgUp, PgDn to move to the top of the current page. (Check the page number in the lower right corner of the screen to make sure that you're on the right page.)

2. **Press the Format key, Shift-F8.**

   You see the blazing Format dialog box.

3. **Press 5 for Header/Footer/Watermark.**

   You see the Header/Footer/Watermark dialog box. You use the first item in the list, Headers, to create a header.

4. **Press H (Headers).**

5. **Press Enter to select Header A.**

6. **Press Enter again to select All Pages.**

   This action tells WordPerfect to make the header appear on every page of the document, exactly the same.

   Next, you are thrown into the Header Editor, which looks like the main editing screen. However, you see Header A in the lower left of the screen.

7. **Type the header.**

   You can change the font, text attributes, and text size; center or flush-right the text; or produce a number of other interesting effects. Try to keep the overall size of the header to less than three lines. Be concise and brief, if at all possible.

   If you want to insert the page number in the header, press the following keys:

   > Shift-F8, P, N, I

   This action inserts a page-number code into the header. The code represents the current page number when the document prints.

If you want to insert the current date in the header, press the following keys:

Shift-F5, 2

This action inserts an updating date marker in the header, which always displays the current date.

8. Press the Exit key, F7, when you're done editing the header.

You return to the document.

✔ The Header/Footer/Watermark menu item in the Layout menu zooms you right to the Header/Footer/Watermark dialog box.

✔ To see the header, refer to the instructions for editing the header in "Editing a header or footer" later in this chapter. You also can use Print Preview, discussed in Chapter 8, to take a look at the header or just print a page of the document.

✔ To stick the header on a specific page, use the Go To command: Press Ctrl-Home and then type the page number at the Go to prompt. Press Enter and you're there. (Also refer to the discussion of the Go to prompt in Chapter 2.)

✔ You can have two headers — an A header and a B header — running on different pages. To create this effect, create Header A as described in the preceding steps. In Step 6, however, select 3 (Odd Pages). Then repeat the steps to create Header B, but in Step 5 press B and in Step 6 press 4 (Even Pages). Header A then appears only on the odd-numbered pages, and Header B appears only on the even-numbered ones.

Preventing a header from appearing on the first page

To prevent the header from appearing on the first page of text (which is usually the title page), follow these steps:

1. Press Home, Home, Home, ↑ to move to the first page in the document.

2. Press Shift-F8, P, U to bring up the Suppress menu.

3. Select what you want to suppress. For example, press 1 and Enter to suppress

header A for the first page. Or press S to suppress everything.

4. Press the Exit key, F7, twice to return to the document.

These commands *suppress* the header for the first page of the document — but only for the first page. The header appears on all the other pages as ordered.

Adding a footer

 A *footer* is text that appears on the bottom of every page. A great footer is *Turn the page, dummy,* although better uses of footers include holding page numbers, listing a chapter or document title, or what have you. You create a footer by using steps similar to the ones you use to create a header. Here are the steps:

1. **Move the cursor to the beginning of the document or to the top of the page where you want the footer to first appear.**

   Press Home, Home, Home, ↑ to move to the top of the document; press PgUp, PgDn to move to the top of the current page (which works sometimes; check the page number to be certain).

   You really should move to the top of the page. Even though you're creating a footer, you should place its code at the beginning of a page of text.

2. **Press the Format key, Shift-F8.**

   The Format dialog box pops up.

3. **Press H for Header/Footer/Watermark.**

   Hey! Isn't that the Header/Footer/Watermark dialog box? Pinch me and tell me I'm not dreaming.

4. **Press 2 (Footers).**

5. **Press Enter to select Footer A.**

6. **Press Enter to select All Pages.**

   This action tells WordPerfect to put the footer at the bottom of every page. After pressing Enter, you arrive in the Footer Editor, which looks just like the Header Editor — and just like WordPerfect, for all that means. You enter the footer's text here.

7. **Type the text that you want to see at the bottom of every page.**

   You can use the character size and attribute commands, center or flush-right the text, and so on. Try to keep the size of the footer small — less than two or three lines. Refer to the preceding section, "Adding a header," for information on inserting the current page number or date.

8. **Press the Exit key, F7, when you're done editing.**

   And keep pressing F7 until you get back to the document.

   ✔ Just like a header, the footer does not appear in the document. To see it, refer to the instructions in the next section on editing a footer. Or refer to the section on Print Preview in Chapter 8 to find out how to visually peruse the footer (but not edit it). Or just print a page of the document.

✔ If you just want a page number at the bottom of the page, don't bother with creating a footer. Refer to "Deciding Where to Stick the Page Number" earlier in this chapter.

✔ Refer to the preceding section for more information on WordPerfect's footers. The same information applies to both headers and footers in a document, although you need to specify F for Footer in the commands, rather than H for Header.

Editing a header or footer

To edit a header or footer you've already created, follow these steps:

1. **Press the Format key, Shift-F8.**

   The Format dialog box is displayed.

2. **Press H for Header/Footer/Watermark.**

   A menu with the same triple-slashed name appears.

3. **Press H for Header or F for Footer, depending on what you want to edit.**

4. **Press A or B to select the appropriate header or footer.**

   For most of us, that's usually going to be A. The Header A dialog box then appears.

5. **Press E to edit the selected header or footer.**

   WordPerfect finds the proper header or footer and then displays a screen that shows you the header or footer's contents.

6. **Edit the header or footer as you see fit.**

7. **Press the Exit key, F7, when you're done editing.**

8. **Press F7 a few times to return to the document.**

If you want to stop using a particular header or footer, move to the page where you want to discontinue using it and then start at Step 1. When you get to Step 5, press F (Off). Press F7 to return to the document. The header or footer no longer appears from that page onward.

Including Footnotes and Endnotes

I must be in a really good mood today because normally this stuff would be considered *advanced* material. Pooh! A great many people need footnotes or endnotes in their documents. Instead of creating them obtusely, follow these handy steps:

1. **Position the cursor in the document where you want the footnote or endnote to be referenced.**

   This is the spot where the tiny number will be displayed, the spot referring to the footnote or endnote. Here is an example.[1]

2. **Press the Footnote key combination, Ctrl-F7.**

   You see the Notes dialog box. Yikes!

3. **Decide whether you want a footnote or an endnote.**

   A *footnote* is a tiny note that appears at the bottom of the current page. *Endnotes* appear after the last line of text on the last page.

4. **Press 1 if you want to create a footnote or 3 if you want to create an endnote.**

   Either way, the following steps remain the same. The difference between the two types of notes is only a matter of appearance or of what your fastidious professor demands of you.

5. **Press C to create the footnote or endnote.**

   You are shipped off to Note Editing Land. The footnote/endnote number appears at the top of the page. *Don't delete it!*

6. **Start typing the footnote or endnote.**

   You can use character formatting, attributes, text size, and so on, in the footnote or endnote. But do limit the paragraph formatting; footnotes don't need to be centered or flushed to the right.

7. **Press F7 when you're done entering the footnote or endnote.**

   You return to the document. The footnote/endnote number appears superscripted in the text.

   ✔ If you want to edit an existing footnote or endnote, follow the same steps but press E (Edit) in Step 5. Then type in the number of the footnote or endnote that you want to edit. Press F7 when you're done editing.

   ✔ To change a footnote's number, follow the same steps but press N in Step 5. WordPerfect asks for the new number. Press the number and then press Enter.

   ✔ *Footnotes* are at the bottom of the page in which they're referenced. *Endnotes* appear at the end of the document, after the last line of text.

   ✔ To delete a footnote or endnote, move the cursor to just before or after the footnote/endnote's number in the document. Press Backspace or Delete accordingly. Thwoop! The footnote/endnote is gone!

_____

[1] This is the tiny number.

✔ If you delete or insert a footnote in the middle of a document, the other footnotes are renumbered automatically.

✔ Footnotes can come in really handy because they give you ultimate control over where readers put their eyes.[2]

---

[2] Made you look!

Chapter 12
Using Tables and Basic Desktop Publishing Stuff

*Y*ou can spice up your text with bold and italics and maybe even use some large characters when your document doesn't run as long as you'd like. Paragraph formatting and page formatting add garlic to your document salad — just a touch, not so much that when you open your mouth and say "Hi," flowers wilt, grown men cry, and women faint. What more can you do? Well, if you're really the daring type, you can pump up your document with fancy tables and formatting that's just one Cicero beneath the official realm of Desktop Publishing. Oh, we've come a long way from the days of word processing with moveable type.

Cobbling Tables Together

A table is this thing with four legs on which you set things — but not your elbows when Grandma is watching. In WordPerfect, a table is a list of items — several rows all lined up into neat little columns. In the primitive days, you'd make this happen by using the Tab key and your handy frustration tool. Face it, making things line up can be maddening. Even in a word processor. Even if you think that you know what you're doing.

Coming to your rescue, of course, is WordPerfect. ("It's TableMan, Ma, and he's here to rescue us!") WordPerfect has an able table command. You use it to create a prison-like grid of rows and columns. Into each cubbyhole or *cell,* you can type information or store society's miscreants, and everything is lined up nice and neat and suitable for framing. The printed result looks very nice and impressive, and if you do things right, your table will even be sturdy enough to eat off.

Creating the table

To create a table in a document, follow these steps:

1. **Position the cursor at the spot in the text where you want to put the table.**

   The whole table will be created at once and inserted into the text — like pasting in a block — a cell block. You fill in the table *after* it's created.

2. **Press the Table command keys, Alt-F7.**

   The Columns/Tables dialog box appears, as shown in Figure 12-1. Welcome to WordPerfect's Lincoln Log menu.

3. **Press T (Tables), C (Create).**

   The Create Table minidialog box appears. You're supposed to enter the number of columns and rows that you want in the table. *Columns* are up and down; *rows* are across. They create the table *grid*. If you don't know how many columns or rows you need, then guess.

4. **Type the number of columns and press Enter.**

   For example, press 3 to have three columns going across.

5. **Type the number of rows and press Enter.**

   For example, press 5 to have five rows marching down.

   You can use the Tab key to move between the various options in this dialog box, and you can change or reenter the numbers if you like. Accuracy isn't a big issue at this stage; you can change the table after it's created if you goof up. (I do this all the time.)

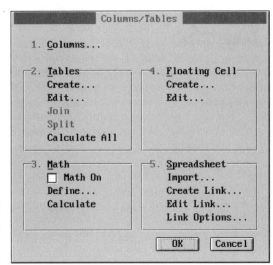

Figure 12-1:
The
Columns/
Tables
dialog box.

6. Press Enter to leave the Create Table minidialog boxlette.

Welcome to prison! After you tell WordPerfect how many rows and columns to make, it builds a table and shows it to you on the screen (see Figure 12-2). The table looks like a spreadsheet, smells like a spreadsheet, and if I weren't afraid of electrocuting myself, I'd tell you whether it tastes like a spreadsheet as well. You're still in WordPerfect, however.

You'll use the Ugly Table Editing Screen to adjust and edit the way the table looks, the number of rows and columns, and the width or height of those rows and columns. But this stuff can wait.

Don't type anything into the table just yet. *Don't even try.*

7. Press the Exit key, F7, to return safely to the document.

This action inserts said same ugly table into the document.

8. Fill in the table.

Refer to the next section.

✔ You also can access the Tables command from the Layout menu. A submenu pops up, from which you can select the Create item to create a table.

✔ Mmmm. Wouldn't some pasta salad be good right now?

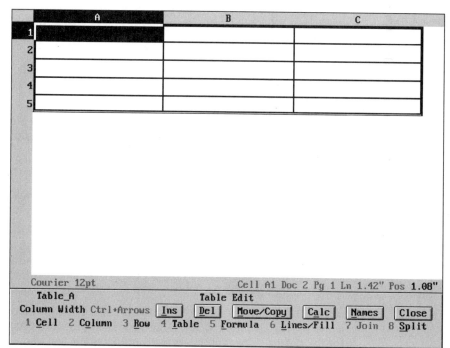

Figure 12-2:
The Ugly
Table
Editing
Screen.

✔ Use a table in a document any time that you have information that needs to be organized into rows and columns. This setup works much better than using the Tab key because adjusting the table's rows and columns is a less-though-still-bitter pill to swallow than messing with tab stops in WordPerfect.

✔ You can always add columns and rows to a table after you create it. Refer to the next section.

✔ The table has an ugly lined border around it and between the cells. You learn how to remedy this situation in "Changing the table" later in this chapter.

✔ Alas, WordPerfect does not have a handy Chair command.

Here are the *I'm in a hurry* emergency 911 table-creation steps:

1. Press Alt-F7, T, C.

2. Type the number of columns and press Enter.

3. Type the number of rows and press Enter.

4. Press Enter, F7.

Putting stuff in the table

An empty table sits in the document. But before you break out the MinWax and clean it up, why not set the table?

The table is divided into rows and columns. Where they meet is called a *cell* — just like they have in prison, but without the TV and metal toilet. Your job is to fill in the various cells with text. Here are some pointers:

✔ Use the Tab key to move from cell to cell. Pressing Enter just puts a new paragraph of text into the same cell. (Each cell is like its own little document.)

✔ The Shift-Tab key combination moves you backward between the cells.

✔ If you press Tab in the last cell on the right in the bottom row, a new row of cells is added.

✔ You can use the cursor-control keys to move from cell to cell as well (how swell). But if the cell has text in it, then the cursor-control keys make the toothpick cursor dawdle through the words. You can still use the cursor-control keys to edit text in the cells, but using the Tab key is best for moving from cell to cell.

✔ Text formatting commands also work in the cells. You can bold, underline, and italicize text, center it, flush it right, and so on. Refer to Chapters 9 and 10 for the details. Note that the formatting affects the text in only one cell at a time or in the cells you collectively mark as a block.

✔ To format a row or column all at once, you need to use the Ugly Table Editing Screen, which is discussed in the next section.

✔ To quickly insert a row in the table, move the cursor to that row and press Ctrl-Insert. The new row is inserted *on top of* the current row.

✔ To delete a row, move the cursor to that row and press Ctrl-Delete. A dialog box asks whether you want to delete the row. Press Y for Yes.

✔ To utterly remove a table from a document, highlight the whole darn thing as a block and then press Delete. Press Y, and the table is blown to smithereens. If pressing Y only erases the table's text, then try starting the block on the line before the one where the table starts. That will kill it, fer sure.

Changing the table

Suppose that you create a card table but really need a dining room table — or one of those long, dual-time-zone tables that rich people eat at. After you create the table, you can change and adjust everything.

To make adjustments in a table, follow these steps:

1. Put the toothpick cursor somewhere on the table.

Anywhere.

2. Press Alt-F7, T, E.

That is, you press Alt-F7 for the Lincoln Log dialog box, T for Table, and E for Edit. The table — and all its contents — go back into the Ugly Table Editing Screen, as shown in Figure 12-3. Here you can do all sorts of interesting things.

✔ The big block cursor is the key to editing the table. You move it with the cursor-control keys or Tab, and it highlights only one cell at a time.

✔ To change the width of a column, move the cell highlight to the column that you want to change and then press Ctrl-← to make the column smaller or Ctrl-→ to make the column wider.

✔ Columns can be only so wide; WordPerfect will not let the table hang off the sides of a page.

✔ To insert columns, move the cell highlight to where you want the new columns. Press the Insert key. Press C (Columns), press H (for how many columns you want to insert), and then type the number of new columns that you want. Press Enter to insert them.

✔ To insert rows, move the cell highlight to where you want the new rows. Press the Insert key, press R (Rows), and then press H (for how many rows you want to insert). Type the number of new rows that you want and press Enter to insert them.

	A	B	C
1	Item	Where found	Comments
2	Interesting black rock	By mailbox	Possibly radioactive; Jordan claims it's from a volcano
3	Bandaid	By yellow Volkswagen across the street	Slightly used; Medical waste
4	Pudding Cup	In front of 27	Empty, was chocolate
5	Tiny dog	Chained to door of 42	Annoying
6	Blackberries	In field	Nummy

C:\PROJECTS\WP6\TRIP   Cell A1 Doc 1 Pg 1 Ln 1.75" Pos 1.08"

Table_A   Table Edit
Column Width Ctrl+Arrows | Ins | | Del | | Move/Copy | | Calc | | Names | | Close |
   1 Cell 2 Column 3 Row   4 Table   5 Formula 6 Lines/Fill 7 Join 8 Split

Figure 12-3:
A table in
the Ugly
Table
Editing
Screen.

✔ To change the borders around the table, press 6 (Lines). WordPerfect displays the Table Lines dialog box. To select a new type of line, press 1 twice and then choose a line from the list that is displayed. The [None] style removes all the lines. Press F7 a few times to return to the Ugly Table Editing Screen.

✔ You cannot edit text in the Ugly Table Editing Screen.

✔ Press F7 when you're done editing the table. When you return to the document, the table wears its new look.

✔ The Table Edit command can also be accessed from the Button Bar. It's the second button from the right.

To apply a character or paragraph format to an entire column, follow these steps:

1. Move the cell highlight to the column that you want to format.

2. Press O.

You see the Column Format dialog box.

3. Press 1 to set the character format, 2 to set the character size, or 4 to set the justification.

4. Press the key that's associated with the formatting you want.

An *X* appears in the box by the format to show that it has been activated.

5. Press F7 to return to the Ugly Table Editing Screen.

Creating Cool Document Titles

Nothing dampens the fire of an exciting paper like a dreary, dull heading. Consider the plight of the hapless garden slug. "The Backyard Gastropod" can be a creative title. *Gastropod* comes from the Latin words for *stomach* and *foot*. Essentially, a slug is a crawling stomach that is lubricated with a thin coating of slime and a built-in fear of salt. But enough biology for now! To make a paper on slugs stand out, you need more than just a title that is creative. You need a title that looks creative!

WordPerfect lets you go wild with text and paragraph formatting. You can select different fonts, text sizes, and attributes; box things in with lines; and apply shading. This colorful stuff really makes your thoughts jump off the page. People will take notice. "Gee, I never thought slugs could be so absorbing," they'll ponder. You don't get that kind of response when you have a dull title.

Figure 12-4 shows various examples of document titles that you can create with WordPerfect. You can mix and match styles to create the ideal title you want. The following sections give details on how you can create each element: formatting text, formatting paragraphs, and producing special effects.

Example 1:

```
              The Slug
       Your Garden's Gastropod
```

Example 2:

Slimey, Sticky, Oozy

SLUGS

In Your Garden

Example 3:

Your Glistening Gastropod Gardening Newsletter

SLUG & SNAIL

Vol II, Issue 6   June 11, 1994

Figure 12-4:
Examples
of
document
titles.

Formatting the text just so

The three steps to formatting text for a title are

1. Selecting a font

2. Selecting a type size

3. Selecting character attributes

To select a font, follow these steps:

1. Press Ctrl-F8.

You see the Font dialog box.

2. Press F for Font.

A drop-down list displays all the fonts known to WordPerfect. The best fonts to use for titles are the blocky, no-frills fonts. These fonts include Helvetica, Arial, Swiss, Univers, Avant Gard, Optima, Futura, and so on. One of these fonts is bound to be available in your list. Select it. (For information on how to select a font, see the discussion on changing the typeface in Chapter 9.)

3. Press S for Size.

Press the down-arrow key to see the font sizes in the drop-down list. Select an appropriately large size for the title from the list or just type a size such as 24 into the box. (For more information on selecting a size, see the discussion in Chapter 9 on changing the font size.)

To make a title big, select a large font size (14pt or more). I like a 24pt title, which is nice and readable from across the hall (with my glasses on).

4. Press A for Appearance.

Bold (press B) and Small Caps (press C) are good attributes to give a title. For example, suppose that you want a title in bold, small caps, and outline formats. Here are the keystrokes:

A, B   **Bold** text first.

A, C   **SMALL** caps

A, O   OUTLINE

Note how the sample text in the bottom of the Font dialog box reflects the changes. (For more information on using character formats, see the discussion in Chapter 9 on text attributes.)

5. Press Enter after you make your selections.

6. Type the title.

✔ Don't worry about centering or shading yet. The character formats come first.

✔ For more information on formatting characters, see Chapter 9.

✔ If you have a multiline title, you can use different type sizes and styles on each line. Avoid the temptation to change the font, however.

✔ In Figure 12-4, Example 1 uses the Courier font, 14pt size, and bold. This formatting is painfully boring, but it's better than nothing.

✔ In Figure 12-4, Example 2 uses the Helvetica font. The first line is 12pt size and bold. The second line is 30pt size and bold (also typed in uppercase). The third line is 18pt size and also bold.

✔ The third example in Figure 12-4 uses the Helvetica font as well. The first line is 18pt size, bold, and italic. The second line is 24pt size, bold, and small caps. The third line is 12pt size and plain old normal text. (Refer to the technical box "Fancy and not required alignment information" to learn how to shove the date to the right side of the box.)

✔ To insert the date in a title, use the WordPerfect date command. Move the cursor to where you want the date to appear and press Shift-F5, 1.

✔ Don't go nuts.

Fancy and not required alignment information

In the third example in Figure 12-4, the volume number is on the left side of the page, and the date is on the right side at the bottom of the title. Both items of text are on the same line. You use WordPerfect's justification feature to slam the volume number against the left margin and smack the date against the right margin. Blithely follow these forbidden steps:

1. Press Enter to start writing text on a new line.

   It's best to start with a blank line. If you're already on a blank line, you don't need to press Enter. (I'm just being safe, that's all. You know, careful instructions are my trademark.)

2. Type the text that you want to line up on the left side of the page.

   Type away, la, la, la.

3. Don't press Enter when you're done!

4. Instead, press Alt-F6, the Flush Right command.

   The cursor hops over to the right side of the page.

5. Type the text that you want to line up on the right side of the page.

   Type away, la, la, la. Or press Shift-F5, 1 to insert the date, as shown in Figure 12-4.

6. Press Enter.

   You're done.

Making the title perfectly centered

After writing the text for the title, you need to line things up on the screen. You use paragraph formatting to center or *justify* titles.

The typical title is centered. To center text that you've already typed, follow these steps:

1. Mark the text that you want to center as a block.

Move the cursor to the block's start, press Alt-F4, and use the cursor-control keys to move the block highlighting to the end of the block.

2. Press Shift-F6.

This action centers the block on the screen.

✔ To center the page from top to bottom, first make sure that the cursor is on the page that you want centered. Press Shift-F8, P, C, F7, F7. (Refer to Chapter 11 for more detailed information on how to center a page.)

✔ Additional information on formatting a block of text is in Chapter 10.

Putting a box around the title

After you center the title, you can draw a nice square box around it if you like. Follow these steps:

1. Mark the entire title as a block.

Move the toothpick cursor to the start of the block, press Alt-F4 to activate block-marking mode, and then move the cursor to the end of the block.

If you want the box to be bigger than the title, then also include the paragraph before and after the title as part of the block.

2. Press Shift-F8, L, B.

You see the Create Paragraph Border dialog box.

3. Press Enter and then press F7 twice: Enter, F7, F7.

The title now has a box around it. The box is similar to the one shown in Figure 12-4, Example 3, but without the shading inside the box. To get shading, refer to "Shading titles" later in this chapter.

✔ You can put a box around any paragraph in WordPerfect — not just around a title.

✔ The Create Paragraph Border dialog box can be accessed from the Graphics menu. Select the Borders menu item and from the submenu that appears, select Paragraph.

✔ To put a border around an entire page, use the Page Border command. Press Shift-F8, P, B, Enter, F7, F7. Use the Print Preview mode to see how it looks (refer to Chapter 8 for information on Print Preview).

Putting less than a box around a title

The box that you put around the title doesn't need to have all four sides. In Figure 12-4, Example 2 has lines only on the top and bottom. To use that setup for a title, follow Steps 1 and 2 in "Putting a box around the title" and then do the following when you see the Create Paragraph Border dialog box:

1. **Press C (Customize), L (Lines).**

   You see the Border Line Styles dialog box. You want to eliminate the right and left lines from the box.

2. **Press L (Left Line).**

   The Line Styles dialog box appears. A scrolling list of line styles is displayed.

3. **Select [None] from the list.**

   Use the arrow keys to highlight [None] and press Enter.

4. **Repeat Steps 2 and 3 to eliminate the right line from the box.**

   Press R (Right Line), select [None] from the list, and press Enter.

5. **Press F7 to close the Border Line Styles dialog box.**

6. **Press F7 again and again, until all the various dialog boxes are gone and you're back to the document.**

You can select one of several line styles from the Line Styles dialog box. For example, if you want thicker lines, you can select the Extra Thick Border option. You can choose from dashed borders, dotted borders, and old Eastern European-style armed border crossings with towers and guard dogs and the whole nine yards.

Shading titles

The neatest effect of them all is to shade the titles, as shown in Example 3 of Figure 12-4. You can shade a title with or without a border around it. Here are the steps you take:

1. **Mark the entire title as a block.**

   Move the toothpick cursor to the start of the block, press Alt-F4 to begin marking, and use the cursor-control keys to move to the end of the block.

   If you want the shaded area to be more than the line that the title is on, also highlight the lines before and after the title.

2. **Press Shift-F8, L, B, F.**

   The Fill Styles dialog box appears. You see a scrolling list of *shaded fill* patterns — from 10% to 100%. The percentage measures the amount of black in the shading. So 50% is equal parts black and white — solid gray. The 100% value is solid black.

   The best values to select are 10%, 20%, or 30%. I prefer 20% because it prints on my laser printer as not too dark to overpower the title text but still dark enough to be recognized as the all-important shading that is so hard to produce with other word processors.

3. **Select the shading you want from the list.**

   For example, use the cursor-control keys to highlight `20% Shaded Fill` from the list.

4. **Press Enter to lock in that shading.**

5. **Press F7 three times to return to the document: F7, F7, F7.**

   The title appears shaded on the screen. This is definitely the coolest way to head up your in-depth slug report.

   ✔ If the shading stinks (and we're all allowed a little latitude for screwing up here), then you can remove it. Just follow the steps outlined for adding it but select the `[None]` Fill Style from the list in Step 3.

   ✔ Shaded titles look best when they're at the top of the first page, not on a page by themselves.

Doing the Two-Column Thing

Columns — especially columns that you can see Right On Your Screen — are one of those features that all the magazines, gurus, and other pseudopundits demanded for word processors. Do we need them? No. Can WordPerfect do them? Yes. Do you want to mess with this? Sure, why not. It will give you something to do while the electric chair recharges.

Before I divulge my WordPerfect column secrets, here's a healthy bit of advice: The best way to do columns is in a desktop publishing package such as PageMaker. Those programs are designed for playing with text, and setting up columns with them is much easier than setting up columns with WordPerfect (although figuring out their instructions is equivalent to an eternal chess match with someone who wears a size-12 hat). In WordPerfect, columns remain more of a curiosity than anything you or I want to spend more than 15 minutes of our time on.

To start columns in a document, follow the steps listed here. If you have already written the text, WordPerfect puts it into column format. Otherwise, any new text that you create is placed in columns automagically.

1. Move the cursor to where you want the columns to start.

2. Press Alt-F7.

This action brings up the Lincoln Log menu that is shown in Figure 12-1.

3. Press C (Columns).

You get to see the Text Columns dialog box, which is shown in Figure 12-5. Everything is set up to create two columns on the page. If you want three columns, press N (Number of Columns) and type the number of columns that you want into the box.

4. Press Enter.

WordPerfect shows you the columns.

✔ You can instantly hop to the Text Columns dialog box by selecting Columns from the Layout menu (it's near the top).

✔ The four types of columns are Newspaper, Corinthian, Dork, and Ironic. Seriously, refer to the techie box "Please don't read this bothersome information on column types" to learn about the various column types.

✔ You can instantly split a document into columns by using the Ribbon. The third item from the left describes how many columns the text has. Normally, you see 1 Col, but you can instantly activate dual-column mode by selecting 2 Col from the list that drops down. To make that selection, you have to use a mouse. (Refer to Chapter 19 for more information on the Ribbon.)

Figure 12-5:
The Text
Columns
dialog box.

```
                     Text Columns
 1. Column Type
      ● Newspaper
      ○ Balanced Newspaper
      ○ Parallel
      ○ Parallel with Block Protect

 2. Number of Columns:          [2  ]

 3. Distance Between Columns:   [0.5"]

 4. Line Spacing Between Rows:  [1.0 ]

 5. Column Borders...


 [Off ] [Custom Widths...] [  OK  ] [Cancel]
```

- ✔ Editing text in columns is a pain. The cursor seems to hop all over the place, and moving from one column to another takes an eternity. (I'm just complaining here because there's nothing else to do.)

- ✔ Using the mouse to poke the cursor to a new spot on a column seems to work nicely.

- ✔ When columns are visible on the screen, normally slow WordPerfect goes into glacier mode. My advice? Write the text first; do the columns last.

- ✔ The three-column text format works nicely on *landscape paper*. This setup is used for most brochures. Refer to Chapter 11 for information on selecting landscape paper.

- ✔ All the text and paragraph formatting mentioned in this part of the book also applies to text and paragraphs in columns. The difference is that the column margins — not the page margins — mark the left and right sides of the text for paragraph formatting.

- ✔ To stop using WordPerfect's Columns feature or to undo Columns, move the cursor to the spot in the text where you want Columns to stop (or where the columns start if you just want to get rid of them). Press Alt-F7, C, F, F7.

Please don't read this bothersome information on column types

Below are my all-English descriptions of various column types. The column type that you probably want to use most often is Newspaper. Mess with the others at your own risk.

Newspaper: The columns flow like columns in a newspaper. When the text reaches the bottom of the first column, the cursor hops up to the top of the next column and keeps going down. Try to make your text not read as badly as the typical newspaper, however.

Balanced Newspaper: This format is like the Newspaper format — but with equal coverage of both Republican and Democratic screw-ups. Seriously, WordPerfect forces the bottom part of each column to end at the same spot on the page. It makes things look neater.

Corinthian: Leafy-looking curly stuff decorates the top of each column.

Parallel: This type of column is best used for organizing vertical information — as in a table. Items in each column are grouped by *rows*. An example is a script where the character's names are in the first column and what they say is in the next column. All of that is considered a row, regardless of how many lines it requires. The next row starts below the longest column in the preceding row. (This list of column types is an example of a parallel column.)

Doric: These columns are bland looking.

Parallel with Block Protect: This format is like the Parallel format, but the rows are always kept together.

Chapter 13
Making Purty Pictures

*I*f your writing isn't flowery enough, try adding a flower to your text. This addition may or may not help the words you've written, but it will be one of those eyebrow-raising things that impress your fellow humans. They'll marvel, "Wow! How did you get that picture of Cindy Crawford into your Midwest Marketing Summary?"

Personally, I have this thing against graphics. I prefer a good book over, say, the visual drivel radiated by the TV every night. So putting a graphics image in text is kind of a compromise. Besides, you can *graphicise* your text without resorting to corny images of clowns with balloons, busy management types wearing ties, and the occasional gorilla. For example, you can draw lines around text and put text into boxes. And if that doesn't make your document graphic enough, just add some raw language and off-color jokes. It works for me.

Adding a Graphics Image

WordPerfect enables you to stick a graphics image into a document — just as you would paste a picture on a piece of paper — and then type text around it. The program takes care of the picture's position and size, lets you write a cute li'l caption, and places the picture at a specific spot on the page. It sounds easy. And at my backyard barbecue last weekend, we all thought pole-vaulting would be easy with that 12-foot piece of PVC pipe. It's funny how you can underestimate things.

From whence commeth thy graphical image?

Before you write anything, you should have a good idea in your head of what you want to write about. (If you don't, and you just stare at the blank screen, then you have what it takes to be a *real* writer!) The same holds true with graphics. You need to have — or have created — the graphics image that you want to use in the text before you paste it in. You can do many things with WordPerfect, but you can't exactly draw with it. Not really.

Graphics images — pictures — come from several places. You can create images in a graphics program, buy a disk full of images, or *clip art,* or use a device called a *scanner* to electronically convert pictures and other printed images into graphics files that you can store in a computer. No matter what, the image must be saved in a file on disk before WordPerfect can use it.

✔ The graphic must be saved as a file on disk before WordPerfect can use it.

✔ WordPerfect can deal with several popular graphics file formats, which are probably all listed somewhere in the manual. As long as a graphic can be saved in a *compatible* format, WordPerfect doesn't balk.

✔ The most common graphics file format is the PCX or PC Paintbrush file. If you can save graphics in that format, you're in business.

✔ WordPerfect's most favorite graphics format is the WPG (WordPerfect Graphics) format. The DrawPerfect drawing program, from the same rancorous people who produce WordPerfect, creates those images.

✔ WordPerfect comes with several dozen graphics images. They're called WordPerfect Graphics files, and their filenames all have the extension WPG. These are somewhere on the hard drive. Refer to Chapter 16 for information on how to find them.

Slapping a graphics image into a document

To stick a graphics image in text, follow these whimsical steps:

1. **Position the cursor at the spot where you want the picture.**

   If any text is already there, the graphic shoves it aside.

2. **Press the all-powerful Graphics command key combination, Alt-F9.**

   You see the Graphics dialog box.

3. **Press Shift-F10.**

   Another dialog box appears — the Retrieve Image File dialog box. Here you type the name of the graphics file that you want to put into the document.

   You need to type the full name — the long and involved DOS pathname. For example, my WPUSER.PCX file is stored on drive D in the IMAGES subdirectory. To retrieve it, I type the following in the box:

   ```
   D:\IMAGES\WPUSER.PCX
   ```

If this DOS pathname stuff makes your eyes cross, you can use the F5 key in the Retrieve Image File dialog box instead. Refer to Chapter 16 for more information on the F5 key. Or if you just don't understand DOS pathnames, refer to Chapter 21 for help with DOS.

4. **Press Enter.**

Splat! The image is pasted into the document, square against the right side of the screen.

✔ If you get an error message, you probably messed up typing the graphics image name. Maybe you forgot a drive letter, colon, backslash, or some other jot or tittle that pleases DOS. Refer to Chapter 16 for instructions on using the handy F5 key.

✔ "Ugh! That wasn't the image I wanted." Hurry and press the Undo key, Ctrl-Z, and try again.

✔ If the graphics image disappears or appears blank, press Ctrl-F3, Enter, which redraws the screen and may invigorate your graphics image.

✔ Select the Retrieve Image item in the Graphics menu to immediately see the Retrieve Image dialog box. Type the graphic's filename and watch that wondrous graphics image appear in the document.

✔ The next section, "Adjusting the graphics image," offers information on modifying the image, adding a border or caption, and so on.

✔ Yes, some images are colorful on the screen. No, unless you have a color printer, they print only in black and white.

✔ Even though I'm admittedly against using graphics in text, sticking a graphic of your signature at the end of a letter is a cool thing to do. Use a painting program, such as PC Paintbrush, to create a graphics image of your John Hancock. Then follow Steps 1 – 4 to insert it at the proper place in the document.

✔ Although they're not really graphics images, WordPerfect has an assortment of oddball characters that you can insert in the text right along with the normal human characters — for example, ☺ or ♥, which is ever popular with teenage girls. Refer to Chapter 9 and Appendix A for more information on WordPerfect's oddball characters.

✔ Nothing slows down WordPerfect like a few graphics images on the screen. Try pasting them in last.

Adjusting the graphics image

I'm not an artist, nor do I play one on TV. Figure 13-1 shows my best efforts at rendering myself sitting at a computer using WordPerfect. Ah, such expression! Can you feel my pain? I'm in the wrong profession. . . .

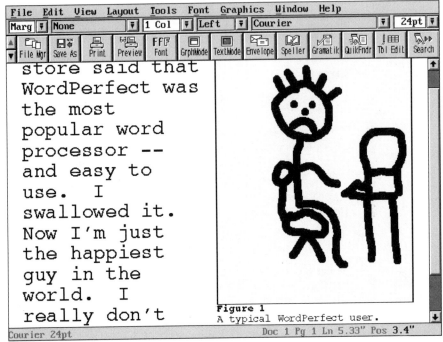

To put a graphics image into text, follow the steps in "Slapping a graphics image into a document" earlier in the chapter. Then you can adjust the image by pressing Alt-F9 again and selecting the image for editing. Keep in mind that you can't use this method to redraw the image — but you can certainly use it to tweak the image a bit.

Here are the basic *I want to tweak my graphics* steps:

1. Move the cursor near the image you want to edit.

If you have a mouse, double-click the mouse on the image and skip to Step 3.

2. Press Alt-F9, B, E.

Alt-F9 is the Graphics command, B is for *Box,* and E is for *Edit.* If you have only one graphic in the document, go to Step 3. Otherwise, you see the Select Box to Edit dialog box.

All the images in the document are numbered — 1 through however many you have. The first graphic to appear in a document is always image 1. Later images have higher numbers. And if you add new images in between old images, the images are renumbered.

Your task in the Select Box to Edit dialog box is to type the number of the image that you want to adjust. Guess. If you guess wrong, you can try again with another number.

Press Enter after you type the box number.

3. The Edit Graphics Box dialog box appears.

The Edit Graphics Box dialog box, which is shown in Figure 13-2, is where you control the graphics image on the screen. You can use this box to do many things, but I've decided to describe only the two most important things.

✔ To adjust the box's position on the screen, press P (Edit Position), H (Horizontal). Graphics boxes are usually put on the right side of the page. You can select another position — Left, Right, Centered, and so on — from the pop-up list. Press F7 to exit this dialog box.

✔ To add a caption to the graphic, press C (Create Caption). The screen changes to what looks like half-a-page editing mode. You see Figure 1 already typed for you — which is nice. Then you can type your own caption. Use the character formatting commands (from Chapter 9) if you want. What you type appears in a tiny box below the graphics image. Press F7 when you're done entering the caption.

✔ Press F7 when you're done messing with your graphics box. This action returns you to the document for editing.

✔ You can move the image around by dragging it with the mouse. Click the mouse on the graphic and keep the button down. The mouse pointer changes to a four-direction arrow, which indicates that you can drag the image to another position in the document.

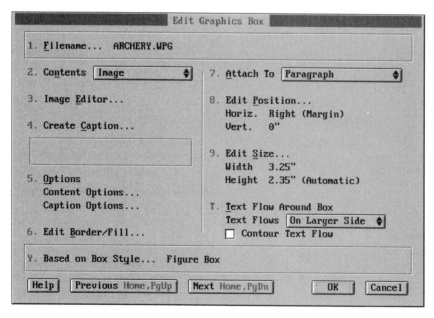

Figure 13-2:
The Edit
Graphics
Box dialog
box.

> ✔ Here's another mouse trick: Click on the image once and then use the mouse to adjust its size. Just hover the mouse over one of the black boxes that appears on the image's borders and drag that box to a new position to resize the image.

> ✔ The image in Figure 13-1 was created using PC Paintbrush. I saved it as a PCX file and then pasted it into WordPerfect using Alt-F9, whatever.

Drawing Lines

WordPerfect comes with its own *Etch A Sketch* program that you can use to draw lines around and over the text. In a way, this feature can be considered graphics. You actually create the graphics on the screen. Unfortunately, you're limited to using lines and characters as opposed to real drawing tools — hence the Etch A Sketch aspect.

To draw lines in and around text, follow these steps:

1. Press Ctrl-F3, L.

WordPerfect shifts into Line Drawing mode. The screen looks similar to the one shown in Figure 13-3, but you see your document.

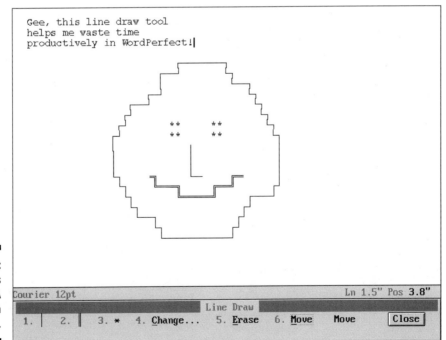

Figure 13-3: WordPerfect's Etch A Sketch mode.

The Line Draw menu at the bottom of the screen lists the line-drawing commands. You use the cursor-control keys to move around and draw the lines:

←	Draw/move to the left
→	Draw/move to the right
↑	Draw/move up
↓	Draw/move down

When you move the cursor around, the line traces the cursor's steps.

Press 1 to draw single lines.

Press 2 to draw double lines.

Press 3 to draw lines that are made with the asterisk character.

2. Press 1, 2, or 3 to draw lines.

When you move the cursor around, you get to play Etch A Sketch on the PC.

To erase mistakes, press 5 and then move the cursor around to remove lines from the screen.

If you want to move around the screen without drawing or erasing lines, press 6. To start drawing again, press 1, 2, or 3.

3. Press F7 when you're done.

✔ If you need to move around without drawing or erasing, press 6.

✔ If you want to draw with characters other than the single line, double line, or asterisk, press 4 and then select a new drawing character to replace the asterisk.

✔ The Line Draw item in the Graphics menu instantly puts you into Etch A Sketch mode.

Part III
Working with Documents

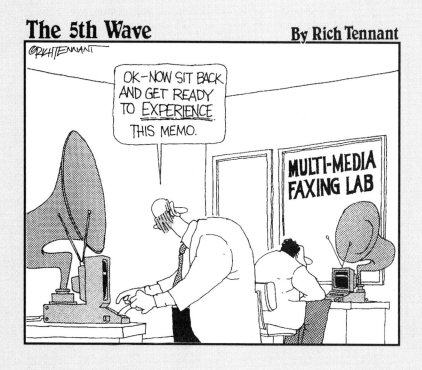

In this part . . .

*D*ocument just sounds so much more important than *that thing I did with my word processor*. It implies a crisp, masterful touch. No, this isn't another dreary report. It's a *document*. This isn't just a letter complaining to the local cable affiliate. It's a *document*. It isn't a note to Michael's teacher explaining his rash. It's a *document*. *Document* sounds professional, so never mind that you had to tie your fingers in knots and print several hundred copies before you got it right — it's a document!

This part of the book explores what you use WordPerfect for: making documents. You learn how to work with documents and files on disk, how to manage files, and how to work with alien documents that were not produced with WordPerfect. You also read the ugly, sordid story of mail merging, which is right up there next to paying taxes as far as mental agony and grief are concerned.

Chapter 14
Working with More Than a File — a Document

* * *

In This Chapter

▶ Working on several documents at one time

▶ Saving a document to disk (for the first time)

▶ Saving a document to disk (after that)

▶ Saving a document to disk and quitting

▶ Saving and starting over with a clean slate

▶ Using the Gang Exit command

▶ Retrieving a document from disk

▶ Loading one document into another document

* * *

A document is what you see on the screen in WordPerfect. It's the *text* you create and edit, the *formatting* you apply, and the *end result* that's printed. But a document is also a file that you store on disk for later retrieval, editing, or printing. Things get rough here because big bully DOS horns in on the action. To work with documents on disk, you need to wrestle with DOS filenames. Personally, I'd rather exist on a diet of birdseed and vending-machine food — but we're all stuck with DOS, so let's try to make the best of things.

Working on Several Documents at One Time

This feature is weird — and handy: WordPerfect enables you to work on more than one document at a time. Some people work on two documents. *Two,* yes, *two.* Some work on four, five, or more — on up to nine at a time (which is the legal limit in most states).

What's the point? The advantage to working on several documents at one time is that you don't have to save one document to disk and start over. You can juggle several documents, copying information between them, editing, and updating. Right now, I have my table of contents in Doc 1, a caption list in Doc 2, and this chapter in Doc 3. I'm a wild man! The multiple-document feature enables me to work on several things at one time without having to keep saving and loading, saving and loading, and on and on.

Send in the Docs

When you want to begin working on another document, you get started in one of two ways:

1. Use the Retrieve command, Shift-F10, to fetch the next document that you want. WordPerfect loads it into its own place — its own *document window* — and you see it on the screen, ready for editing action.

2. Use the New command in the File menu to start working on a new document. WordPerfect gives you a fresh, blank screen, and you're off and typing.

✔ To figure out which document you're working on, look at the clue that's scribbled in the lower right corner of the screen. If you see Doc 1, you're in Document 1; if you see Doc 2, you're in Document 2. If you're very busy, you may see Doc 9, which means you're in Document 9 — and nine documents is the most you can work on at one time.

✔ The goings on of one document are independent of the other: printing, spell-checking, formatting, and so on, affect only the document that is currently visible on the screen.

✔ When you're working with multiple documents, pressing F7 only closes the current document — just as if you'd used the Close command. You do not exit WordPerfect; instead, you see another document on the screen.

✔ To truly quit WordPerfect, you use the Home, F7 key combination. Refer to "Using the Gang Exit command" tucked away later in this chapter.

Switching from one document to another

Not only can you work on several documents at one time, but you can switch between them while you're working. You don't need to close any one document before working on another one. It's as if WordPerfect is giving you several typewriters to use, each of which has its own piece of paper. You just need to switch typewriters to start working on something else.

To switch from one document to another, use the Switch To command, F3. Pressing F3 displays the Switch to Document dialog box, which is shown in Figure 14-1. Press the number key (1 through 9) that corresponds to the number of the document that you want to work on. WordPerfect instantly switches to that document.

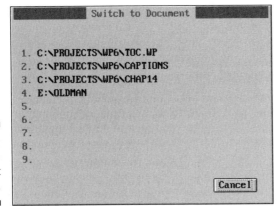

Figure 14-1:
The Switch
to Document
dialog box.

✔ The Switch To command is found in the Window menu.

✔ You can copy a block from one document to another. After you highlight the block and press Ctrl-C to copy it, press F3 and zoom to the other document. In that document, press Ctrl-V to paste in the block. This method makes moving information between several documents easy. (Refer to Chapter 6 for detailed block action.)

✔ I like to keep *core* documents in the same Doc number. For example, I always keep my table of contents in Doc 1. I put other stuff that I work on into other documents. However, when I need to get back to my table of contents, I press F3, 1 (switch to Doc 1) to get there quickly.

✔ If a document has been saved to disk, then its cryptic DOS pathname appears by its document number in the Switch to Document dialog box. Otherwise, you see (Untitled) listed.

If you know which document number you want to switch to, use these quick steps:

1. Press F3.

2. Type the document number.

Switching between this and that document

To quickly switch between the current document and the one you just left, press Shift-F3.

For example, if Doc 1 is on the screen and you press Shift-F3, Doc 1 goes away and you are presented with Doc 2 (which is a new blank page). You can switch back to Doc 1 by pressing Shift-F3 a second time.

If you pressed F3, 4 to move to Doc 4 from Doc 1, then you can press Shift-F3 to get back to Doc 1. If you press Shift-F3 again, you return to Doc 4.

✔ You can use the Switch item in the Window menu to move between this document and that one.

✔ You can use the Ctrl-Y key combination to "cycle" through all your document windows — not just this and that one. Keep pressing Ctrl-Y until the document you want is on the screen.

✔ The Shift-F3 key switches you between the current document and the one that you just came from. To switch to a specific document number, use the F3 key as described in the preceding section, "Switching from one document to another."

✔ When a block is marked on the screen, the Shift-F3 key combination is used to change the case of the text in the block. For example, you may change the text from uppercase letters to lowercase letters. Refer to the discussion on converting uppercase and lowercase letters in Chapter 9.

Saving Documents

You don't save a document to disk only when you're done with it. In fact, you should save it almost *immediately* — as soon as you have a few sentences or paragraphs. Save! Save! Save!

As you're working on the document, save it again!

When you're done, be extra sure to save it one last time!

Saving documents is about the most important thing you can do in WordPerfect. And it involves only a minor level of drudgery — so no complaining!

Saving a document to disk (for the first time)

To save a document that hasn't already been saved to disk, follow these steps (if you've already saved the file, skip to the next section):

1. Press the Save key, F10.

You see the Save dialog box.

If you see the Document Summary dialog box instead, press F7 twice: F7, F7. Document Summaries are required by some large organizations that don't believe any one individual can be responsible for anything. Fill the box out if you have time to waste. Otherwise, pressing F7, F7 gets rid of it. Then you see the Save dialog box. (Refer to the technical box, "Ridding yourself of the Document Summary hex," later in this chapter to learn how to switch off the Document Summary feature.)

2. Type a DOS filename for the document.

This part is tricky. DOS filenames can contain only letters and numbers, and they can be no more than eight characters long. You have to be brief and descriptive (which rules most lawyers out from effectively naming files).

3. Press Enter.

If everything goes right, then the disk drive churns for a few seconds, and eventually you see the filename — plus a few cryptic DOS characters — in the lower left corner of the screen. The file has been saved.

If there is a problem, you're likely to see an error message dialog box. You are most likely to see a tiny dialog box that says

```
Replace filename?
```

This message tells you that the disk already contains a file with the name you have chosen. Press N and then skip back up to Step 2 and type another name. If you press Y instead of N, the current file replaces the file on the disk — which is probably not what you want to do.

You may see one of these other error message dialog boxes:

```
Invalid drive/path description
Invalid filename
```

These two error messages mean that a problem occurred when you tried to save the file to disk. Most likely, you used a naughty symbol in the filename. Go back to Step 2 and use only letters and numbers in the filename.

✔ The Save item in the File menu performs the same function as pressing F10. And it even says *Save,* which is remarkable because F10 sounds more like a shoe size.

✔ Save your documents!

✔ After you save, save again. To save again, see "Saving a document to disk (after that)."

✔ Additional rules for naming files are in Chapter 16.

✔ You should organize files, storing them in special places on the disk called *subdirectories.* Chapter 16 tells you how to store files in subdirectories, and Chapter 21 contains some technical mumbo-jumbo on subdirectories.

Ridding yourself of the Document Summary hex

I hate Document Summaries. One of the reasons I originally became a WordPerfect user was because it lacked this time-wasting feature. Now it's back. Ugh.

To switch off the Document Summary feature, follow these steps:

1. When you see the Document Summary dialog box, press Shift-F1.

   You see a configuration dialog box. The third item in that box is Create Summary on Exit/Save. That item has an X in its check box, meaning that WordPerfect bothers you for the unnecessary summary information each time you save a document to disk.

2. Press 3.

   The X disappears from the check box, and WordPerfect will no longer bug you for a Document Summary.

3. Press F7 once or twice until the Document Summary dialog box goes away — for good.

Saving a document to disk (after that)

The instructions in this section assume that you've already saved your file to disk once. So why save your file again (and again)? Because it's smart! You should save your file to disk every so often — usually after you write something either brilliant or so complex that you don't want to retype it. (If you haven't yet saved your document to disk, refer to the preceding section.)

Saving a document to disk a second time updates the file on disk. This process is painless and quick:

1. **Press Ctrl-F12.**

   Crunch, crunch! Done!

2. **Continue working.**

   ✔ You can quickly save a document to disk by selecting the Save command from the File menu.

   ✔ I recommend pressing Ctrl-F12 every so often as you continue to toss words down on the page.

   ✔ If you've already saved a file to disk, its name appears in the bottom left of the screen.

   ✔ If you haven't yet saved the document to disk, then pressing Ctrl-F12 has the same effect as pressing F10 to save a document the first time. Refer to "Saving a document to disk (for the first time)" earlier in this chapter.

Saving a document to disk and quitting

You're done for the day. Your fingers are sore; your eyes are glazing over. Everywhere you look, you see Doc 1 Pg 4 Ln 9.49" Pos 3.53" off to your lower right. You blink and rub your eyes, stretch out your back. Ah, it's Miller time. But before you slap your buddies on the back and walk into the sunset on a beer commercial, you need to save your document and quit for the day:

1. **Press F7, the Exit command key.**

   A dialog box appears, asking whether you want to save the document.

2. **Press Y to save the document.**

   If the document hasn't yet been saved, you see the Save dialog box. Follow the steps outlined in "Saving a document to disk (for the first time)" earlier in this chapter.

   Eventually you see one of two messages in a dialog box. The first one will probably be

   ```
   Exit WordPerfect?
   ```

3. **Press Y to quit and return to DOS.**

   If you've been working on more than one document, you see the following message:

   ```
   Exit Document n?
   ```

   The *n* will be a document number — 1 through 9. What the message means is that you've been working on more than one document and the F7 key will quit (actually, close) only the current document. Press Y to exit that document. Then skip back to Step 1 and repeat these quitting steps for the other document(s).

   ✔ When you exit WordPerfect, you find yourself at the DOS prompt. Or, if you were running a menu system, you see the menu. Or, if you're a gutsy type and run Windows, then Windows happily bounces back up on the screen.

   ✔ You can find the Exit command loitering near the bottom of the File menu.

   ✔ Always use the F7 key to quit WordPerfect. Never turn off your PC or reset it when WordPerfect is on the screen.

   ✔ "Using the Gang Exit command," later in this chapter, explains how to quit WordPerfect quickly when you're working with several documents.

Press these quickie keys to save a document and quit WordPerfect (provided that you've already saved the file to disk):

F7, Y, Y

Saving and closing (starting over with a clean slate)

When you want to save a document, clear it off the screen, and start over with a clean slate, you use the Close command. To close a document, follow these absorbing steps:

1. Press the Exit key, F7.

A dialog box appears, asking whether you want to save the document.

2. Press Y to save.

You go through the Save procedure if you haven't yet saved the document to disk. The steps are outlined in "Saving a document to disk (for the first time)" earlier in this chapter. Follow them with vigor.

3. At the next dialog box prompt, press N.

You stay in WordPerfect but start over again with a clean slate.

✔ The Close command in the File menu offers an easier way to close a document and start over. The prompt from Step 1 appears, asking whether you want to save the document. Press Y to save it. When you press Y to save the document, WordPerfect automatically rations you a new blank page. You don't have to mess with the second dialog box.

✔ You don't have to quit WordPerfect and start it over to begin working with a blank slate.

Press these quickie keys to save a document and start over again with a clean slate (provided that you've already saved the file to disk):

F7, Y, N

Using the Gang Exit command

When you really need to quit, and you don't want to stop by to visit all your documents and wave good-bye with the F7 key, use the more powerful Home, F7 key combination. Remember that Home is the *big* key. So if F7 is the *good-bye* key, then Home, F7 is the *big good-bye* key.

Follow these steps to quit WordPerfect quickly when you're working on several documents:

1. Press Home, F7.

Press the Home key. Release it. Press and release the F7 key. You see what I call the Gang Exit dialog box, which is shown in Figure 14-2.

```
┌─────────────────────────────────────────────────────┐
│▓▓▓▓▓▓▓▓▓▓▓▓▓  Exit WordPerfect  ▓▓▓▓▓▓▓▓▓▓▓▓▓        │
│                                                       │
│      Save      Filename                               │
│   A. ☒   1. │C:\PROJECTS\WP6\EAT03          │         │
│                                                       │
│   B. ☐   2. │C:\PROJECTS\WP6\ALIEN         │          │
│                                                       │
│   C. ☐   3. │C:\PROJECTS\WP6\STORY         │          │
│                                                       │
│   D. ☐   4. │C:\PROJECTS\WP6\GOATS         │          │
│                                                       │
│   E. ☒   5. │                              │          │
│                                                       │
│   [ (Un)mark All ]      [ Save and Exit ]  [ Cancel ] │
└─────────────────────────────────────────────────────┘
```

Figure 14-2:
The Gang
Exit dialog
box.

The dialog box lists all the documents you're working on, by both number and filename. If a file hasn't yet been saved, its filename box is blank (like the box for Document 5 in Figure 14-2), and an X appears in the little Save check box. You see the filenames of documents that have been saved, and if they've been modified, you see an X in the little Save check box (see the X in the little box for Document 1 in Figure 14-2).

2. **To save everything and exit, press Enter.**

   Documents that haven't been saved are saved. You are asked to type filenames for documents that need them.

   There's the DOS prompt! You're outta WordPerfect.

✔ The Gang Exit command's real name is Exit WP, and it lives at the bottom of the File menu.

✔ WordPerfect is actually smart about the Home, F7 command. This command saves files that need saving and doesn't bother with the files that are up to date.

Grabbing Documents from Disk

After you have saved your documents from certain peril by saving them to disk, you can pull them back into WordPerfect. You can get them back right away, or, more likely, you'll want to retrieve them at a later point in time. As long as a document has been save, save, saved to disk, retrieving it is only a matter of knowing the proper and unintuitive key combinations.

Opening a document

When you first start WordPerfect, or after you clear away one document and start over again with a clean slate, you have the option of opening a previously saved document from disk into WordPerfect for editing.

To grab a file from disk — retrieve it — follow these steps:

1. **Holler, "Here document! Here, boy! Come on! Here!"** *(Whistle.)*

2. **Press the Open command, Shift-F10.**

   The Open document dialog box pops up in an unfriendly manner.

3. **Type the name of a document stored on disk.**

4. **Press Enter.**

   WordPerfect finds the document and loads it on the screen for editing. You may see one of the following messages:

   ```
   Converting for printer
   Converting DOS text file
   ```

   That's OK; the document file on disk is being made kosher for WordPerfect.

5. **Go!**

   ✔ Mouse alert! Handy Open command lives in File menu. Pass it on.

   ✔ If the document isn't found, you see an error message and are given the chance to try again. Edit the document filename, if you want, using the ← and → keys and the Delete and Backspace keys, or type a new filename. If you still get an error message, refer to the discussion on finding lost files in Chapter 24.

   ✔ You also can use the miraculous F5 key to hunt down a file on disk and load it into WordPerfect. Refer to Chapter 16 to learn how to work a miracle.

   ✔ Argh! If the screen fills with scary-looking stuff, then what you tried to load from disk probably wasn't a WordPerfect file. Press these keys to get rid of the stuff: F7, N, N.

   ✔ Chapter 15 has additional information on loading alien document formats, including Text, ASCII, and other word processors' documents.

   ✔ You can keep opening files all the do-dah-day. WordPerfect puts each one in its own document, or Doc, but you can have only nine documents open at one time. Refer to "Working on several documents at one time" earlier in this chapter.

✔ If you want to load a document when WordPerfect first starts, type that document's filename after you type **WP** and a space at the DOS prompt. Refer to the discussion of editing a document on disk in Chapter 1 for more information.

Quickly opening the last stuff you've worked on

Suppose that you're just starting WordPerfect for the day — or after you've been out. You want to pick up with the last thing you worked on — the last document you saved before you quit WordPerfect. Here are the handy steps:

1. Press the Open command, Shift-F10.

2. Press the ↓ key.

   A list of files that you've recently saved to disk drops down.

3. Press Enter to retrieve the last file that you saved to disk.

   Or use the ↓ key to highlight one of the other three files you've most recently saved, immediately loading the file of your choice into WordPerfect for editing.

This trick is an extremely handy shortcut. Unfortunately, however, WordPerfect recalls only the last four files you saved. (This trick almost makes up for the Document Summary feature that I hate so much.)

Loading one document into another document (retrieving)

You can use the Open command to stick one document into another one that is already on the screen. Instead of putting the second document into its own *Doc,* WordPerfect performs something similar to a massive block-paste operation. Inserting one document into another one is not a problem, so long as that's what you intend to do.

To load one document into another, follow these steps:

1. **Position the cursor in the current document where you want the other document's text to appear.**

2. **Press the Open command, Shift-F10.**

3. **At the prompt, type the name of the file that you want to paste into the current document.**

4. **Press Shift-F10.**

5. **Press Enter.**

   The text of the new document appears right where the cursor is.

✔ If you select the Retrieve command from the File menu, you don't have to press Shift-F10 as you do in Step 4; just press Enter to retrieve the file.

✔ If you goof, you may be able to undo the insertion by pressing Ctrl-Z.

✔ The resulting, combined document has the same name in memory as the original document, already saved to disk.

✔ You can retrieve any number of documents into the current document. There is no limit. (But avoid retrieving the huge hulking cow document if possible.)

✔ These steps enable you to retrieve a block of text that was saved as a file and then stick that block into another document. (Slapping a commonly used piece of text into several documents is often called *boiler plating*. *Boiler plating* is also the way cheap romance novels are written.)

Chapter 15

Working with Other Documents, Alien and ASCII

*W*ordPerfect is not the only word processor in the world. (Lucky for the world.) Other folks use other word processors, and occasionally you may tangle with the files they create. Or you may need to give someone a file in ASCII format. At moments like these, you have to deal with non-WordPerfect documents — what I call the *alien file formats.*

Loading a DOS Text File

A *DOS text file* is a special, nondocument file that you can load into WordPerfect for editing. It's a nondocument file because it contains no formatting, boldfacing, underlining, centering, headers, or footers. It's just plain old text.

To open a DOS text file, follow these steps:

1. Press the Open command, Shift-F10.

The Open Document dialog box appears.

2. Type the name of the DOS text file that you want to load.

3. Press Enter.

Because the file isn't a WordPerfect document, you see the File Format dialog box that is shown in Figure 15-1. WordPerfect guesses the file format, which is probably ASCII Text (Standard). That format is high-lighted in Figure 15-1.

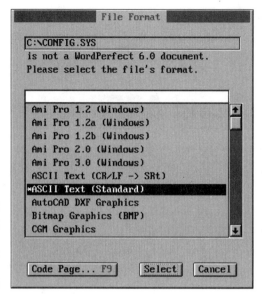

Figure 15-1:
The File
Format
dialog box.

4. Press Enter again to select ASCII Text (Standard).

The DOS text file appears on the screen, ready for editing just like any WordPerfect document.

🖝 If you save the file to disk again, it becomes a WordPerfect document, complete with any formatting changes that you may have added. However, most of the time you are directed to save the file back to disk as a DOS text file. This procedure is covered in the next section.

🖝 DOS text files are also called *ASCII files*. ASCII is an acronym that basically means *a DOS text file*. You pronounce it *ASK-ee*.

🖝 Information on opening WordPerfect document files lurks in Chapter 14.

🖝 The only critical thing about dealing with a DOS text file is saving the file back to disk in the DOS text format. The steps that you need to follow to save it in the DOS text format are in the next section.

Saving a DOS Text File

WordPerfect normally saves documents to disk as WordPerfect document files, which keeps all the formatting and special stuff intact for the next time you work on the document. But WordPerfect is capable of saving files in the DOS text format, which is also known as *saving a file in ASCII format*.

To save a document in the DOS text, or ASCII, format, follow these steps:

1. **Press the Save command, F10.**

   You must press F10 here. Do not press Ctrl-F12. You need the Save As command, not the quick Save command.

2. **If the Document Summary dialog box noses its way onto the screen, press F7 twice: F7, F7.**

   This action gets rid of the lousy document summary information, which isn't required for saving a DOS text file to disk. (Refer to Chapter 14 for much-needed instructions on turning this *feature* off permanently.)

   The typical Save Document dialog box appears.

   Normally, you type a filename here, and WordPerfect saves the file as a document on disk. But you want to save the file as a DOS text file. To do that, you have to change the format, which appears in the box below where you type the filename.

3. **Press Esc, 2.**

   A list drops down, showing you the file formats under which WordPerfect can save documents.

4. **In the list, look for the ASCII Text (Standard) format.**

   Use the ↑ and ↓ cursor-control keys to move through the list and highlight the ASCII Text (Standard) format.

5. **Press Enter.**

6. **Press 1 to highlight the Filename box again.**

7. **Type a filename for the DOS text file.**

8. **Press Enter to save the file to disk.**

   If a file with the name you've entered already exists, WordPerfect asks whether you want to replace that file; press Y to replace it or N to try another name.

✔ Saving a DOS text file may be a requirement in some instances — for example, if you're ever asked to edit the special CONFIG.SYS or AUTOEXEC.BAT files. You can load those files the same way you load any WordPerfect document, but you have to save them back to disk as DOS text files.

✔ You can save a document as both a DOS text file and a WordPerfect document file. First, save the file to disk as a WordPerfect document. Then save the file to disk as a DOS text file, using a different name. (Some users put the extension TXT on a DOS text file.) Then they have both a DOS text file, which is what DOS wants, and a WordPerfect file that contains secret codes and prints out really purty.

Understanding the ASCII thing

WordPerfect saves its documents to disk in its own special file format. That format includes the text — the basic characters you type — plus information about formatting, boldfacing, underlining, graphics, and anything else you toss into the document. All that stuff is saved to disk so that the next time you use WordPerfect, you get the formatting back for editing, printing, or whatever.

Every word processor has a different document file format. WordPerfect documents are considered *alien* to other word processors, which use their own non-WordPerfect format. It has been this way since the dawn of the PC. So to keep the confusion low, a common text format was developed — the *ASCII* format.

ASCII is an acronym for something I need not mention here because you are not going to be tested on this material, and, besides, you'd probably forget what the acronym stands for two minutes after you read it. What's more important than knowing what it represents is knowing how to pronounce it: *ASK-ee*. It's not *ask-two*. It's *ASK-ee*.

An ASCII file contains only text. It does not contain formatting codes, boldface, underlining, graphics, or anything else. Just text. The ASCII format is also called the *plain text format* or sometimes the *DOS text format*. Whatever you call it, an ASCII file contains only text.

Because ASCII files aren't littered with word processing code, their text can be read by any word processor. In a way, ASCII files are the Esperanto of document files. Any word processor can read an ASCII file and display its contents. The text looks ugly, but it's better than nothing. Also, to maintain compatibility, WordPerfect can save your files in ASCII format, as described in "Saving a DOS Text File" earlier in the chapter.

Loading Documents Created by Alien Word Processors

Suppose that crazy Earl gives you a disk full of his favorite limericks. Of course, Earl is crazy, but not that crazy. He uses Windows and the Ami Pro word processor. Without thinking about it, Earl has handed you a disk full of Ami Pro documents, and it's making you silly.

First antipanic button: Don't worry about the Windows aspect. Although Earl uses Windows, you don't have to use Windows to be able to load his files. A PC disk is a PC disk. No problems there.

Second antipanic button: WordPerfect can safely read Earl's limerick files, even though he saved them in that whacko Ami Pro file format. To retrieve the files, just follow the steps in "Loading a DOS Text File." Yes, the same steps. The only difference is that WordPerfect will recognize the Ami Pro documents and automatically highlight Ami Pro 3.0 (Windows) in the Format list.

✔ Not only can WordPerfect read Ami Pro documents, but it also recognizes several other popular document formats instantly. Just use the Open command to open alien word processor documents.

✔ Nothing's perfect. The alien document that you open into WordPerfect may require some fixing up — font adjustments and whatnot. At most, this is a minor bother; at least you don't have to retype anything.

✔ After the file is in WordPerfect, you can save it to disk in the WordPerfect format. Just use the Save command as you normally do.

✔ Occasionally, WordPerfect finds something so utterly bizarre that it doesn't recognize it. When that happens, you can try to open the document, but asking the person who created the document to save it in ASCII format is probably a better idea.

✔ Another common document format is *RTF,* the *Rich Text Format.* This format is better than ASCII because it keeps track of underlining, boldface, and other formatting things. If you find that you'll be sharing files often with other weirdo word processors, try to get everyone to settle on a common format, such as RTF. Better still, get everyone to settle on WordPerfect.

Saving Documents in Alien Formats

The time has come for you to give Earl your collection of leper jokes. Alas, they are saved to disk in WordPerfect 6.0 format. You could be lax like Earl and just hand him a floppy disk full of WordPerfect documents. But then he'd call you up and complain or ramble on and on about some new word processor conversion program he found. You don't have time for that, so just do him a favor and save the file in his own word processor's format.

This task is simple. Follow the steps outlined in "Saving a DOS Text File" earlier in this chapter. In Step 4, however, select the proper alien word processor format from the list. For Earl, you select Ami Pro 3.0 (Windows). The file is saved in the alien format.

Users on Venus prefer Word for Windows. Users on Mars prefer WordStar, but, hey, they've always been behind the times.

Chapter 16
Managing Files

In This Chapter

▶ Naming files

▶ Finding a place for your work

▶ Using a new directory

▶ Understanding the miracle of QuickList

▶ Using the marvelous F5 key

▶ Looking at documents on disk

▶ Copying files

▶ Deleting files

▶ Renaming files

▶ Finding text in files

The more you work in WordPerfect, the more documents you create; because you always save those documents to disk, the more files you make. This is how a hard drive gets full of stuff; you create it. In a way, your hard drive is like your closet. It's full of stuff. And unless you have a handy closet organizer — like the one I bought for three low, low payments of $29.95 — things are going to get messy. This chapter tackles the subject of using and organizing files. (I'd carelessly toss in a joke about women's shoes in closets here, but my wife would hit me.)

Naming Files

When you save your precious work to disk (which is always a good idea), you need to give it a filename. But naming files isn't all that much fun, and it has nothing to do with WordPerfect; point the finger of blame at DOS.

  ✔ DOS is the one that has such restrictive filenames!

  ✔ DOS is the one that limits you to eight measly characters!

  ✔ DOS is the one that lets you use only numbers and letters!

  ✔ DOS is the scourge upon which . . . OK. Let's not get carried away.

To save a document to disk, you need to use a DOS filename. Here are the rules:

- ✔ A DOS filename can be no more than eight characters long. It can be less, sure. A one-character filename is OK but not very descriptive.

- ✔ You can use any combination of letters or numbers to name your file. Extra points are awarded for being clever. Uppercase and lowercase letters are the same to DOS.

- ✔ A DOS filename can start with a number. In fact, the name of this file, the document that contains the text for this chapter, is 16 (a one and a six). That's a perfectly legit DOS filename — and descriptive too because it tells me what this file contains. (A filename like CHAP16 is more descriptive and also legit; CHAP14.WP is even more so.)

- ✔ A DOS filename cannot have spaces.

- ✔ A DOS filename cannot contain symbols. OK, that's a half truth. But why clutter your brain with the symbols it can and cannot have? It's just better to name files by using only letters and numbers.

- ✔ A DOS filename can have an optional filename extension. An *extension* follows the filename and can contain one, two, or three characters. A period separates the filename from the extension, and that's the only time you see a filename with a period in it. Filenames do not end in periods.

- ✔ Sometimes filenames are displayed with spaces in them. Ignore the spaces. The spaces are used for lining up the filenames and extensions on the screen. You don't need to type the spaces to enter a filename.

- ✔ A *pathname* is a super-long filename, describing exactly where a file is on a disk drive. The pathname contains a colon, letters, numbers, and backslash characters. For more information, refer to the next section.

- ✔ Examples of good and bad filenames are provided in Chapter 1, in the section on saving your stuff.

Finding a Place for Your Work

A hard drive can be a rugged and unforgiving place — like the parking lot at Nordstrom's during a shoe sale. Trouble looms like it does when the last pair of off-white pumps is priced under $10. Unless there is some semblance of organization, chaos rules.

To work the hard drive right, you need organization. It's a big deal: organization. Special places called *directories* are on the hard drive; sometimes the nautical term *subdirectories* is used instead. These places are like holding bins for files. All files of a certain type are stored in and retrieved from their own directories.

Chapter 21 covers organizing and setting up directories. Your guru or the person responsible for setting up your computer should have built some of these directories and arranged them for your use. (If not, you can create directories as needed; refer to Chapter 21.)

Each of these directories is known by a specific name. That name is called a *pathname*. The pathname includes the disk drive letter, a colon, a backslash, and then a directory name. If you have a directory within another directory (a subdirectory), then its name is also included in the pathname, along with extra backslash characters to make it all look confusing.

Table 16-1 lists some common pathnames. Please write in any additional pathnames you use, along with their purposes. If all this stuff has you shaking your head, have your guru fill in the pathnames for you.

Table 16-1	Some Common Pathnames
Pathname	*Contents/Description*
C:\	Drive C, main root directory
A:\	Drive A, main root directory
C:\WP	WordPerfect's directory (may also be WP60)
C:\DOS	DOS's directory

✔ You can use pathnames with the File Manager command key, F5. Directing WordPerfect to use a specific directory is covered in the next section.

✔ A better way to put your pathnames to use is with WordPerfect's miraculous QuickList feature. This is covered in an upcoming section.

✔ You can combine a pathname with a filename for use with the Save (F10) and Open (Shift-F10) commands. This is a long and complex thing to do, however, with great potential for typos. I recommend using the F5 key to change directories instead of typing a pathname. (Only those well versed in DOS-talk usually mess with pathnames anyway.)

✔ Yes, the complete pathname for your document is what you see in the lower left corner of the screen after you save a file. If you can read it, great. Otherwise, consider it similar to those meaningless numbers and letters that appear on an airplane ticket.

Using a New Directory

To use a specific directory on the hard drive with WordPerfect, follow these steps:

1. Press F5, the File Manager key.

The Specify File Manager List Whatever dialog box appears.

2. Press the equal (=) key.

This action tells WordPerfect to switch to a new directory so that you can use files in that directory. You see the Change Default Directory dialog box.

3. Type the name of the new directory you want to use.

For example, suppose that you need to use the C:\WP\WORK directory. You type that exactly as follows:

```
C:\WP\WORK
```

That is, press C and type a colon (:) to specify drive C. Then type **\WP** to specify the \WP directory and **\WORK** to specify the WORK subdirectory under the \WP directory.

Don't put any spaces in there and don't end the line with a period. Also, don't type any filenames; this is a directory-only command. (Filenames work with the Save and Retrieve commands.)

4. Press Enter.

This action causes WordPerfect to switch over to the new directory. The directory name always appears when you press the File Manager command key, F5. WordPerfect saves files to that directory and always looks in that directory for files to open.

5. Continue using the File Manager dialog box or press F7 to return to your document.

✔ After you switch to the new directory, you can use WordPerfect's Save (F10) and Open (Shift-F10) commands to save and open files only to and from that directory.

✔ If you type the name of a directory that doesn't exist, WordPerfect asks whether you want to create it. Press N if you meant another directory. (If you want to create a directory, refer to Chapter 21.)

✔ If you don't press the F5 key to switch to another directory, you are putting all your files into the same, cluttered closet-like directory. It's best to create a number of directories for your files to keep your work well organized.

Understanding the Miracle of QuickList

Talking about subdirectories and pathnames is unavoidable when you use a program that runs under — yuck — DOS. (Ick, ack!) It comes with the territory, just like when you visit your insurance agent and talk suddenly shifts to "term, vested, dismemberment" and "Are there any 16-year-olds who drive your vehicle?" Chilling, isn't it?

Fortunately, WordPerfect provides an easy way to get around the DOS talk. You can use WordPerfect's QuickList feature to help you organize your stuff. And with QuickList, you can use cute names instead of subdirectories and paths — names that actually reflect what you do with WordPerfect.

Before you start, a word of advice: QuickList is one of those features you might want to have your guru configure for you. I'll walk you through it, but for this brief tutorial you'll be sticking more than a cautious big toe into the swirling cesspool of DOS. Hold your nose!

Setting up QuickList

With the QuickList feature, you can instantly access DOS subdirectories that contain WordPerfect documents and so forth without needing to know cryptic DOS pathnames. Unfortunately, to set up QuickList, you *do* need to know the pathnames. Follow these steps:

1. **Press the F5 key.**

   This action brings up the introduction-to-the-File Manager dialog box, called the Specify File Manager List dialog box. Ignore it.

2. **Press the F6 key.**

   This action selects the QuickList button. You'll see the QuickList dialog box displayed, similar to the one shown in Figure 16-1. The list you see describes, in very English-like terms, subdirectories or storage places on the hard drive for your files and other WordPerfect folderol. (How QuickList works is covered in the next section.)

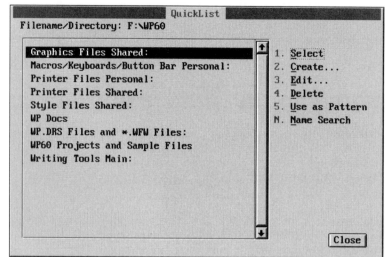

Figure 16-1:
The
QuickList
dialog box.

3. Press C (Create).

Press C to create a new item in the QuickList dialog box. You see the Create QuickList Entry dialog box, as shown in Figure 16-2.

4. Type an English-like description for a subdirectory on the hard drive.

For example, if you store all your letters in a \LETTERS subdirectory, type **All my letters**. Use a descriptive name that tells you what type of files are stored in a particular subdirectory. (Figure 16-2 shows that I typed **PCs for Dummies** in that field, indicating the subdirectory where I keep all my documents for the *PCs For Dummies* book.)

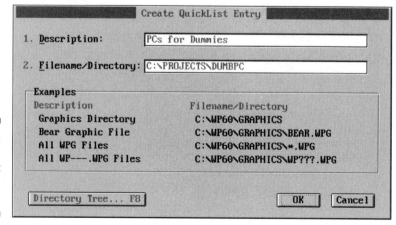

Figure 16-2:
The Create
QuickList
Entry dialog
box.

5. Press Enter.

The cursor moves to the Filename/Directory text box. Here you enter the pathname for the files described in the first box. For my *PCs For Dummies* files, that's the C:\PROJECTS\DUMBPC directory.

6. Type the pathname to your document files.

You may want to refer to "Finding a Place for Your Work" earlier in this chapter for a list of popular pathnames and subdirectories you've used on your PC. Or take advantage of the handy F8 key (the *Directory Tree* command) to see a graphical representation of the hard drive. Use the ↑ and ↓ keys to locate your directory. Or press O to switch to another drive.

7. Press Enter after typing the pathname.

8. Press the F7 key to exit from the Create QuickList Entry dialog box.

Your new entry appears in the list along with all the others. You can now use QuickList, as described in the next section, to switch between subdirectory storage places on the hard drive without needing to memorize a DOS pathname.

✔ WordPerfect automatically creates several QuickList items when WordPerfect is set up. These items can help you easily get to where WordPerfect stores some of its documents, graphics files, and other stuff; just select the appropriately phrased item from the list, as described in the next section.

✔ You can delete an entry in the list by highlighting the entry, pressing D, and then pressing Y.

You can make some entries generic — for example, *Current Project.* You can switch the subdirectory assigned to that entry by highlighting the entry and pressing E (Edit). Type a new subdirectory name in the Edit QuickList Entry dialog box; then press the F7 key to save it.

Using QuickList

You can use the QuickList tool only from certain dialog boxes: Save, Open, File Manager, and other places where you need to access files on disk. The primary clue indicating whether QuickList is available is a button labeled QuickList in the dialog box. The function key assigned to that button is always F6. Follow these steps to access the QuickList feature from one of those dialog boxes:

1. Press the F6 key.

The QuickList dialog box is displayed.

2. Use the ↑ or ↓ key to highlight an item in the list.

3. Press Enter to select that item as your subdirectory.

This causes WordPerfect to use that subdirectory for selecting files to open, save, or view. The idea here is that the English-like description you choose is much more memorable than a pathname. That's it! QuickList is just a shortcut, and a good one.

The QuickList command key, F6, works only in dialog boxes that you use for accessing disk drives. When you're editing, the F6 key is used to make your text bold. (Chapter 9 has information on formatting characters.)

Using the Marvelous F5 Key

The F5 key has a powerful and interesting command attached to it: File Manager. This is as close to DOS as you dare come while using WordPerfect. Indeed, you can skip DOS altogether if you become dexterous with the F5 key. Here's how it works:

Press the F5 key. You see the Specify File Manager List dialog box displayed, as shown in Figure 16-3. But that's not it. It's simply a precursor, the foyer to the File Manager's lobby — actually, it's more like the elevator. Inside the Specify File Manager List dialog box, you see the Directory prompt and then a DOS pathname that looks something like this:

```
C:\WP60
```

This pathname is the name of the directory where WordPerfect is currently storing files. (This murky subject is hammered out in Chapter 21.)

This dialog box gives you the opportunity to look at the current directory, to look at another directory on disk, or to change WordPerfect's directory. Changing the directory is covered in "Using a New Directory" earlier in this chapter. Because this is just a look-see exercise, press Enter to see the current directory.

Figure 16-3:
The Specify File Manager List dialog box.

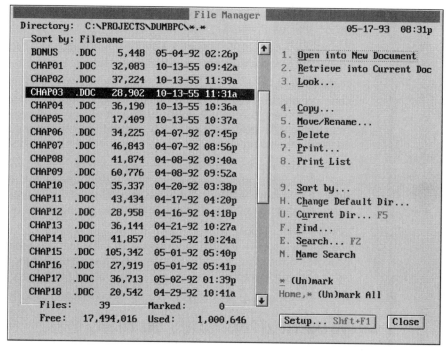

You'll see a crowded display on your screen, similar to that shown in Figure 16-4. Busy! Busy! Busy! I could take all day telling you what's going on. Instead, read the following list for the high points:

- Say, isn't that the current date and time in the upper right corner of the screen? Too bad it isn't updated every minute.

- All the files, WordPerfect documents and such, are listed on the left side of the screen. The display has the filename and optional extension lined up in columns. Keep in mind that the filenames don't really have spaces; the spaces you see here are just for show.

- Look at the right side of the screen. It's a menu!

The rest of the sections in this chapter detail how the commands in the File Manager menu/window/contraption work.

- Press F7 to exit the File Manager's crowded and overdone screen.

- Use the ↑ and ↓ keys to move the highlight bar on the screen. More files may be available; keep pressing the ↓ key to check. The commands in the menu on the right side of the screen affect the highlighted file.

- Mark several files and treat them as a single unit. You *mark* files by highlighting the file and pressing the asterisk key (*). Highlight another and then press the asterisk again. After a group of files is marked, you can copy, delete, rename, or print the group by selecting the proper command at the bottom of the screen.

✔ To unmark files marked with asterisks, press Home, * (asterisk).

✔ To load a file from disk, highlight the file and press O (Open). That's the same as using the Shift-F10 key command in WordPerfect, but with the File Manager screen you can peruse through several files — even peek into them to see what golden nuggets they contain; refer to the section "Looking at documents on disk."

✔ Know the differences between *opening* and *retrieving* a file! If you highlight a file and choose the *Open into New Document* command, that document is placed into its own window. But if you press R to retrieve a file, WordPerfect puts the file into your current document at the toothpick cursor's position.

✔ The *current directory* is the directory that WordPerfect is currently using. To switch directories, press the F5 key again and type the new directory name; then press Enter.

Looking at documents on disk

Wouldn't it be nice if you could look into a document before you loaded it, like getting a sneak preview? Doing so is entirely possible with the File Manager key, F5.

Press F5 and then press Enter. You see the File Manager dialog box on your screen. A list of files appears on the left side of the screen.

Use the ← and → cursor-control keys to highlight a filename. When the filename is highlighted, press L. This activates the Look command, allowing you to examine a file — to x-ray it.

✔ Use the ↑ and ↓ keys or the plus and minus keys on the numeric keypad to peruse the file.

✔ Let out a primal scream if you see the waste-of-time document summary information displayed. Press L again to see the document.

✔ Press Esc when you're done looking at a file.

✔ If the file is a WordPerfect document, you'll see its text. Other files may show up as text only. Weird files consisting of cryptic computer instructions and gunk show up equally weird on the screen.

✔ Do not try to load any of the weird files into WordPerfect. Although WordPerfect will choke, it won't die. If you do load a weird file (and I don't know why you would, seeing how I just warned you), press F7, N, N to clear it away and start over.

Copying files

You can use the File Manager screen/menu/whatever to copy files to and from directories in the system. After you press F5 and Enter to bring up the File Manager screen, follow these steps to copy files:

1. **Select the file you want to copy.**

   Move the highlight bar to that file. If you want to do a gang copy, move the highlight bar using the cursor-control keys and press the asterisk key to mark each file.

2. **Press C to activate the Copy command.**

   You see a Copy dialog box, with the prompt `Copy Highlighted File to` followed by a DOS pathname. Ignore the pathname. Skip to Step 3.

   If you marked a group of files, you see a dialog box asking whether you want to `Copy marked files`. Press Y for Yes. You see the Copy dialog box, but the prompt is `Copy Marked Files to`.

3. **Enter the _destination_, the place where you want to copy the file or files.**

   For example, if you want to copy them to a disk in drive A, type **A:** (that's the letter A and a colon). If you want to copy the file or files to another directory, type the complete pathname.

4. **Press Enter.**

   The file or files are copied to the specified destination.

   ✔ Press F7 when you want to exit the File Manager screen/menu/scrambled eggs on brain.

   ✔ Make sure that you have a formatted disk in drive A or drive B before you copy files there. Refer to the section on formatting disks in Chapter 21 for more information.

   ✔ If a file by the same name already exists at the destination, you are asked whether you want to replace it. My advice is to press N unless you're absolutely certain that you're not overwriting something important. Try the Copy command again but use a different destination or another disk.

   ✔ For help on copying files, specifying destinations, and such, refer to _DOS For Dummies,_ 2nd Edition, published by IDG Books Worldwide. The information provided on file fitness in that book's Chapter 3 applies to WordPerfect's Copy command as well.

Deleting files

You can use the File Manager menu/screen/atrocity of organization to pluck unworthy files from the hard drive. Before you begin your acts of utter destruction and lay the files at peace, here's a warning: *Don't delete anything you need.* However, deleting older copies of files, backups, or just plain old junk (junk files happen) is OK.

Start with the File Manager screen in front of you (Press F5, Enter). When you're ready to destroy, follow these steps:

1. **Select a file to blow away.**

   Move the highlight bar to that file. If you're feeling particularly feisty, use the cursor-control keys to move the highlight bar and press the asterisk key to mark one or more files.

2. **Press D (Destroy).**

   OK, the D stands for the Delete command. You see a dialog box asking whether you really want to delete your file. Skip to Step 3.

   If you marked a group of files for slaughter, you see a message that asks whether you want to delete the marked files. Press Y for Yes. You then see a message asking you to confirm that you want to delete the files.

3. **Press Y.**

   The file or files are no more. Gone! Gone! Gone! Purge dem files!

   ✔ Instead of pressing D for delete, you can press the Delete or Backspace keys.

   ✔ Press F7 when you want to exit the File Manager menu/screen/host of atrocities.

   ✔ Oops! If you want to undelete a deleted file, refer to Chapter 24.

   ✔ Die Lust der Zerstörung ist zugleich eine schaffende Lust! (M. Bakunin)

Renaming files

The File Manager also comes in handy if you want to rename files on disk. Although you can rename a group of files, I recommend doing only one file at a time; dealing with groups here gets complicated fast.

With the File Manager menu/screen/happening displayed (press F5 and then Enter), follow these steps to slap a new name on a file:

1. **Select the file you want to rename.**

   Use the cursor-control keys to move the highlight bar until it highlights the file you want to rename.

2. **Press 5 (Move/Rename).**

   You'll see a dialog box where you can enter the new filename.

3. Type a new name.

You can use the ← and → arrow keys or Backspace and Delete keys to edit the filename displayed.

4. Press Enter after you've typed a new name for the file.

✔ Changing a file's name does not change its contents.

✔ You cannot give a file a name used by another file; no two files can have the same name. If you try to give a file an existing filename, you see a Replace *filename?* prompt. Press N and then start over with Step 1, choosing another name.

✔ You must follow the proper rules for naming a file when you use the Rename command. Refer to "Naming Files" earlier in this chapter. If you use a forbidden character in the filename or commit some other DOS sin, you see the error message Can't rename file. Try again.

Never rename files that have COM, EXE, BAT, or SYS extensions!

Finding text in files

At last, something most excellent with which to end this dreary chapter. You can use the File Manager to locate text in WordPerfect documents. This is a great feature for document fishing — those times when you have forgotten a document's name but don't want to tediously load a bunch of files individually to scan for text. Instead, follow these steps to search for specific text in files:

1. Press F5 (File Manager) and press Enter.

2. Press F (Find).

You see a pop-up list of options displayed on-screen.

3. Press E (Entire document).

The Find Word in Entire Document dialog box appears. This action directs WordPerfect to scan all the files in the current directory for the text you're about to type.

4. Type the text you want to scan for.

Be specific and be brief. For example, scan for a name or a key word — something particular to the document you're hunting down.

5. Press Enter.

WordPerfect scans all the files, looking for the specified text. This may take some time. Don't think that WordPerfect is dead if it spends eternity-minus-one looking through your files.

When the search is done, WordPerfect displays only those files that contain text matching the text you specified in the File Manager window/thing. Or if you are lucky, only one file will be displayed — the file you want. If you're not so lucky, you can narrow down the number of files even further. Simply search the abbreviated list of files using a different word. If a match isn't found, you see a Not Found dialog box.

✔ To search another directory, press F5, type that directory's *pathname,* and press Enter. WordPerfect then displays only files found in that directory and subsequently searches only those files.

✔ To open a found document, use the cursor-control keys to highlight the filename and press O.

Chapter 17
Mail-Merging
(Mind-Blowing Stuff)

In This Chapter

▶ Getting an overview of mail merge

▶ Preparing the primary document

▶ Preparing the secondary document

▶ Merge mania!

Mail merge. Ugh. What it is: a way of producing several customized documents without having to individually edit each one. We're talking form letters here — but sneaky form letters that you can't really tell are form letters.

Mail merge. Ugh. What it isn't: easy. In fact, the Mail Merge key, F9, isn't even marked on your *WordPerfect 6 For Dummies* keyboard template. The reason is that you have to look in the manual anyway, so why bother? But, instead of picking up the manual (and we don't want anyone injuring his or her spine here), read this chapter, which contains the basic, need-to-know steps to mail-merging.

Getting an Overview of Mail Merge

There are two ways to handle WordPerfect's mail merge feature:

1. Read this chapter.

2. Start drinking heavily.

I'll outline the first approach here. The second approach you can attempt on your own. (If you've been through this before, go to the section "Preparing the Primary Document" in this chapter.)

Mail merge is the process of taking a single form letter, stirring in a list of names and information, and then merging both to create several documents. Each of the documents is customized with the list of names and information you provide.

The file that contains the names and other information is called the *secondary document.* The file that contains the form letter is referred to as the *primary document.*

You start by creating the primary document in WordPerfect. Create it as you would any other document, complete with formatting and other mumbo-jumbo. But, where you would put *Dear Mr. Blather,* you put a fill-in-the-blanks special code, which is called a *field.*

Continue creating the primary document, putting in fields where you later want customized information. This is similar to working Mad Libs, but in WordPerfect you usually provide fields for nouns instead of writing in verbs, adverbs, and adjectives. When you're done, you save the primary document to disk.

The secondary document contains the names, addresses, and other information you want to merge into the primary document. But unlike the primary document, the secondary document is created using a special format. It's almost like filling in information in a database program. (In fact, that's exactly what it is.)

Each of the names, addresses, and other information in the secondary document composes what's called a *record.* WordPerfect creates a custom letter using the primary file as a skeleton and fills in the meat by using a record in the secondary file. I know — totally gross. But nothing else I can think of now describes it as well.

Because no one commits this routine to memory (and for good reason), the following sections provide outlines to follow so that you can create a mail merge document by using primary and secondary document files. Cross your fingers and check the kids; we're goin' mail-mergin'.

- The primary document is the one with the fill-in-the-blank items.
- The secondary document contains the names, addresses, and other information you need to fill in the blanks.
- Each blank item is filled in using the field found in the secondary document.
- The collection of all the fields for a document is called a *record.*
- Don't memorize any of this.

Preparing the Primary Document

The primary document is the fill-in-the-blanks document. Create it as you would any document. Type away, inserting formatting and such as necessary. Only leave certain key items blank. Actually, you don't leave them blank; instead, you type *fields*.

Fields represent information to be read from the secondary document and plugged into the primary document. Here's how to create a field:

1. Position the cursor to where you want the field.

Position the cursor just as you'd position it before typing a name, an address, or another key element in a document.

2. Press Shift-F9.

If this is the first field in your document, WordPerfect displays a major Merge Codes dialog box. The dialog box asks whether this is the primary document or the secondary document. The first item in the dialog box, Form, should be selected. If Form is selected, press Enter. If Form is not selected, press 1.

The Merge Codes (Form File) dialog box is displayed. Hmmm. Looks interesting.

3. Press F for Field.

You'll see the Parameter Entry dialog box. Sigh heavily.

4. Type a field name.

The field is the fill-in-the-blanks part of your document. Each field (or blank) must have a unique name. Type in the name, being brief and specific. Use lowercase letters.

Examples of fields include *name, address, title, company, city, zip, salutation,* and so on. Make the fields describe what goes in your document. In Figure 17-1, the field names are *name, apt, day, month,* and *agency.*

5. Press Enter after typing the field name.

The field name is inserted into your document in the following format:

```
FIELD(name)
```

Look at that cryptic code as a blank that will be filled in later. Do not delete the FIELD, parentheses, or any part of the field unless you want to remove it from your document.

6. After creating a field, continue typing.

Press Enter to start a new line, type a comma or a period — do anything you have to in order to make the field fit in. To create additional fields, repeat the preceding steps.

7. When you're done creating the primary document, save it to disk.

To help give you an idea of what's going on, I've set up a primary document in Figure 17-1. This is a form letter — the primary document — that is later *merged* with the secondary document.

✔ Remember your field names. Print your primary document and highlight the names or jot them down on a piece of paper. You need to know the names when you create the secondary document.

✔ Type the field names in lowercase. You can use numbers in them if you like — for example, *address1* and *address2*.

✔ You can use the same field name a number of places in your document. Just follow these steps and insert the field again, just as you would a name, address, company name, and so on, into a document.

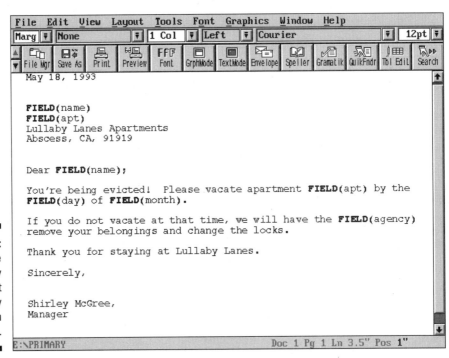

Figure 17-1:
A sample
primary
document
with many
fields in
place.

Here are the quick steps for entering a field into a document:

1. Press Shift-F9, F.

2. Type in the field name.

3. Press Enter.

Preparing the Secondary Document

The secondary document is a database file of sorts — not a traditional WordPerfect document. It starts with the list of fields — the names of the blanks in the primary document that need to be filled in. The secondary document contains several lists, or *records,* of information that WordPerfect will merge into those fields. The end result is many customized documents.

Start the secondary document as a blank slate. Switch over to Doc 2 or save and clear away the primary document. (Refer to Chapter 14 for information on switching documents or starting over with a clean slate.)

To create a secondary document, follow these steps:

1. **Press Shift-F9.**

   You'll see the Merge Codes dialog box, which is the same box you saw when you initially created the primary document. If you see the Merge Codes (Form File) dialog box displayed instead, then you'll need to start over.

2. **Press 2.**

   This selects the Data [Text] item, which defines what you're working on as a secondary merge document.

   The Merge Codes (Text Data File) dialog box appears.

   This is the secondary document's version of the Merge Codes (Form File) dialog box.

3. **Press N for Field Names.**

   You'll see the Field Names dialog box displayed. Your task is to type in all the field names used in the primary document. The field names can be entered in the same order they appear in your primary document. Type in each name and press Enter. For example, you may type the following:

   ```
   name
   company
   address1
   address2
   ```

Type in each of the names you jotted down from the preceding section. Type the names exactly as they were entered into the primary document, including any numbers.

4. After you've entered the last name, press the F7 key twice.

You'll be returned to your document. The field names will be placed at the top of your screen. Note the following things:

- ✔ The field names start with a FIELDNAMES doohickey.
- ✔ Each of the names is listed between a set of parentheses and is separated by a semicolon.
- ✔ The field names end with an ENDRECORD doohickey and a hard-page break (double line of death).

At the bottom left of the screen, you'll see a Field prompt that is followed by the name of your first field. WordPerfect is waiting for you to put information into the various fields — the items that will fill the related blanks in the primary document. WordPerfect is waiting for you to create a *record*.

Each group of fields is called a record. For each record, you need to fill in the various fields. This is like filling in a response card or one of those endless forms at a government bureaucracy. Here's how that works:

1. Type the text you want to fill in for the first field.

The field name will appear at the bottom of the screen. Here is an example:

```
Field: name
```

Type in the name or the proper data you want for that field.

2. Press the F9 key.

Do not press Enter unless you want the Enter key as part of your field!

The F9 key displays ENDFIELD on the screen and drops you down to the next line. Notice the new field name at the bottom left corner of the screen.

3. Repeat Steps 1 and 2 for each of the fields in your document.

When you get to the last field, don't press F9. Instead, go to Step 4.

A clue that you're at the last field is that the Field prompt at the bottom changes from a name to a number. If you carelessly reach that point, backspace to erase the last ENDFIELD marker and then go to Step 4.

4. Press Shift-F9, E.

After the last field, you don't press the F9 key. (If you did, press Backspace and erase the ENDFIELD jobbie.) Pressing Shift-F9 inserts the ENDRECORD thingamabob plus a double line of death into your document. You're now ready to type in the next record and all its fields.

5. **Repeat Steps 1 through 4 for the next set of information you want plugged into the primary document.**

   Keep doing these steps for all your information, entering data for all the people to whom you'll be mailing letters, resumes, reports, pyramid schemes, and so on.

6. **When you're done entering fields and records, save the secondary document to disk.**

✔ The FIELDNAMES item should be the first record in your secondary document. That's how WordPerfect matches up names and other information you have entered into the secondary document to the correct spaces in the primary document. Do not edit or alter this text in any way! If you mess up, start over again with a new document.

✔ Remember to press F9 to end each field. Do not press Enter! If you do press Enter, press Backspace to delete it and then press F9 instead.

✔ Press Shift-F9, E after the last field to end the record and start a new record.

Here are the steps you follow to create the first record in the secondary document:

1. Type in the information for each field. The field name appears at the bottom of the screen.

2. Press F9 when you're done typing the information for a field. Do not press the Enter key!

3. After the last field in the record, press Shift-F9, E.

Merge Mania!

After creating the primary and secondary documents, you're ready to merge away! Ensure that both primary and secondary documents have been saved to disk. Doing so is very important!

1. **Press the Merge Mania key, Ctrl-F9.**

2. **Press 1 to select Merge.**

   You'll see the Run Merge dialog box on your screen, as shown in Figure 17-2.

```
┌─────────────────────────────────────────────────────────┐
│                        Run Merge                         │
│                                                          │
│   Form File:  [_                                    ][▼] │
│                                                          │
│   Data File:  [                                     ][▼] │
│                                                          │
│   Output:  [Unused Document  ◆]                          │
│                                                          │
│   Repeat Merge for Each Data Record:  [1    ]            │
│   Display of Merge Codes       [Hide Merge Codes    ◆]   │
│                                                          │
│   [Data File Options...]                                 │
│                                                          │
│   [File List... F5]   [QuickList... F6]    [Merge] [Cancel] │
└─────────────────────────────────────────────────────────┘
```

Figure 17-2:
The Run
Merge
dialog box.

3. Type in the name of your primary document.

4. Press Enter.

5. Type in the name of your secondary document.

6. Press Enter.

7. Press Enter again to start merging.

After a few moments — maybe longer, depending on how detailed the merge is and how many records you have — you'll have a complete, merged document.

The primary file will appear several times on the screen and will have information from the secondary files plugged into each copy. All the files will be separated by hard page breaks (double lines of death).

✔ Always examine the results of the merge. Some things may not have fit properly, and there will doubtlessly be some editing involved.

✔ Sometimes things don't work in a merge. This involves some adding or editing of the fields between the primary and secondary documents. Make sure that your field names match in both documents. Double-check to ensure that for each blank field in the primary document there is something to fill in that blank in the secondary document.

✔ No, there isn't any way they could have made this harder.

✔ Save the completely merged files as a document on disk. WordPerfect doesn't do this automatically. In the end, you'll have your primary file, the secondary file, and the resulting merged files — three files on disk.

✔ You can print right from the merged file to get those custom, uniquely crafted documents out to the foolhardy who actually think that you took the time to compose a personal letter. Ha! Isn't mail merge great?

Part IV
WordPerfect's Bootiful Interface

The 5th Wave   By Rich Tennant

Prior to releasing WordPerfect 6.0, WordPerfect developed a graphical user interface known as "SkiLight."

Why'd they call it "SkiLight?"

The price went through the roof.

In this part . . .

Once upon a time, WordPerfect was a really ugly stepsister of a program. Yikes! Then along came the graphical fairy prince. He kissed WordPerfect on her blemished text interface, and, lo and behold, WordPerfect became a thing of beauty. Well, actually more *thing* than *beauty,* but the old gal certainly has improved over her old, incredibly confusing, and chaotic text mode.

This part of the book waxes poetic on WordPerfect 6.0's graphical interface — the *bootiful* interface. Although it's now possible to see your text on-screen exactly as it will print, you still must contend with the way WordPerfect does things. So the grimalkin may look good, but she still smells the same.

Chapter 18
Using the Graphical Interface

Striving to make WordPerfect easier to use, the folks at WordPerfect World Headquarters decided to bestow a graphical interface on you. Hip-hip! And the WordPerfect folks let you use a mouse. Yeah! And they added happy, friendly pull-down menus, dialog boxes, and other gadgets. Rah! And, if using these new features only made logical sense, we'd consider ourselves emphatically lucky.

This chapter chews slowly on WordPerfect's graphical interface — using the mouse, menus, and dialog boxes. Sometimes, this stuff makes sense to you — like if you've ever been chained to a chair and forced to endure several hours of Microsoft Windows. (In some places this is considered abuse or even torture outlawed by the Geneva Convention.) Other times, you'll have to do a lot of head scratching and mouse monkeying to make what you want happen. This chapter helps reduce that drudgery.

Mickeying with the Mouse

A computer mouse is a furless, eyeless, faceless, cold medical-plastic beast that has a long tail, which is plugged into your PC's rump. The typical computer mouse (scientific name *mousius computarus*) is beautifully illustrated in Figure 18-1.

It's a serious waste of time if you're using WordPerfect 6.0 in its graphical mode without a mouse. Although most of what goes on in WordPerfect involves typing at the keyboard (which herds of old hands are adept at), a lot more can get done with the mouse. Further, there are some things you can do by mouse that just can't be done without one.

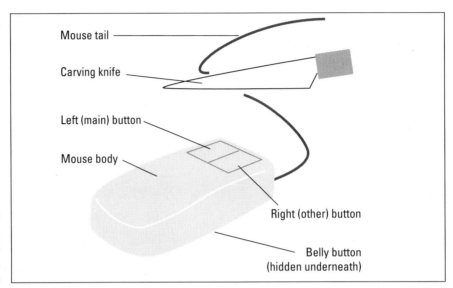

Figure 18-1:
Mousius
Computarus.

Mouse tail

Carving knife

Left (main) button

Mouse body

Right (other) button

Belly button
(hidden underneath)

✔ Now is the time for all good men (and ladies, too) to rush out and buy a mouse for their computer. You need one. If you don't have one yet, then you'll be getting one soon. More and more DOS programs can use a mouse, so there is a mouse hanging by its tail in some computer store right now, squeaking "Buy me" followed by your name.

✔ If you don't have a mouse, then the subjects covered in this part of the book are of no concern to you.

✔ It doesn't matter which mouse you have. Microsoft's and Logitech's are the best. Other mice, as long as they claim some type of compatibility with those two brands, are OK. But, hey, why waste money? Buy a Microsoft or Logitech mouse and you won't be sorry.

✔ The mouse requires software to *drive* it. This software must be installed in your PC's CONFIG.SYS or AUTOEXEC.BAT file. Force your computer guru to do this task for you. (If you already have a mouse, then this task has already been done.)

✔ If you're a southpaw and would like to use your mouse in the lefty mode, press these keys: Shift-F1, M, L, F7, F7. This should save wear and tear on the left side of your brain.

✔ Additional information on a computer mouse, including how to use it, is offered in the book *PCs For Dummies,* published by IDG Books Worldwide. Please refer to that book if you're totally lost here.

Telling All about Mr. Menu

Most, if not all, of WordPerfect's commands are accessed through a menu thing that appears at the very top of the screen. The menu thing itself is referred to as the *pull-down menu* according to WordPerfect's Department of Coming Up with New Names. I like to call it the *menu bar* because it has the happy *bar* term in it.

Across the menu bar are various menu titles. Each title represents a category of commands that do something in WordPerfect (see Table 18-1).

Table 18-1		Menu Titles and Commands
Menu Title	*Key*	*Type of Commands*
File	Alt-F	File commands: open, close, and manage files; file your nails; quit WordPerfect; and so on.
Edit	Alt-E	Basic text editing: cut, copy, paste, glue, block, search, replace, lose, and so on.
View	Alt-V	Screen control: what you see and what you don't. Better views imply higher resale value.
Layout	Alt-L	Formatting stuff.
Tools	Alt-T	The *things that we couldn't think of anywhere else to put them* menu.
Font	Alt-O	Character formatting stuff.
Graphics	Alt-G	Commands that deal with graphics.
Window	Alt-W	Control over the document window — the great white space you write in.
Help	Alt-H	Nauseating attempts to overwhelm you with kindness.

The menus are pretty dumb by themselves. What's important is the list of commands that appear — that actually *drop down* — when you select a menu title.

✔ You can activate the menu bar by pressing the Alt-= key combination or the right mouse button. This action highlights the File menu title. You can use the ← and → keys to highlight the other menus.

✔ After a menu is highlighted, press the Enter key to pull it down.

✔ To instantly pull down a menu, press and hold the Alt key. Then press the key underlined in the menu title (the second column of Table 18-1 lists the Alt-key combination to use).

Using the mouse, click on a menu title to instantly pull down that menu.

With each menu are various WordPerfect commands. The commands appear below the menu bar. On the left is the command's name, and on the right is a key combination you can use to avoid the menu or a triangle (▶), which indicates a submenu.

✔ Use the ↑ or ↓ cursor-control key to highlight a command in a menu. Press Enter to select the command.

✔ You can instantly select a command by clicking on it with the mouse.

✔ As with the menu titles, some commands have underlined letters in them. Press that letter to instantly select a command.

✔ Some commands appear *dimmed* and cannot be selected. This means that the command doesn't apply to whatever you're doing in WordPerfect. For example, you can't use the Cut command from the Edit menu to cut a block of text if that block isn't marked on the screen. I mean, duh!

✔ When a menu has been pulled down, you can use the ← or → cursor-control key to see another pull-down menu. In fact, you can use all the cursor-control keys to have a little pull-down menu show in your idle moments.

✔ If you select a submenu command, marked with a ▶, then another menu appears to the side of the first menu. You can select an item from the submenu just as you would from a main menu.

✔ Menu items with a check mark (✔) by them indicate something that can be switched on or off — like a character attribute. The check mark means that the item is on; selecting the item again switches it off.

✔ Press the Esc key to make the menu go away. You may have to press Esc a few times to get back to your document for editing.

✔ Press the right mouse button to make the menu go away.

✔ Personally, I prefer the keyboard commands.

Using the Confusing Dialog Boxes

When a command offers you more than one option, you'll often see a *dialog box* displayed, listing options, commands, places to type text, buttons, and other graphical mayhem. There are four things a dialog box accomplishes:

1. A dialog box allows WordPerfect to graphically display various commands and options.

2. A dialog box lets you make selections, change settings, or input information.

3. A dialog box adds to WordPerfect's graphical look.

4. A dialog box overwhelms you with options and makes you feel like a monkey in some lab experiment trying to figure out which level shocks you and which one dispenses the M&M.

✔ The dialog box looks like a big gray panel that appears somewhere on your screen — like what happens when you're driving behind an overloaded pickup truck on its way to the dump, and a wet piece of paper flies off and attaches itself to your windshield. A blue border lines the top of the dialog box. The dialog box's title is centered in the middle of the blue border.

✔ Some dialog boxes are very tiny. Other dialog boxes cover the entire screen.

✔ Your document sits and waits peacefully behind the dialog box.

✔ On the dialog box are many handy gadgets that you can manipulate by using the keyboard or the mouse. This is how you make choices, select options, and type stuff in.

✔ Selecting an option in a dialog box sometimes displays another dialog box.

✔ You can make most dialog boxes go away by pressing the Esc key.

✔ Unlike with Microsoft Windows and other graphical environments, you cannot move WordPerfect's dialog boxes.

Making selections in a dialog box

A dialog box presents you with a list of items you can select, like choosing from a menu. There are special doodads in the dialog box you can manipulate with the mouse, but most of the stuff can be accessed from the keyboard.

Note how each dialog box is divided into various areas. As an example, consider the Font dialog box. (Refer to Figure 9-1 in Chapter 9 or press Ctrl-F8 to see the Font dialog box on your screen.)

Each area in the dialog box is roped in by a thin white-and-gray line. In the Font dialog box, there are six of these areas, and they are numbered 1 through 6 in blue. Pressing the proper number key activates that area and displays more options. You can also press the underlined letter in the name next to the number key (F for Font, for example) or click on the name with the mouse.

Somewhere, either along the bottom or along the right side of the dialog box, is a set of buttons. The two mains buttons are OK and Cancel. If you select OK, you're saying that you want all the settings in this dialog box applied to the document.

If you select Cancel, you're telling WordPerfect to never mind. Sometimes other buttons appear in the dialog box instead of Cancel — like Close.

To select a button, you can press the underlined key in the button's title, press the key combination that's displayed on the button in blue characters, or click on the button with the mouse.

A special deal with buttons is the *chain of blue dots* that may lasso a button's title. You can activate that button by pressing the Enter key. You can move the lasso to another button by pressing the Tab key.

Figure 18-2 shows each of the different types of buttons you may see. The first one is named Belly; pressing B activates this button because the B is underlined. The second button has a blue chain around it, and you activate it by pressing the Enter key. You activate the third button by pressing the F13 key, WordPerfect's Button command.

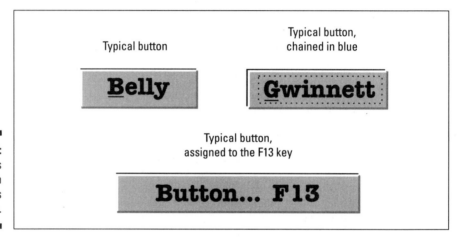

Figure 18-2:
Various buttons in WordPerfect's dialog boxes.

Typical button

Typical button, chained in blue

Belly

Gwinnett

Typical button, assigned to the F13 key

Button... F13

✔ To select an item in a dialog box, press the number key next to that item. You can also press the key associated with the underlined character in the item's name or click on the item's name using the mouse.

✔ The Tab key can be used to move around and highlight various options and commands in a dialog box. You can select the highlighted option, outlined in a blue polka dot chain of agony, by pressing the Enter key.

You can stab at any command in a dialog box using the mouse. With the mouse, click on the command or button to select it.

Buttons, doodads, and dialog box gizmos

In addition to having items with numbers by them and buttons, a dialog box has other interesting gizmos. You manipulate these gizmos using the mouse or keyboard.

Figure 18-3 shows a collection of check boxes. These are items that can be switched on or off. When an X appears in the check box, then the option is on.

For example, you can have bold text or text that is not bold. If a check appears in a check box next to Bold, then that character attribute is on and happy.

Figure 18-3:
Check
boxes.

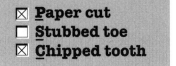

You can switch check boxes on or off in two ways. One way is to press the character key associated with the underlined letter in the check box's name — for example, B for Bold. You can also click on the check box using the mouse.

Radio buttons, like check boxes, can be either on or off (see Figure 18-4). When the radio buttons are on, they're black. When they're off, they're white. Unlike with check boxes, only one radio button in a *family* can be on at a time. The idea here is like the old car radios, which had a row of buttons for changing stations. Only one button could be pressed at a time because, unlike today, you only wanted to listen to one station at a time. When you see radio buttons in WordPerfect, it's because you can have only one option on in a set at a time.

Figure 18-4:
Radio
buttons.

To switch a radio button on or off, press the character key associated with the underlined letter in the radio button's name — N in Normal, for example. Or you can click on the radio button using the mouse.

A special type of button is the pop-up list (see Figure 18-5), which gets its inspiration from your toaster. When you select the pop-up list button, a list of items appears. From that list, you select Yes, No, Maybe, Ask me tomorrow, and so on. The item currently selected appears as the button's name. Two triangles pointing up and down tell you that the button is a pop-up list button.

Figure 18-5:
A pop-up
list button.

My answer is | **Yes** ⬍ |

To select an item from a pop-up list, press the character key that's underlined in the name displayed — for example, N for Co_n_tents. Then use the cursor-control keys to highlight an item in the list. Or you can click on the button with the mouse — but keep the mouse button down to see the items in the list — and then drag and release the mouse over the item you want.

The drop-down (not *drop-dead*) list works like pop-up lists, but the list drops down and doesn't pop up (see Figure 18-6). See? The list appears *below* the button. For example, all the items on the Ribbon are drop-down lists. You select a new font from a drop-down list. The down arrow with the crew cut is your signal that a drop-down list lives beneath it.

Figure 18-6:
A drop-down list.

To select an item from a drop-down list, press the key represented by the underlined character in the name displayed — for example, F for _F_ont. The list drops down (duh), and you can use the cursor-control keys to highlight an item. With the mouse, you can click on the down-arrow thingy and then scroll through the list using the scroll bar attachment. Then click on the item you want.

Another aspect of drop-down lists is that you can type into the box to the right of the down-arrow-bar button. For example, type in the font you want in the Font dialog box. It's much easier to type in **Souvenir** than to scroll through a long list of fonts.

Finally, there are text boxes in dialog boxes (see Figure 18-7), which are areas where you can type something in. Usually this something is a cryptic filename, although it may also be text to search for, a caption on a graphic, or whatever.

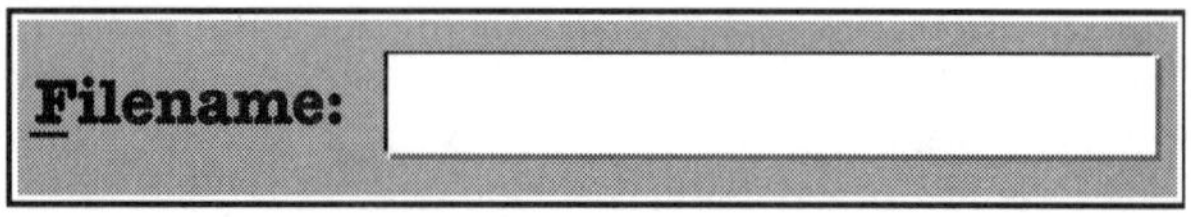

Figure 18-7:
A text box.

_F_ilename: [   ]

To work the text box, press the key represented by the underlined character in the box's name — F for _F_ilename, for example. Or you can click on the box with the mouse.

When you type into the box, an underline cursor appears to guide you. All WordPerfect's cursor-control key commands work in the box.

- Normally, you press the Tab key to end input in a text box. Pressing Enter is the same as ending your input and pressing the OK button in the dialog box. Sometimes this is what you want, but I usually press the Tab key to be sure.

- Text boxes may also be called *input boxes*. That's their Macintosh name.

- Many of these gadgets have counterparts in the text mode of WordPerfect. The gadgets look and operate in a similar manner, although I don't recommend that anyone use the text mode.

Yes, it's a lot easier to click on things than to look for underlined characters on the screen. But, when you use a command frequently, the underlined character shortcuts can be a lot quicker.

Chapter 19
Using Buttons and Bars

*I*t's easy to get slaphappy with WordPerfect's graphical interface. WordPerfect has a whole armada of optional gizmos, scroll bars, and upsie-downsie things that you poke and cajole — but only if you have a mouse. If you do, then you can use these goodies: the Button Bar, Ribbon, and Outline Thingy. Without a mouse, using these items is as futile as understanding how WordPerfect does tabs or trying to teach your dog to drive (and he drinks from the toilet fer goodness sake).

Using the Button Bar

There are some WordPerfect commands you use more than others. WordPerfect sort of apologizes for making them difficult to use — unmemorable and crude key combinations, difficult-to-find menu items — by giving you quick access to the commands via the *Button Bar*.

Figure 19-1 shows what the Button Bar may look like if it's visible on your screen. You should be able to see 13 picture buttons, each of which has a cutsie picture and garbled text description representing one of WordPerfect's gazillion or so commands. Table 19-1 describes the buttons available in WordPerfect's normal "I haven't messed with it" configuration.

Figure 19-1:
The Button
Bar.

Table 19-1		Button Bar Options
Button Name	*Key Equivalent*	*Command*
File Mgr	F5	File Manager
Save As	F10	Save As
Print	Shift-F7	Print
Preview	Shift-F7, 7	Print Preview
Font	Ctrl-F8	Font/Character format
GrphMode	Ctrl-F3, G	Change to graphics mode
TextMode	Ctrl-F3, T	Change to text mode
Envelope	Alt-F12	Print Envelope
Speller	Ctrl-F2	Spell Check
Gramatik	Alt-F1, 3	Grammatik
QuikFndr	F5, F4	Quick Finder
Tbl Edit	Alt-F7, T, E	Table Editor
Search	F2	Search down

Some of these are handy: Click on the Speller button with the mouse and you see the Speller dialog box; click on the Search button to see the search dialog box; click on Font to see the Font dialog box, and so on. Other buttons are silly: The Text Mode button switches WordPerfect to text mode, and who wants to go there? The Table Edit button edits only tables that you've already created. What's more important is that these buttons, though handy, are probably not the commands you use most often. Fortunately, you can change them — if you dare.

- ✔ To activate a button, click on it with the mouse. There is no way you can do this from the keyboard.

- ✔ In the Spanish language version of WordPerfect, the Button Bar is called the *Cantina Butòn*.

- ✔ You may see more than 13 buttons on your screen if you're running WordPerfect in a high-resolution graphics mode.

- ✔ WordPerfect may have more buttons available than you can see on the Button Bar at any one time. To the left of the Button Bar are two triangles. Click on ▼ or ▲ to see more buttons. If both triangles are is dimmed, then no more buttons are available.

- ✔ The "Building your own Button Bar" section later in this chapter describes how you can customize the Button Bar.

- ✔ To make the Button Bar visible on your screen, select the Button Bar item from the View menu (press Alt-V, B).

Custom-made Button Bars courtesy of WordPerfect HQ

Realizing that most of the commands on the regular Button Bar are rather torpid, the folks in WordPerfect's Department of Buttons and Taverns devised some other Button Bars with different commands for you to use. There are seven different Button Bars you can load from disk and use in WordPerfect. They're listed in Figure 19-2, the Select Button Bar dialog box, which you can see on your screen by selecting the View menu, the Button Bar Setup submenu, and the Select item (quick keystrokes: Alt-V, S, S).

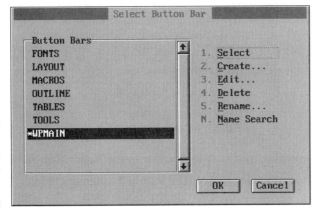

Figure 19-2:
The Select Button Bar dialog box.

The items in the Select Button Bar dialog box represent various Button Bar configurations, each with a fun set of buttons that are geared toward a specific something: fonts, tables, text layout, and so on.

To select an item from the Button Bars list, use the cursor-control keys to highlight the item and press Enter. You'll see the new Button Bar with its unique buttons displayed.

✔ Most of the Button Bars have many more buttons than can be displayed on the screen at once. Use the up or down triangles at the left side of the Button Bar to display more of the buttons.

✔ You can create your own Button Bars and save them to disk, or modify those you load and then resave them. This is all mulled over in a section later in this chapter, which . . . Oh. Here it is.

Building your own Button Bar

Food-loving tip of the day: Salad bars are always set up so that you get to the best stuff last. They put the lettuce and broccoli and cheap stuff first because they know everyone will pile that on their plates like the greedy gluttons they are. Then, when they come to the good stuff at the end of the salad bar, there's no room for it on their Mt. Everest-sized plates. Oh, well. There's always seconds.

WordPerfect understands mankind's basic frustration with the self-serve salad bar. No, they won't encourage you to dart behind slow-moving, elderly patrons or the lumbering tumid. Instead, they let you customize WordPerfect's own Button Bar, enabling you to place your most favorite and prized commands first.

To create a new Button Bar of your very own, you can start with an existing Button Bar and add or replace buttons, or you can roll your own. Refer to the preceding section for instructions on using one of WordPerfect's own Button Bars. To roll your own, follow these steps:

1. **Select the Button Bar Setup option submenu from the View menu and from the submenu, choose the Select item.**

   Use the mouse to do this or press Alt-V, S, S.

   The Select Button Bar dialog box appears, as shown in Figure 19-2.

2. **Press C for Create.**

3. **Type a name for your new Button Bar in the Button Bar Name text box.**

   Keep it short and descriptive. The Button Bar name is the first part of a filename. I named mine BBB for Better Button Bar.

4. **Press Enter.**

   The Edit Button Bar dialog box appears, as shown in Figure 19-3. If you're editing a new Button Bar, the final two items, Delete Button and Move Button, are dimmed.

5. **Select option 1, 2, or 3 to add a button to your Button Bar.**

   For example, suppose that you want to add the Quick Save command, Ctrl-F12, as the first button in your Button Bar. You press 1 to add a menu item and then select the Save command from the File menu. A Save button then appears on the Button Bar, complete with title and icon. You can continue to select menu items to add as buttons; press F7 when you're done.

   If you select option 2, WordPerfect displays a long scrolling list of its features in the Feature Button List dialog box. From here you can select some commands you won't find on the menus — for example, Grammatik, to go right to that utility; Paper Size, to go right to the Paper Size dialog box; and so on.

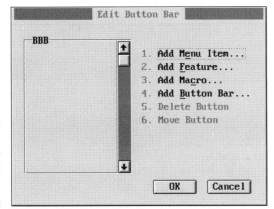

Figure 19-3:
The Edit
Button Bar
dialog box.

The final option, 3, is useful if you or someone more adept at these things has created WordPerfect macros. If so, you can assign the macros to a button to quickly access what they do.

After adding buttons, you may want to move a few. Highlight the button title in the dialog box; then press M for move. Use the cursor-control keys to move the highlight to a new position; press Enter to paste the button.

6. **When you're done, press the F7 key.**

You return to the Select Button Bar dialog box.

7. **Highlight your new Button Bar in the list and press S to select it.**

This locks in your Button Bar for use in WordPerfect.

✔ To change the Button Bar in the future, follow the preceding steps. Or create a new Button Bar and select it by following the instructions in the preceding section, "Custom-made Button Bars courtesy of WordPerfect HQ."

✔ Put the buttons you use most often to the left side of the Button Bar. This applies the same philosophy as the menu bar, where the most commonly used commands appear on the left (because we read from left to right).

✔ Remember that you can add more buttons to the Button Bar than can be displayed on the screen at once. Use the up or down triangles and the mouse to see the additional buttons.

TIP

Favorite buttons for the Better Button Bar

The buttons I use in my personal Button Bar are all commands compiled from the menus (which means I used the 1 key in the Edit Button Bar dialog box to add them). Here they are, in case you want to use them as well:

Menu Button	Command	Reason
1	New	To quickly start a new, blank document. (There really is no key equivalent for the New command.)
2	Save	To quickly save an existing document
3	Open	To open a document
4	Close	To close a document
5	File Manager	Quick access to the File Manager
6	Print	Quick access to the Print dialog box
7	Cut	Good for cutting a block you've selected with the mouse
8	Copy	Copying a block you've selected with the mouse
9	Paste	Pasting a block you've selected with the mouse
10	Bold	Makes bolding text easier when you've selected something with the mouse
11	Italics	Ditto here, but with italics
12	Switch To	I'm always switching documents
13	Exit WP	Grand-slam exit button

My purpose in selecting these particular items for buttons was to be as mouse-happy as possible. Because the Button Bar is a mouse-only thing, you have to assume the only time you'll need it is when you're using the mouse. Therefore, adding the Cut, Copy, and Paste commands makes sense after you've selected text with the mouse. The same goes for Bold and Italics and the other commands as well.

Refer to Figure 20-2 in the next chapter to see how these buttons look on the screen.

Toying with the Button Bar

Playing with WordPerfect's interface is covered in detail in the next chapter. Before moving on, I thought I'd mention that the Button Bar isn't glued to the top of the screen. You can change its position to the bottom of the screen or place it vertically along the left or right sides of the screen. Wherever you want to place the Button Bar, WordPerfect puts it there. To change the Button Bar's home office, follow these steps:

1. **From the View menu, select the Button Bar Setup item and from the submenu, select the Options item.**

   That is, press Alt-V, S, O. The Button Bar Options dialog box is laid out for you. Options 1–4 are for selecting the position for the bar; options 5–7 are for selecting the style.

2. **To change the Button Bar's location, press 1, 2, 3, or 4 to put it on the top, bottom, left, or right of the screen.**

3. **To change the Button Bar's look, press 5, 6, or 7.**

   Option 5 is normally selected, which shows both text and pictures. Options 6 and 7 show only the icons or text, respectively. If you choose either 6 or 7, then the Button Bar gets thinner at the top of the screen, allowing more buttons to be displayed at once.

4. **Press the F7 key when you're done.**

   I prefer both the names and pictures on my Better Button Bar. I mean, why make WordPerfect more cryptic than it is already? Still, after you know your buttons, having a smaller Button Bar (selecting option 6 or 7 in the Button Bar Options dialog box) means you get to see more of your document — and more buttons — on the screen at once.

Print Preview's Button Bar

Another Button Bar used in WordPerfect appears when you activate the Print Preview command. The buttons there are unique to the Print Preview command and can be changed just as the main Button Bar can be changed. However, the commands you can put on Print Preview's Button Bar can be selected only from the menus available in that mode.

   ✔ Refer to Chapter 8 for more information on Print Preview.

   ✔ You can modify the Print Preview Button Bar if you like (though I don't recommend it). The steps are similar to those outlined in the "Building your own Button Bar" section.

Working with the Ribbon

The Ribbon is another mouse-only strip of gadgets hanging below the menu bar. It's depicted in Figure 19-4, the way it probably looks on your screen most of the time.

There are six items on the Ribbon, all pull-down menus and all accessible only with the mouse (though menu item commands and key combinations can access most of the features as well). The purpose of the Ribbon is to offer you some decent control over your text. Supposedly. The following list describes each item accessible from the Ribbon:

Figure 19-4:
The Ribbon
in all its
glory.

| Marg ▼ | None | ▼ | 1 Col | ▼ | Left | ▼ | Courier | ▼ | 12pt ▼ |

✔ **The zoom/view drop-down box, Marg**

This drop-down box affects how big your document looks on the screen. Normally, *Marg* is selected, meaning that you see the page from margin to Marge Simpson — I mean, margin to margin. Other various items in this box contain various "zoom values," which are fully described in Chapter 20.

You can change this item's contents also by selecting the Zoom item from the View menu or pressing Alt-V, Z.

✔ **The outline viewing drop-down box, None**

This drop-down box has to do with WordPerfect's outline mode, which isn't covered in this book. You can collapse or expand the outline by using this drop-down box or by accessing the Outline command from the Tools menu. (This book's sequel, *More WordPerfect For Dummies*, available soon, covers the Outline command in detail.)

✔ **The column drop-down box, 1 Colonel**

This drop-down box tells you how many columns you have on a page. Unless you're messing with columns in WordPerfect, you'll always see *1 Col* displayed, meaning that text appears only one column wide — in other words, normal.

Refer to Chapter 12 for more information on columns.

✔ **The paragraph justification drop-down box, Left**

This drop-down box can be used to change a document's justification between Left, Flush Right, Centered, and Full Justification. If a block is highlighted, then only that block's justification is affected.

I use this drop-down box and personally find it a lot handier than wading through all the different line formatting dialog boxes. For more information on justification and flushing right, refer to Chapter 10.

✔ **The current font drop-down box, Courier**

This is another handy drop-down box on the Ribbon. You can use this box to quickly change the font, which is better than doing the exact same thing in the Font menu (Ctrl-F8). Just drop down the list, highlight the font you want, and click on it with the mouse. Or you can quickly type the font's name into the text box right on the Ribbon. This is most convenient.

More information about fonts and such is covered in Chapter 9. It also covers selecting a font size, which is what happens in the next drop-down box.

✔ **The font size drop down box, 12 Pints**

This drop-down box can be used to set the size of the font you're using. The size is measured in *points*, which is abbreviated *pt* on the screen (it's not really pints). You can select a new point size from the drop-down list or type the numbers right in the box.

✔ Again, the Ribbon is fairly useless if you don't have a mouse. However, it may be handy to have because it always lets you know which font you're using.

✔ To make the Ribbon visible on your screen if it isn't there already, select the Ribbon item from the View menu or press Alt-V, R.

✔ Refer to Chapter 18 for more information on operating drop-down boxes.

The Outline Thingy

A third hash line of happiness you can display on WordPerfect's screen is what I call the Outline Thingy. Figure 19-5 illustrates said thingy.

This book does not cover WordPerfect's outlining function, though it can be handy, and, I must admit, all good writers need an outline program — which is built into WordPerfect. Cool.

✔ To make the Outline Thingy visible, select the Outline Bar item in the View menu or press Alt-V, O.

✔ If you don't have a mouse or don't plan on using WordPerfect's outline feature, then you don't need the Outline Thingy taking up space on the screen.

✔ All the commands on the Outline Thingy have equivalents in the Outline submenu of the Tools menu.

✔ This book's long-awaited sequel, *More WordPerfect For Dummies* (available soon), covers using the Outline Thingy and outlining in general. Look for it in a bookstore near you, probably sometime around Christmas '93.

Figure 19-5:
The Outline
Thingy.

Chapter 20
Viewing Your Document

. . . .

In This Chapter

▶ Understanding WordPerfect's modus operandi

▶ Now you see it; now you don't want to see it

▶ Zooming about

▶ Doing WordPerfect's Windows

▶ Messing with the screen

. . . .

Welcome to using a PC in the '90s. Forget that boring old text interface! WordPerfect has joined the rest of the crowd with a *graphical user interface*, the GUI (which proper PC etiquette determines is pronounced *gooey* — from the medical term of the same name). Gone, gone, gone is the boring old text interface. If you're not old enough to remember it, let me tell you — hurl! Ugly colors and splotches represented underline and italics. It was horrid!

The old WordPerfect interface is gone (but not forgotten) and has been replaced by a new way of looking at your document, one even the color-blind amongst us will appreciate. Text is displayed the same way on the screen as it is when it's printed. And you can customize the screen itself with various and sundry doohickeys and gizmos. It's all presented here in old-fashioned, yet highly readable, text.

Understanding WordPerfect's Modus Operandi

There are three, count 'em three, modes for viewing your document in WordPerfect:

1. Text

2. Graphics

3. Page

The Text mode is very similar to older versions of WordPerfect. Character formats are shown using different colors. The menu is still there, as are the dialog boxes, and you can use a mouse. So much for investing in all that VGA graphics hardware. Ho-hum.

The Graphics and Page modes look identical; I was working in these modes when I made my illustrations for this book. The only difference is that the Page mode shows you an entire page — headers and footers, footnotes, right side of the page to left side of the page. This information is a bit much, so most people opt for the gentle Graphics mode.

You can change WordPerfect's operating mode through the Ctrl-F3 key. Pressing Ctrl-F3 brings up the Screen dialog box, as shown in Figure 20-1. You select one of the three different modes by pressing T for *Text,* G for *Graphics,* or P for *Page.*

You can also change the screen mode by selecting the Text, Graphics, or Page items from the View menu.

- ✔ The Graphics mode may really S-L-O-W D-O-W-N your computer. Graphics take a lot of PC brain muscle, and some older computers may not be up to that mental task.

- ✔ If the Graphics mode on your screen works with glacier-like speed, then consider doing your typing in the Text mode. You can then do your final editing and apply character and paragraph formatting in the Graphics mode.

- ✔ You can adjust what you see and how much of what you see by using WordPerfect's Zoom command in the Graphics mode. Refer to the "Zooming About" section later in this chapter.

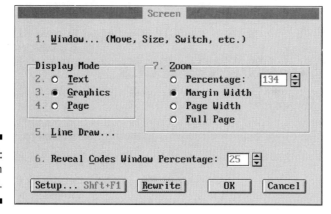

Figure 20-1:
The Screen
dialog box.

Now You See It; Now You Don't Want to See It

WordPerfect can toss up many graphical gems on the screen to make your editing easier — or just make the screen look clunky. All these gems are controlled from the mighty View menu. That's where you switch on and off a number of WordPerfect's GUI options. And that number is six:

1. Ribbon

The Ribbon is a bar-like thing that lives just beneath the menu bar. To switch it on or off, select Ribbon from the View menu (press Alt-V, R).

2. Outline Thingy

The Outline Thingy (actually, Outline Bar) lives beneath the Ribbon and is used to manipulate WordPerfect when it's in the outline mode. To switch it on or off, select Outline Bar from the View menu (press Alt-V, O).

3. Pull-Down Menus

The Pull-Down Menu item in the View menu controls whether or not the menu bar is visible all the time. You can temporarily see the menu by pressing Alt-= (Alt and the equal sign keys) or the right mouse button. Or press Alt-V, P to turn it on and off using the keyboard.

4. Button Bar

The Button Bar is a row of buttons you can click with the mouse to quickly perform some common WordPerfect functions. To switch it on or off, select Button Bar from the View menu (press Alt-V, B).

5. Horizontal Scroll Bar

The Horizontal Scroll Bar is a scroll bar along the bottom of the screen, used to slide your document left or right. This option is useful only if you magnify your document using the Zoom command, as covered later in this chapter (in this section "Zooming About"). To switch on the Horizontal Scroll Bar, select it from the View menu (press Alt-V, H).

6. Vertical Scroll Bar

More useful than the Horizontal Scroll Bar is the Vertical Scroll Bar, which you activate by selecting the Vertical Scroll Bar item from the View menu (press Alt-V, V). You can use the mouse with this scroll bar to move around in your document.

✔ When an option is on and visible on the screen, a check mark (√) appears next to its command in the View menu. Selecting an item already marked with a check mark turns that option off.

- ✔ Yes, most of these doohickeys are useless if you don't have a mouse. You can still use the menus, but you can't use the keyboard to toy with the other gizmos.

- ✔ The words *horizontal* and *Zontar*, the thing from Venus, are not related.

- ✔ Chapter 19 contains more information on using the Ribbon and Button Bar.

- ✔ Also refer to the "Doing WordPerfect's Windows" section later in this chapter for information on viewing several documents all at once in little, adjustable windows.

Zooming About

When you're working in the Graphics mode, you can use the Zoom command to tell WordPerfect how much of the document you want to see at once. This command works like a zoom lens, as opposed to using the zoom "going fast" definition. You can *zoom in* to see your text very large on the screen, like looking through a zoom lens at some sizzling, sunbathing goddess by the pool from your 15th floor hotel room. Or you can *zoom out* to see your document the way it would look from outer space.

The Zoom command is found in the View menu. It's a submenu that contains several items; three are in English, and the rest are percentages.

The percentage items, from 50% up through 300%, are magnification factors, like they used on the bridge of the old Starship Enterprise:

Capt. Kirk: Put it on the viewer, Mr. Spock.

[Bleep! We see nothing on the viewer.]

Capt. Kirk: Magnification factor 2.

Spock: Alt-V, Z, 2.

[Large text looms in front of the ship.]

Table 20-1 describes the items in the Zoom submenu and how each affects the way your document looks on the screen.

✔ A 100% zoom means the text you are editing is the same size on the screen as it is when printed — like when you were sitting in front of a typewriter. Remember them?

✔ The 300% zoom factor shows your text very big! Grandpa may bellyache about not seeing the menus, but he'll be working text like a 14-year-old with 300% Zoom on.

✔ Margin Width is the handiest size. You'll see each line of text, from the right margin to the left, which all fits nicely on the screen.

✔ Margin Width is the best zoom size.

✔ The Full Page option lets you look at the entire page all at once on the screen — sort of like Print Preview. However, in the Graphics mode (not Page) you still won't see any headers, footers, or footnotes.

✔ Some zoom modes display more than an entire page, showing you a dull gray background where the page ends. Don't be alarmed; that's just the raw fabric of the universe bleeding through in a computer program. Don't click in there with the mouse, or you may poke a hole in the space-time continuum.

✔ You can also change Zoom from the Ribbon. The first drop-down list is the Zoom list, containing the same items — though horridly truncated — as in Table 20-1.

✔ If you use the Zoom item on the Ribbon, you can also type in your own magnification factors. For example, type in **500** to see your document magnified 500 percent.

Table 20-1	View Menu Zoom Option
Zoom Factor	_Your Text Is Displayed..._
50%	Half as big as it will be when printed (minute)
75%	¾ as big as it will be when printed (tiny)
100%	As big as it will be when printed
125%	1¼ times as big as it will be when printed (big)
150%	1½ times as big as it will be when printed (large)
200%	Twice as big as it will be when printed (gargantuan)
300%	Three times as big as it will be when printed (humongous)
Margin Width	From the right margin to the left margin
Page Width	From the right side of the page to the left side of the page
Full Page	On the whole page (microscopic)

Doing WordPerfect's Windows

Chapter 14 touches on the idea of working with multiple documents in Windows. Now, here's a secret: each document is really a *window*. The reason you don't see it that way is that WordPerfect displays the document using the whole screen — minus real estate occupied by the menu, Button Bar, Ribbon, and so on (see Figure 20-2). If you like, you can see the document windows and even view multiple documents all at the same time.

There are two ways to window-ize WordPerfect, both of which access the Frame command:

1. **Press Ctrl-F3, W, F.**

   or

2. **Select the Frame item from the Window menu; use the mouse or press Alt-W, F.**

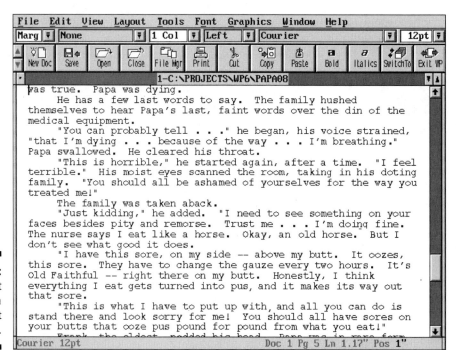

Figure 20-2:
A document
in a
WordPerfect
window.

After using either method, the document appears with a *frame* around it instead of full screen in WordPerfect. This adds some gizmos to the screen, particularly at the top of the frame.

✔ The box with the dot in it, at the upper left corner of the frame, is used to close the window. You can either click on this box with the mouse or just use the Close command from the menu to close the window.

✔ The down triangle at the upper right corner of the frame reduces the Window to tiny, credit-card size. This provides more space on the screen for viewing other documents at the same time — the *tiled* window effect.

✔ The up triangle at the upper right corner of the frame enlarges the window to fill the entire screen (or what's left after you add the Button Bars). This is the same as selecting the Maximize option from the Window menu.

✔ You can change the window size by dragging any of its four corners or the left or right sides with the mouse.

✔ When the window is displayed in a reduced size, you can move it by dragging the window around the screen with the mouse; click and drag on the window's title bar, which is the bar displaying the filename.

✔ No, WordPerfect's windows have nothing to do with Microsoft Windows. You did not buy WordPerfect for Windows — a separate product. Instead, WordPerfect is borrowing a good idea by stealing from Windows' presentation. The bad side is that it looks like Windows. The good side is that if you know Windows, you'll be at home. Then again, the good side is that you don't have to use WordPerfect's windows at all.

✔ To un-windowize WordPerfect, select the Maximize item from the Window menu or press Ctrl-F3, W, A.

Viewing Several Document Windows at Once

With WordPerfect's windows, you can easily view several documents at once. This comes in handy when you're comparing documents or when you just want to have two or more available so you can see them both — like looking at two sheets of paper for reference.

To simultaneously display several documents in the windows, press Ctrl-F3, W, T or select the Tile option from the Window menu. This places all your documents into their own window frames on the screen. (Of course, you need to be working on more than one document to see the net effect.) In Figure 20-3, I have shown four documents displayed on the screen. Each appears in its own li'l window (and each uses a different zoom factor).

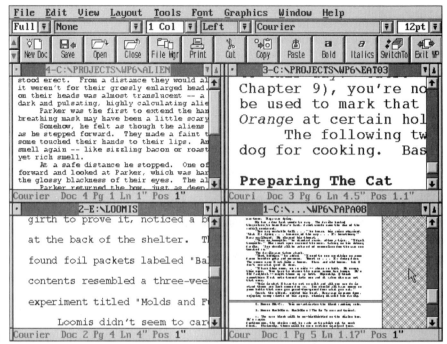

Figure 20-3:
Tiling
several
documents
on the
screen.

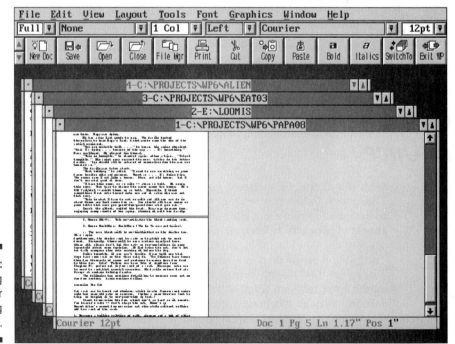

Figure 20-4:
Cascading
or
overlapping
windows.

Another approach to displaying information is to *cascade* the windows. With cascading, the windows overlap.

To cascade, press Ctrl-F3, W, C or select the Cascade option from the Window menu. Figure 20-4 shows the same four documents as Figure 20-3 but cascaded. An advantage to cascading is that you can adjust each window's size individually.

You can switch windows by either using the F3 key or clicking on the window you want to activate with the mouse.

I recommend avoiding the windows unless you really need to view two (or more) documents at once. The maximized mode that WordPerfect normally displays your document in displays more text on the screen and doesn't overwhelm you with the graphical interface.

Messing with the screen

Sick of those dull, gray colors? Want to see more text on the screen? *¡No problemo!* WordPerfect is flexible. You can change the way the colors look on the screen and change the screen *resolution* to suit your tastes. All it takes is the following keystrokes:

Shift-F1, D, G

This displays the Graphics mode Screen Type/Colors dialog box — a place you don't have to go to, but it's nice to visit when you're in the mood. Figure 20-5 shows what the dialog box may look like.

The commands you type in the Graphics mode Screen Type/Colors dialog box affect WordPerfect's overall look. This is something you don't want to change often but can if you like.

To select a new graphical resolution for WordPerfect, press the S key. This displays a list of video graphics hardware that may be installed in your PC. Your current hardware should be highlighted. Press Enter to select your current hardware; then you can select a different graphical resolution from the next screen. For example,

you can switch from normal VGA (known as 640 x 480) to a *higher* resolution, something like 800 x 1,000,000 — or whatever you see on the screen.

To select new colors for WordPerfect, press C. WordPerfect's normal color set — the one used in this book — is called *[WP Default]*. (Can't you just see some WordPerfect geek telling his house painter, "Yes, I want the bedroom done in WP Default"?) You can select other colors — including the insipid *Clown Town*—from the list. Or you can press C if you want to create your own color scheme. I won't bother going through the steps because if you're into this, you probably won't read what I have to say anyway.

- ✔ Press F7 to exit the Graphics mode Screen Type/Colors dialog box; then press F7 twice more to return to your document.

- ✔ Not all PCs can switch to a higher resolution graphics screen.

- ✔ If you change to a higher resolution screen, then you can see more text on the screen, more buttons on the Button Bar, and so on.

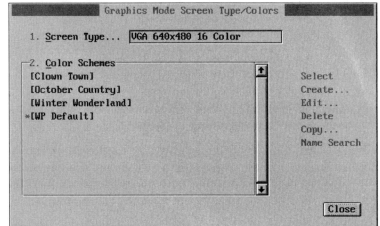

1. Screen Type... VGA 640x480 16 Color

2. Color Schemes
[Clown Town]   Select
[October Country]   Create...
[Winter Wonderland]   Edit...
*[WP Default]   Delete
                                          Copy...
                                          Name Search

                                          Close

Figure 20-5:
The
Graphics
mode
Screen
Type/Colors
dialog box.

Moving around in WordPerfect with the monitor set at a lower screen resolution is definitely faster than using the higher resolutions. If WordPerfect seems stubbornly slow, consider switching to plain ol' VGA resolution.

Part V
Help Me,
Mr. Wizard!

The 5th Wave
By Rich Tennant

"YOU MEAN TO TELL ME YOU KNEW THIS WAS SACRED INDIAN BURIAL GROUND AND YOU BUILT THE COMPUTER ROOM HERE ANYWAY?! YOU FOOL! YOU FOOL!"

In this part . . .

WordPerfect is not the sole cause of your woes. When you use a computer, you have several things to contend with: the computer, DOS, the printer, phases of the moon . . . It's like starring in a bad French farce with too many villains. Fortunately, some humans — yes, humans — really like computers. When you're in dire straits, you can call on their expertise. Call them wizards. Call them gurus. Call them when you need help. And when you can't call on them, refer to the chapters in this part of the book to help you through your troubles.

Chapter 21
Dealing with DOS

In This Chapter

▶ Organizing files

▶ Creating a new directory

▶ Putting WordPerfect on the path

▶ Making a WordPerfect batch file

▶ Formatting disks

▶ Backing up

*I*f WordPerfect is set up just so, you never have to mess with DOS, the computer's disk operating system. Yeah, right. And the check is in the mail, your kid really doesn't know who broke the lamp, and I'm from the government and I'm here to help you. Fortunately, it's possible to avoid DOS *most* of the time you're using WordPerfect. During those few times when DOS and WordPerfect do clash, however, turn to this chapter for the help you need.

This is seriously optional reading for the typical WordPerfect beginner. Only peer into these pages if you're stuck and have nowhere else to turn.

Organizing Files

DOS's main job is to put files on disk. It gobbles up WordPerfect documents in memory and spits them out on your hard drive for later retrieval, editing, and printing. This is immensely handy, and I recommend that you save all your documents to disk; refer to Chapter 14 for details.

The drawback to using the hard drive is that it gets cluttered quickly. To help you avoid the clutter, DOS enables you to organize files on the hard drive into separate storage places called *directories*. Each directory contains its own, separate set of files, and yet all the files are stored on the hard drive. The directories keep you organized.

I recommend that you use directories to organize your various projects. You can even have directories within directories for two and three levels of organization. It can be fun, but it's not without its cryptic aspect.

  ✔ The subject of naming files and storing them on disk is covered in Chapter 16.

  ✔ If your guru has organized the hard drive, refer to the section on finding a place for your work in Chapter 16. Use the table there to write down the names of the various subdirectories your guru may have set up for you.

Creating a New Directory

Creating a new directory is like making a new garage or closet. Suddenly, you have all the storage space you dreamed of. Think of your power tools neatly organized and no more boxes piled waist high. And, for you men out there, think of all the shoes you could put into that closet! Too bad real life isn't as handy as a computer. When you need new space for organizing your documents, or you want to start a new project, you can create a new directory on disk.

To create a new directory for storing documents and files — but no shoes — follow these steps in WordPerfect:

1. Press the File Manager key, F5.

This displays the Specify File Manager List dialog box on your screen. A DOS *pathname* is highlighted in the box; this is WordPerfect's current directory.

2. Press = (the equal key).

You see another dialog box, the Change Default Directory.

3. To create a new directory, type its full pathname.

For example, suppose that you want to create a directory named WORK on drive C. Type **C:\WORK** at the prompt.

4. Press Enter.

You'll see yet another dialog box, this one with the briefest of messages, `Create C:\WORK?`

5. Press Y (Yes).

The directory is created, but you're not using it yet. To use the directory, repeat Steps 2, 3, and 4. This action logs you to the new directory, where you can start using it at once.

  ✔ You can find more information on using a directory in the section about using a new directory in Chapter 16.

  ✔ Directories are named just like files: you can use from one to eight characters — letters and numbers only.

✔ You use these steps to create subdirectories as well as directories. Just type the complete pathname for the directory you want to create. For example, to create a directory named POEMS in the WORK directory, type the following at Step 3:

```
C:\WORK\POEMS
```

Putting WordPerfect on the Path

The *path* in the title of this section does not refer to that rose-lined walkway that extends from your front door to the mailbox. Nope. This is DOS, and nothing is charming. A path is an involved list of subdirectories that DOS searches for files. It's like a list of places DOS searches in the garage for missing garden tools. But, in this case, the tools are programs.

The advantage to putting WordPerfect on the path is that you can type **WP** at any DOS prompt anywhere in the computer system, and WordPerfect immediately runs. DOS can always find the WP tool in its garage full o' stuff. This setup helps you avoid that odious Bad command or file name error message.

If you're a total DOS beginner, and you want to put WordPerfect on the path, you need to know a few things. First, you need to know where the WordPerfect program files are located. For most of us, that's in the following directory:

```
C:\WP60
```

If your copy of WordPerfect is in a different directory, you need to specify its pathname in the PATH command. The path is how DOS finds the WordPerfect program when you type **WP.**

To put WordPerfect on the path, follow these steps:

1. **Start with a new document in WordPerfect.**

   Save your stuff if you need to and then start over with a clean slate. Refer to the section on saving and starting over with a clean slate in Chapter 14.

2. **Load the AUTOEXEC.BAT file for editing.**

   This is a special file DOS uses each time you start the computer. Press Shift-F10 (Open); at the prompt, type the following:

```
C:\AUTOEXEC.BAT
```

   If the AUTOEXEC.BAT file appears on the screen, go to Step 4.

If nothing appears on the screen, your PC lacks an AUTOEXEC.BAT file. Gasp! How could you do such a thing? Never mind; type the following before anyone else notices:

```
PATH=C:\WP60
```

That is, type **PATH,** an equal sign (=), the letter **C,** a colon (:), a backslash (\), and **WP60**. This is the location of WordPerfect on the system. If WordPerfect is in a different directory, type that pathname rather than C:\WP60. Then press Enter and skip to Step 6.

3. **Make sure that ASCII Text (Standard) is highlighted in the File Format dialog box and press Enter.**

4. **Look for a line in the AUTOEXEC.BAT file that starts with the word** *PATH.*

For example, you may see the following:

```
PATH=C:\DOS
```

If you already see WordPerfect listed on the path — a directory similar to C:\WP60, hidden somewhere on that line — there's nothing else to do here. Skip to Step 7.

If you don't see C:\WP60 or anything similar after the word *PATH,* move the cursor to the end of the PATH line by pressing the End key.

5. **Type a semicolon (;) and the pathname for WordPerfect.**

For example, type the following at the end of the PATH line:

```
;C:\WP60
```

That is, type a semicolon (;), the letter **C** and a colon (:) for drive C, a backslash (\), and **WP60.** If your copy of the WordPerfect program is in a different directory, type its pathname rather than WP60.

6. **Save AUTOEXEC.BAT back to disk.**

But you must save AUTOEXEC.BAT as a DOS text file. Carefully press F10 (Save). Press Esc twice if you see the Document Summary dialog box.

In the Save Document dialog box, be sure that the second line down reads ASCII Text (Standard). If it does not, press Esc, R and select the ASCII Text (Standard) item from the drop-down list. The file *must* be saved in ASCII format — plain text, no icing, real-man stuff.

Press Enter to save the file. You are asked whether you want to replace C:\AUTOEXEC.BAT; press Y (Yes).

7. **Exit the document and start over again with a clean slate.**

Press F7, N, N to close the document and get ready to work on something else.

✔ These steps put everything into place, but they don't turn the ignition switch. You have to quit WordPerfect and reset your computer for the magic to happen. **Remember:** Reset the PC only when you see a DOS prompt on the screen.

✔ Boy! This is sure complex. If you agree, have your guru do it all for you. But the advantage to taking these steps is that they enable your computer to always find WordPerfect when you type WP and press Enter at a DOS prompt.

✔ If you made a mistake, or something doesn't work right after you follow these steps, contact your guru for assistance. Explain that you tried your best on your own before calling him or her. Your guru will appreciate hearing that.

✔ If you put the WordPerfect directory on the path, then there's no need for you to create a WordPerfect batch file, as described in the following section.

Making a WordPerfect Batch File

Batch files are — stand back! — *programs* you can create for DOS. Yes, this is programming. So what is the topic of programming doing in a *...For Dummies* book? Well, you asked: chapter 1 probably directed you here, suggesting that you take a peek to see what a batch file can do to help you run WordPerfect.

Before reading any further, you should know that if you followed the steps for putting WordPerfect on the path in the previous section, there's no need to create a WordPerfect batch file. Therefore, what remains of this section is for the stout hearted and for true batch-file believers.

A batch file can help you run WordPerfect in a painless and quick manner, just as a plugged-in toaster in the bathtub can kill you in a painless and quick manner. This stuff requires some guts you may not be willing to forsake here.

Here are the as-painless-as-possible steps for creating a WordPerfect batch file. Follow these steps to the letter:

1. Start over with a clean slate in WordPerfect.

Refer to the section on saving and starting over with a clean slate in Chapter 14 for details.

2. Type the following text, pressing Enter at the end of each line:

```
@ECHO OFF
C:\WP60\WP %1
```

There are only two lines to type: The first starts with an @ (at sign), the word **ECHO**, a space, and the word **OFF.** There is no space between @ and ECHO.

The second line is a pathname, indicating the location of WordPerfect on your hard drive. For this example, type the letter **C**, a colon (:), a backslash (\), **WP60**, another backslash (\), **WP**, a space, a percent sign (%), and the number **1**. (Reads like a secret code, no? Better go get the Captain Marvel decoder ring.)

If you have WordPerfect in a different location (on a different drive or in a different directory), specify that pathname as the first part of line 2. The second half of the line — the space and %1 — stays the same.

3. **Save the batch file creation to disk.**

The file must be saved as a DOS text file. Press the F10 key to save then press Esc twice if you're forced to look at the hideous Document Summary dialog box.

In the Save Document dialog box, press Esc, R. The file format list drops down. In that list, find the ASCII Text (Standard) item, highlight it, and press Enter.

Press F to highlight the Filename text box. In the box, type **C:\WP.BAT** as the filename. That's the letter **C** and a colon (:) for drive C, a backslash (\), and **WP.BAT,** the name of the file. Then press Enter.

4. **Close the batch file document.**

Press F7, N, N.

✔ Here's a suggestion: Direct your DOS guru to do this stuff for you. Show him or her this book and point to the following paragraph, which is directed right at your guru:

Hello, Mr. Guru! I want you to create a WordPerfect batch file for my computer. Stick it in a directory on the path. Make sure that you specify the proper location for WordPerfect on my system. Refer to the preceding example for what I want. Don't get too fancy; I'm a WordPerfect beginner. Thank you. Your pizza is in the mail.

✔ If you're adept at these types of things, put the WP.BAT file in the DOS directory. Or put it in a special batch-file subdirectory if you've created one.

Formatting Disks

Formatting disks is something we all have to do. Disks begin life naked. All the disks in a new box are blank, like blank audiocassettes and videotapes. But unlike when recording music or a TV program, you must *format* a computer disk before you can use it. Here's how to do that in WordPerfect:

1. **Press Ctrl-F1.**

This action activates the Shell command, which normally displays a lovely seafood and pasta platter. But because you probably have just a regular copy of WordPerfect, you see a boring dialog box displayed instead. (I won't show it to you here because it's right there on your screen.)

2. **Carefully press 6 (DOS command).**

   You want to select the sixth item, the DOS command.

   If you accidentally press 1, ignore what you see on the screen. Type the word **EXIT** and press Enter to return to WordPerfect.

3. **Type the following:**

   ```
   FORMAT A:
   ```

   That is, type the word **FORMAT**, a space, the letter **A**, and a colon (:).

4. **Press Enter.**

   This action directs DOS to run its FORMAT command, which prepares a floppy disk for use. The screen clears, and you see something like the following displayed:

   ```
   Insert new diskette for drive A:
   and press ENTER when ready...
   ```

5. **Stick a new floppy disk into drive A.**

   For the larger 5¼-inch disks, close the drive's door latch.

6. **Press the Enter key.**

   DOS usually displays something mildly interesting while formatting takes place. Think of it like that annoying band of stock-market quotes that crawls along the bottom of the screen on *CNN Headline News* during the weekdays.

   After formatting is complete, you see the following:

   ```
   Format complete.
   Volume label (11 characters, ENTER for none)?
   ```

   The second line is DOS asking you to enter a volume label for the disk.

7. **Press Enter.**

   You may see some interesting yet entirely meaningless statistics displayed.

   DOS finally asks whether you want to format another disk:

   ```
   Format another (Y/N)?
   ```

8. **Press N.**

   At the bottom of the screen is a `press any key to continue` prompt.

9. **Press Enter and you're back in WordPerfect.**

- ✔ DOS uses two floppy disk sizes: the small and compact 3½-inch disks and the larger and floppier 5¼-inch disks. Buy the right size for your computer. Compare sizes by measuring the floppy disk drive's gaping maw.

- ✔ There are also two disk capacities. Always buy the largest capacity the system can handle. For most of us, that's high capacity or high density. As long as you use these disks, formatting won't be a problem.

- ✔ Sometimes you can buy preformatted disks. They're a tad more expensive than the other disks, but they save you time and the hassle of repeating these steps every time you want to use a floppy disk.

- ✔ If you see a message along the lines of `Cannot save UNFORMAT information`, go ahead and press Y to continue formatting the disk.

- ✔ If you see any other type of message claiming the disk can't be formatted, use another disk.

- ✔ *DOS For Dummies,* 2nd Edition, published by IDG Books Worldwide, goes into great detail on buying, formatting, and using floppy disks.

Backing Up

Backing up your stuff is as important as saving a document to disk. When you back up, you create duplicate documents on a second disk, usually a floppy disk. That way, if anything ever happens to the computer or its hard drive, you can recover quickly by using the backup copy.

You can back up in one of two ways. The first is to run a special backup program, such as DOS's BACKUP command or the new DOS 6 MSBackup program — definitely something your guru needs to set up for you. Your guru should also give you a list of instructions on how and when to back up.

The second way you can back up is to use WordPerfect's File Copy in the File Manager window. In the File Manager window, you mark the files you want copies of and then copy them all to a floppy disk in drive A. Follow the steps outlined in the section on copying files in Chapter 16 for more information.

- ✔ You should back up your files every day. If you use the File Manager key, F5, to mark and copy files, check the file dates and copy everything that has today's date on it (all the files you worked on today). When WordPerfect asks whether you want to replace files already on the backup disk, press Y; you always want newer files to replace older ones.

- ✔ To use a floppy disk, you must format it. Refer to "Formatting Disk" earlier in this chapter for additional information.

- ✔ If you accidentally delete a file, you may be able to undelete it without having to resort to a backup copy of the file. Refer to the section on accidentally deleting documents in Chapter 24.

Chapter 22
Using WordPerfect in Windows

In This Chapter

▶ Setting up WordPerfect in the Program Manager

▶ Starting WordPerfect in Windows

▶ Switching to graphics mode

▶ Temporarily getting out of WordPerfect

▶ Associating files in the File Manager

*T*his chapter is about using WordPerfect in Windows. It's not about using WordPerfect *for* Windows, which is an entirely different program. Instead, this chapter offers soothing words of advice to the handful of readers who are doomed to be enslaved in a sluggish graphical environment, laden with mouse buttons and fancy graphics and . . . Hey! Doesn't WordPerfect 6.0 sound a lot like Windows? Maybe they were made for each other. Or maybe they're what happens when cousins marry.

If you don't have Windows or don't use WordPerfect in Windows, then you can freely skip this chapter. (It's not like there's going to be a test on it or anything.) There are lots of Windows sayings and conventions used in this chapter. If you really need help with Windows, consider reading *Windows For Dummies*, published by IDG Books Worldwide.

Setting Up WordPerfect in the Program Manager

You can't just walk into Windows and work with WordPerfect. No way! Windows is as ignorant of WordPerfect as WordPerfect is ignorant of Windows. You must deliberately set up a Windows computer to run WordPerfect. Here's my advice:

Have someone else do this stuff. Seriously. There are plenty of Windows wizards out there who will gladly configure your PC to have WordPerfect ready and available as an icon in Windows.

If you fail to find someone to do it for you, do the following steps. Note that I'm assuming you know how to use a mouse in Windows, that you know what the Program Manager is, and that you really want to go through 12 steps to use WordPerfect in Windows. Take a deep breath and begin.

1. **Activate the Program Manager.**

   Click somewhere on the Program Manager window to bring it to the top.

2. **Locate the group into which you want to place WordPerfect 6.0.**

   The group is one of the Program Manager's miniwindows. Put WordPerfect into a WordPerfect group if you already have one. Otherwise, find the Main group and place it in there. Click the mouse on the group after you've found it.

3. **Select the New command from the File menu.**

   The New Program Object dialog box appears. Make sure that the Program Item radio button is darkened; if it's not, click on that button.

4. **Click on the OK button.**

   The Program Item Properties dialog box appears. This is where you tell Windows about WordPerfect 6.0.

5. **Click on the Browse button.**

   This brings up a handy file-finding dialog box, Browse. Use the file controls in this dialog box to locate the WordPerfect directory. It's most likely on drive C, in the WP60 subdirectory.

6. **Select the file named WP60.PIF in the WordPerfect directory.**

   The WP60.PIF file is a configuration file, built by the kind folks at WordPerfect HQ. It tells Windows exactly what to do with WordPerfect. Find that file in the Browse dialog box and highlight it.

7. **Click on the OK button.**

8. **Click on the Change Icon button in the Program Item Properties dialog box.**

   Ignore the warning box that appears; click on OK.

9. **Click on the Browse button in the Change Icon dialog box.**

   The Browse dialog box appears. This time your job is to hunt for the file named WPICONS.DLL, which can be found in the WordPerfect directory. Highlight that file.

10. **Click on the OK button.**

11. **Click on the OK button in the Change Icon dialog box.**

12. **Click on the OK button in the Program Item Properties dialog box.**

    WordPerfect 6.0 now appears in the Program Manager with its own icon.

Technically avoidable drivel about Windows, WordPerfect, and icons

If you're obsessed with Windows, then I can't help you. However, it's possible to build your own Windows group in the Program Manager; the folks at WordPerfect HQ, despite their Microsoft-ward sneer, have made it easy for you. WordPerfect comes with several fun, flashy, icon files, so you can easily install several of WordPerfect's programs and utilities for easy Windows access. Because this isn't a Windows book, you're on your own to set up your WordPerfect group.

✔ Isn't Windows easy to use? No, seriously, if you use the PC only for WordPerfect, dispense with Windows. Just run WordPerfect from DOS when the computer starts.

✔ These instructions do not apply to other Windows shells, such as the Norton Desktop, or anything else that's funky and new and runs under Windows.

✔ Here is the shortcut step for setting up WordPerfect in Windows: consider having someone else set up WordPerfect to run under Windows.

Starting WordPerfect in Windows

After WordPerfect is squared away and sitting as an icon in the Program Manager, you're ready to run it. Here's how that works in Windows:

1. Find the WordPerfect icon in the Program Manager.

It is probably a plain, old, ugly MS-DOS icon with *WordPerfect* displayed underneath it, though it may also appear as its own WordPerfect icon.

If you can't readily find the WordPerfect icon, look for the group named Applications. Or look in the Main group. Double-click on a group to open it and examine its iconic contents.

2. Double-click on the WordPerfect icon.

This action runs WordPerfect on the screen as you're used to it: full-screen graphical fun and frivolity.

✔ Use WordPerfect in Windows just as you do in DOS. The program appears in the graphics mode on the screen, just as you're used to seeing it. Feel free to wipe those droplets of sweat from your furrowed brow.

✔ Do not run WordPerfect 6.0 in a Windows window. If you attempt to do so, Windows grouses and complains, and everything slows down even more than normal. Press Alt-Enter to return WordPerfect to the full-screen mode.

✔ When you're done using WordPerfect, press the F7 key as you normally would to quit. When WordPerfect vanishes from the screen, you are returned to Windows' blazing, graphics interfaceological glory.

Temporarily Getting Out of WordPerfect

Unlike with DOS, when you use Windows, you can do several things at once. If you just need to break away and play a game — er, do some financing — you can temporarily exit WordPerfect by pressing one of the following key combinations:

Ctrl-Esc | Pressing this key combination brings up the Task List dialog box. You see a list of the programs Windows is running — all at once. Double-click on the program in the list you want to run next. For example, if you were running another program, double-click on the WordPerfect item when you want to return to it.

Alt-Esc | This is the task-switching key combination. When you press Alt-Esc, you switch to another program running in Windows. It's anyone's guess which program this is, which is why I recommend pressing Ctrl-Esc.

Alt-Tab | Press and hold the Alt key and press the Tab key. *Do not release the Alt key.* This key combination clears the screen and displays the name of another program running in Windows. You can continue to press the Tab key to see every program's name. Only when you release the Alt key are you zapped into another program.

✔ When you press Ctrl-Esc or Alt-Esc to switch from WordPerfect, Windows takes over the screen. WordPerfect is reduced to a small icon at the bottom of the screen. To get back to WordPerfect, double-click on that icon.

✔ Even though you leave WordPerfect to do something else, you haven't quit the program. WordPerfect is still running; it's just not up on the screen. To return to WordPerfect, use one of the three key combinations listed and select WordPerfect as the program you want to run.

✔ If WordPerfect is already running and you try to run it again, you see the message `Are other copies of WordPerfect currently running?` If you see this message, or anything similar, press Esc to immediately cancel. Then use one of the three key combinations listed here to locate the already-running copy of WordPerfect.

Associating Files in the File Manager

A handy way to run programs in Windows is to associate them with their files in the File Manager, which means that you tag a certain type of file as belonging to a certain program. For example, you can earmark all files with the WP extension as documents that belong to WordPerfect.

Why associate WP files with WordPerfect? So that you can use the File Manager to locate documents and then double-click on them to both start WordPerfect and load said document. At times this stuff actually works in Windows. Follow these steps to associate files with the WordPerfect program:

1. **Use the File Manager to locate a WordPerfect document on disk.**

    The document file must have the WP extension or some other extension common to all (or most) document files.

2. **Click once on the filename to highlight it.**

3. **Select the Associate item from the File menu.**

4. **In the Associate dialog box, type the full pathname of the WordPerfect program:**

    ```
    C:\WP60\WP.EXE
    ```

    This is the same pathname as specified in "Setting Up WordPerfect in the Program Manager" earlier in this chapter. Normally, the pathname is typed exactly as shown here. If you have WordPerfect's WP.EXE file on another drive or in another subdirectory, adjust the pathname accordingly.

5. **Click on the OK button.**

    All files with the WP extension, or those matching the extension on the file you selected, are now associated with WordPerfect. To automatically run WordPerfect and load one of those files, select an associated file in the File Manager and double-click on it.

✔ Associated files appear in the File Manager with teeny horizontal lines on their icons. Unassociated files appear with blank icons.

✔ Associating files isn't magic. It works only by the common file extension. So if you, like me, don't always give files a WP extension, the association doesn't work. Gee, isn't Windows easy?

✔ If you see the message Are other copies of WordPerfect currently running? when WordPerfect starts, press the Esc key. You already have a copy of WordPerfect running in Windows. Exit the File Manager and press Ctrl-Esc. From the list of programs displayed, double-click on WordPerfect. Then use the Shift-F10 command in WordPerfect to retrieve the document the old-fashioned way.

✔ If you created a PIF file for WordPerfect, you can type **WP.PIF** rather than the longer C:\WP60\WP.EXE pathname in Step 4 of the steps.

Chapter 23
Thinking of the Printer as Your Friend

. . . .

In This Chapter

▶ Feeding it paper
▶ Unjamming the printer
▶ Getting rid of incessant double spacing
▶ Replacing ribbons and toner
▶ Getting rid of weird characters
▶ Setting up a new printer
▶ Changing printers
▶ Selecting a network printer

. . . .

*I*s the printer your friend? Perhaps. Unfortunately, friend or foe, the printer is just as stupid as the computer. This means that you must beat it with a stick a few times to get it to behave, or else you wind up hitting yourself in the head with the same stick. But give yourself a second to repose; consider leafing through this chapter before causing yourself or your printer any physical harm. (The subject of printing in WordPerfect is covered in Chapter 8 of this book.)

Feeding It Paper

The way the paper feeds into the printer depends on the printer you have. Some printers eat paper a page at a time. Other printers may suck up continuous sheets of fan-fold paper directly from the box (the spaghetti approach). And laser printers delicately lift one sheet of paper at a time from their paper trays and weld the image to the page by using dusty toner and inferno-like temperatures. Printing can be quite dramatic.

Whichever way the printer eats paper, make sure that you have a lot of it on hand. The end result of a word processor's labors is the printed document. So buy a box or two of paper at a time. I'm serious: you save money and trips to the store in the long run. As a suggestion, look for a huge paper store or supplier and buy printer paper from it rather than from an office supply or computer store. The prices are better.

- ✔ Try to get 20-pound paper. The 18-pound paper is too thin. I like 25-pound paper, which is thicker and holds up very well, but it's more expensive. Paper that's too thick, such as card stock, may not go through your printer.

- ✔ Colored papers and fancy stuff are OK.

- ✔ Do not print on erasable bond paper. This paper is awful. After all, the point behind erasable bond is that you can erase it, which doesn't happen much with paper run through a computer printer.

- ✔ Avoid using fancy, dusted paper in a laser printer. Some expensive papers are coated with a powder. This powder comes off in a laser printer and gums up the works.

- ✔ Only buy two-part or three-part fan-fold paper if you need it. This kind of paper contains carbon paper and is commonly used for printing invoices and orders. Also, the old green-bar paper makes for lousy correspondence. It has *nerd* written all over it.

- ✔ If you need to print labels in the laser printer, get special laser-printer labels. I recommend Avery labels.

- ✔ Laser printers can print on clear transparencies but only those specially designed for use in a laser printer. Anything less than that melts inside the printer, and you're forced to clean out the gunk.

Unjamming the Printer

Next time you're in San Francisco, there's a little psychic you can visit in The Haight. She'll do a chart for your printer, to explain why it jams on some days and not on others. This is the best solution I can offer to the question "Why can't the paper always go through the printer like it's supposed to?"

If you have a dot-matrix printer and the paper jams, cancel printing in WordPerfect. (Refer to the section in Chapter 8 on canceling a print job.) Then turn off the printer. Rewind the knob to reverse-feed the paper back out of the printer. Don't pull on the paper or it will tear, and then you'll have to take apart the printer to get the paper out. (If that happens, call someone else for help.)

If the paper jams in a laser printer, you have to pop open the lid, find the errant piece of paper, remove it, and then slam the lid shut. Watch out for various hot things inside your printer; be careful about what you touch. You don't need to cancel printing here because laser printers have more brain cells than their dot-matrix cousins. However, you may need to reprint the page that jammed in the printer. Refer to the section in Chapter 8 on printing a specific page.

✔ If using thick paper caused the jam, then retrying the operation probably won't work. Use thinner paper.

✔ Sometimes WordPerfect may halt printing. If so, press Shift-F7, C and look for the Action prompt in the Control Printer dialog box. Do what it says there, which is usually `Type G to continue`.

Getting Rid of Incessant Double Spacing

Nothing is quite as disenchanting as a printer that constantly produces double-spaced documents whether you want double-spaced documents or not. This is a terribly annoying problem; fortunately, it has a handy, one-time solution, provided that you kept the printer manual when you bought the printer.

Somewhere on the printer is a tiny switch. That switch controls whether the printer double-spaces all the time or only single-spaces. If the printer is double-spacing all the time, the switch is set to double-space no matter what. You need to find that switch and turn it off.

✔ Sometimes the little switch is on the back or side of the printer; sometimes it's actually *inside* the printer.

✔ Turn off the printer before you flip the switch. This rule of thumb is especially important if the switch is inside the printer. Turning off the printer also prevents people from printing while your fingers are in the way of the printer's buzz-saw-like gears.

✔ The switch may be referred to as *LF after CR* or *Line feed after carriage return* or *Add LF* or *Life after LA* or *Stop double spacing!* or something along these lines.

Replacing Ribbons and Toner

Always have a good ribbon or toner cartridge in the printer. *Always!* Most printers use ribbons; laser printers use toner cartridges. Never skimp on ribbons or toner cartridges lest the printer pixies come to you in your dreams and smear ink on your fingers.

✔ Keep a supply of two or three extra ribbons or toner cartridges on hand. This supply holds you in case you need a new one over a working weekend.

✔ When the ribbon gets old and faded, replace it. Some places may offer reinking services for ribbons. This approach works, provided that the ribbon fabric can hold the new ink. If the ribbon is threadbare, buy a new one.

✔ You can revitalize an old ribbon by carefully opening up its cartridge and spraying some WD-40 on it. Reassemble the cartridge and put the ribbon on some paper towels. Let it sit for a day before reusing it. This should give the ribbon some extra life, but it can be done only once.

✔ Ink printers use ink cartridges. Replace them when they run low on ink just as you replace a ribbon or toner cartridge.

✔ When a laser printer's toner cartridge gets low, you see a flashing toner light or the message `Toner low` displayed on the printer's control panel. Take the toner cartridge out and rock it a bit, which makes it last about a week longer. When you see the message again, replace the toner cartridge immediately.

✔ There are services that offer toner recharging. For a nominal fee, they refill old toner cartridges with new toner. Then you can use the toner cartridge again and squeeze some more money out of it. Nothing is wrong with this, and I recommend it as a good cost-saving measure. But never recharge a toner cartridge more than once, nor should you do business with anyone who says doing so is OK.

✔ Some new toner cartridges (Hewlett-Packard's for certain) come with UPS mailing labels for you to use to send the cartridge back to the factory for proper recycling. I had Al Gore over the other day for my annual chain-saw tree-cutting contest and wild-animal slaughter barbecue, and he told me that he thought this was an environmentally great idea.

Getting Rid of Weird Characters

If strange characters appear on your output — almost like the printer burped — it's a sign that WordPerfect may not be set up to use the printer properly. Those stray @ and # characters that appear on the paper but not on the screen indicate that the printer driver may be improperly installed.

Refer to "Changing Printers" later in this chapter. Check the current printer (the one with the asterisk by it) and make sure that it has the same name as the printer hooked up to the PC. If not, select the proper printer from the list. And if the printer isn't on the list, refer to the next section, "Setting Up a New Printer," for information on getting the printer to work properly with WordPerfect.

Setting Up a New Printer

Setting up the printer is both a physical and mental activity. The physical part involves connecting a cable to both the PC and the printer. The part that makes you mental is the software part, where you gracefully grab WordPerfect by the throat and scream, "Look, bud, this is my printer! And I paid lots of money for it! Use those special fonts I paid for!"

Hopefully, someone else has set up the printer for you. This procedure is done when you first install WordPerfect. One of the many questions the installation process asks is "Which printer do you have?" Of the thousands of possibilities, WordPerfect knows about 800. This isn't something to poke fun at; of all PC software available, WordPerfect supports more printers than any other product. Chances are, you'll get to use all the printer power you paid for.

If WordPerfect isn't set up to use your printer, or if you've changed printers and need to reset everything for the new printer, follow these steps:

1. **Run the INSTALL program that came with WordPerfect.**

   This program is located in the same directory as WordPerfect. Chances are, you can type **INSTALL** at the DOS prompt, press Enter, and run the WordPerfect Installation program. If this approach doesn't work, scream out loud right now for help.

2. **Follow the directions on the INSTALL program's screen.**

   Press Y or N if you see the colorful boxes. Then you'll see the WordPerfect 6.0 Installation screen.

3. **Press 4 for Device Files.**

4. **Press Enter at the** Install files from **prompt.**

   This selects drive A as the place where you'll put your WordPerfect installation disks, should you need them. (If you installed from drive B, type **B:** in the box.)

5. **Press Enter in the next box.**

6. **Press 4 to select** Printer Files.

   You'll be prompted to insert the disk labeled *Install 1* that came with WordPerfect.

7. **Insert the Install 1 disk.**

   Close the disk drive door if you're using a 5¼-inch floppy disk.

8. **Press Enter.**

   WordPerfect displays a printer selection list. Find your printer in the list and highlight it.

9. **Press Enter yet again.**

10. **Press Y.**

    Obey any further instructions on the screen. If you're asked to insert another floppy disk, do so. When you're asked whether you want to install another printer, press Y if you do or N to quit.

WordPerfect runs.

(Do you get the impression that this is a lot to do? The pain price is awfully high when you have to deal with 800 printers.)

11. Select a printer port.

Into which hole in your PC's rump do you plug in the printer cable? Chances are, if you have only one printer, the printer port is LPT1. If you're using a second printer or a network printer, it's probably LPT2.

12. Almost done.

13. Select an initial font.

This is the font WordPerfect uses when you have that printer selected. Some printers have more fonts than other printers. The standard, dull Courier font is WordPerfect's (and the Post Office's) favorite. I like the Roman font because it makes me feel like I'm wearing senatorial robes while I write.

14. You're done.

Back to DOS. You now can run WordPerfect again and enjoy the benefits of the new printer.

✔ When setting up printers for WordPerfect, install every possible printer that you think you'll ever use. For example, I set up WordPerfect for every printer in the office, even though my PC has always used the same printer. I even added a few printers I'd like to buy but can't afford. That way, if I ever switch printers in the future, I won't need to go through these steps; I can go to the steps in the next section, "Changing Printers."

✔ If you can't find a disk for the printer you want to set up, call WordPerfect's printer support line. The number can be found in the manual. Of course, I can't find it there. If you can't either, dial 1-800-555-1212 and ask for WordPerfect printer support or just WordPerfect technical support. The 800 operator will give you the number. Write it down.

✔ Some manufacturers provide additional printer drivers for WordPerfect. Your printer may have come with a disk that contains WordPerfect drivers. Scour the piles of junk around your desk for that disk.

Changing Printers

The multiple-choice printer game is necessary because a single PC can be connected to or have the potential of using several different printers. For example, you may change printers in the future or one day walk into your office and find that someone else has changed the printer for you. (How nice.) When that happens, you need to tell WordPerfect that you're using another printer.

To select another printer for WordPerfect, follow these steps:

1. **Press Shift-F7 to display the Print/Fax dialog box.**

2. **Press S to select a new printer.**

   The screen clears, and you see a list of printers WordPerfect knows about. (These printers were selected when WordPerfect was initially installed.)

   The printers are listed by name and model number. For example, the Hewlett-Packard LaserJet 4 is listed on the screen as HP LaserJet 4.

   The printer currently selected is highlighted and has an asterisk next to its name.

3. **Press the ↑ or ↓ cursor-control key to highlight the printer you want to use.**

4. **Press Enter.**

5. **Press the F7 key.**

You're done. WordPerfect is now set up to use the new printer.

   ✒ Selecting the proper printer in WordPerfect is a requirement. It means that WordPerfect will talk to the printer in a language they both understand, and if the entrails are favorable that day, things print as beautifully as you intended.

   ✒ There's no point in changing printers unless you have the new printer hooked up and ready to use with the computer. If that's not the case, don't mess with things.

   ✒ If the printer you want to use isn't listed, refer to the preceding section, "Setting Up a New Printer."

Selecting a Network Printer

If your computer is shackled to a network, the odds are pretty good that you use a network printer. This is the type of occasion worth wearing black for. When you use a network printer, it usually means the printer isn't there, tied directly to your computer via the printer umbilical cord. Instead, the printer is elsewhere, somewhere *out there*, in the network ether.

Printing to a network printer works just like printing to a regular printer. You still press Shift-F7 to bring up the Print/Fax dialog box, and all WordPerfect printer commands and whatnot work the same. The difference is that the printer may not be in the room with you. You have to walk over to the printer room or to the boss's office to pick up your stuff from the printer.

✔ Follow the instructions in the preceding section, "Changing Printers," for information on selecting a specific network printer. You may also need to contact your network human to see which printer is in which office (although it may say so right on the screen; you never know).

✔ Why is it that only bosses (or the biggest PC crybabies — often both one and the same) always get to have the printer in their offices? Why can't we people who really use the printer have it in our offices? Revolt! Revolt!

The 5th Wave By Rich Tennant

"LARRY, LISTEN VERY CAREFULLY TO ME-TURN...OFF...THE...PRINTER!"

Chapter 24
Help Me — I'm Stuck!

. . . .

In This Chapter

▶ I can't find WordPerfect!

▶ How do I find lost files?

▶ Where did my document go?

▶ Where am I now?

▶ It's not printing!

▶ Oops! I deleted my document!

▶ Oops! I just reformatted my disk!

▶ What's a nonhyphenating hyphen?

▶ The screen looks weird!

▶ The darn thing's run amok!

. . . .

*T*here I was, minding my own business, when all of the sudden — for no apparent reason — WordPerfect *(fill in the blank)*.

Where is my baseball bat?

It happens all too often. And it happens to everyone. "It worked just great when I did this yesterday. Why doesn't it work today?" Who knows? Retrace your steps. Check the grounds for signs of gypsies. But in the end, read this chapter for some quick solutions.

I Can't Find WordPerfect!

Nothing induces that sensation that you've just stepped through a door marked *Twilight Zone* better than typing **WP** at the DOS prompt and seeing `Bad command or file name`. Uh-oh. Looks like WordPerfect found the car keys and is gone, gone, gone. But where did it go?

You may have tried to run WordPerfect from an alien hard drive. Type the following at the DOS prompt:

```
C:
```

Typing **C:** and pressing Enter logs you to drive C, the main hard drive. Now try typing **WP** at the DOS prompt.

If the *C:* trick doesn't work, try typing in this command:

```
CD \
```

That is, type **CD**, a space, and then the backslash character (not the forward slash you find under the question mark). Press Enter and then type **WP** to start WordPerfect again.

If you *still* can't find WordPerfect, reset your computer by pressing Ctrl-Alt-Delete. That is, press and hold the Ctrl and Alt keys and then press the Delete key. Release all three keys. Your computer will reset. When it's done, start over by typing **WP**.

- ✔ You might also try to find the WP.EXE file. Refer to the section "How Do I Find Lost Files?" later in this chapter for details.

- ✔ If you consistently have this problem, contact your guru. You can also refer to the sections about putting WordPerfect on the path and making WordPerfect a batch file in Chapter 21.

How Do I Find Lost Files?

Sometimes DOS has a hard time bolting files down on a disk. Because the disk is constantly spinning, I assume that centrifugal force flings the files outward, plastering them to the inside walls of the disk drive like gum under a school desk. That's the mental picture I get. Whatever the case, you can find a lost file quite easily. It just takes time. A putty knife is optional.

If you're in WordPerfect, press the F5 key, the File Manager command. This command is covered in detail in Chapter 16. You may think that you need to use the down-arrow key to view extra files not displayed in the dialog box. This is a common mistake. Just press the plus key on the numeric keypad to see the next screenful of files.

Another trick you can use in the File Manager window/thing is choosing the N command. Press N to display the Name Search text box at the bottom of the screen. Type the first letter of your filename, type the second letter, and so on. As you type, WordPerfect highlights a filename in the File Manager that starts with those letters. If you see your filename on-screen, use the arrow keys to highlight it.

If the F5 key doesn't help you locate your file, you need to use DOS. Exit WordPerfect. (Refer to the section in Chapter 14 on saving a document to disk and quitting.) At the DOS prompt, type the following command:

```
DIR \LOSTFILE /S
```

That is, type **DIR**, a space, the backslash character, and the name of the file you're looking for. In this example, I'm using LOSTFILE as a sample filename. You type the complete filename you're looking for, including any file extensions. Be exact. Follow the filename with a space, the forward slash character, and an S.

Confirm that you typed everything properly. Then press Enter. If the file is found, you see something like the following on the screen:

```
Directory of C:\BERMUDA\TRIANGLE
LOSTFILE   1313 11-13-92 13:13p
  1 file(s)  1313 bytes
```

In this example, DOS located the lost file in the subdirectory named C:\BERMUDA\TRIANGLE. Look on your screen for the line that starts Directory of. The rest of the line lists the directory in which your lost file was found. Use that directory with DOS's CD command so that you can pinpoint the file. Here is an example:

```
C:\> CD \BERMUDA\TRIANGLE
```

Type the **CD** command, a space, and the name of the directory you see on-screen to change to the subdirectory that stores the lost file. From there you can start WordPerfect and load the document or, better still, use DOS's COPY command to copy the file to where it belongs.

- ✔ If more than one matching filename appears, you may have to check several directories to find the document you're looking for.

- ✔ If the file isn't found, it may be on another disk drive. Type the drive letter and a colon and then press Enter to log to another disk drive. Then use the DIR command to hunt for your file.

✔ Consider that you may have saved the file under a different name.

✔ Additional information on the DIR and CD commands, and DOS in general, can be found in the book *DOS For Dummies*, 2nd Edition, published by IDG Books Worldwide. (Buy it now, just in time for my balloon payment.)

Where Did My Document Go?

Ever get the sensation that the computer is making faces at you when you turn away? Sometimes, when you look back, the computer won't even have your document on-screen. In the rush to hide its sneering grin, the computer may have put DOS on the screen. Or your document may be there, but none of the text is on-screen.

First, try pressing Shift-F3. This key combination is the Switch command you can use to switch between two WordPerfect documents. You may have accidentally pressed Shift-F3 while trying to type another key combination. If so, you can press Shift-F3 again to get back to Document 1. (For more information on the Shift-F3 command, as well as the F3 Switch To command, refer to the switching documents section in Chapter 14.)

If you see the DOS prompt, try the EXIT command. If your screen looks something like

```
Enter 'EXIT' to return to WordPerfect
C:\STUFF>
```

type **EXIT** and press Enter. WordPerfect instantly returns with your document intact. (This trick also deserves a major *Whew!*)

In the last case, try moving the cursor up and down a few pages by pressing the PgUp or the PgDn key. You may have a blank page in the document, and you're only seeing the blank part on your screen. Fiddling with the cursor-control keys should get you reoriented.

✔ If you're running Windows, refer to Chapter 22. The section on temporarily getting out of WordPerfect describes how to return to WordPerfect if it vanished entirely from your screen.

Where Am I Now?

If the keyboard keys seem to be too close together or your fingers suddenly swell, you may find yourself accidentally pressing the wrong cursor-control keys, and, lo, you're somewhere else in your document. But where?

Rather than use your brain to figure things out, press Ctrl-Home twice. Ctrl-Home is the Go To command; press Ctrl-Home, Ctrl-Home to move to the previous cursor position and reset the document as you remember it. (Also refer to Chapter 2.)

It's Not Printing!

Golly, the printer can be a dopey device. You tell WordPerfect to print, and the printer just sits there — deaf as a post! "Doe, dee, doe," it says. "Aren't you glad you paid twice as much money for a laser printer? Yuck, yuck, yuck!"

Believe it or not, the printer is not being stupid. In fact, you should check to make sure that the printer is turned on and working, that it has paper to print on, and that the printer cable is still connected. Only then can you slap it for not printing.

But wait! Before slapping it, try pressing

Shift-F7, C

to display the Control Printer dialog box. Read the Message line in the dialog box to see whether WordPerfect knows what's wrong. Then read the Action line to find out what to do about the problem.

✔ Do not try printing again. Don't even try pressing harder on the keys. When the printer doesn't work, it doesn't work. This problem requires more attention than telepathy.

✔ Refer to Chapter 8 for additional information about printing.

Make sure that both the computer and printer are turned off before you plug in a printer cable.

Oops! I Deleted My Document!

Deleting files, just like stepping on cockroaches, is necessary. But what if you found out that a dead cockroach had really been a reincarnation of your Aunt Shirley? Wouldn't you want her back? You may find yourself with the same "wish" for a deleted file. If you accidentally delete a file, follow these steps to reincarnate your file in WordPerfect:

1. Panic. Hate yourself. Say a dirty word.

2. **Press Esc to exit the File Manager window.**

(I'm assuming here that you deleted the file in WordPerfect's File Manager. If not — if you're at the DOS prompt — skip to Step 4.)

3. **Press Ctrl-F1, 6.**

4. **In the DOS Command text box, type**

```
UNDELETE
```

You see a bunch of interesting stuff on-screen; at the bottom, you see a line that starts with a question mark and ends with the prompt

```
Undelete (Y/N)?
```

The question mark appears instead of the deleted filename's first character.

5. **Is the filename that starts with the question mark the file you want to undelete? If so, press Y.**

If not, press N and repeat this step until your filename appears.

6. **After you press Y, a prompt asks you to type the first letter in the filename. Do so.**

You know what the first letter was better than I do. When you type the letter, you see the message

```
File successfully undeleted.
```

It lives! It lives!

7. **Press Enter to return to WordPerfect.**

If you started all this at the DOS prompt, type **WP** and press Enter to start up WordPerfect.

✔ *Don't save anything to disk after deleting a file!* The next thing you do in WordPerfect is press Ctrl-F1. This key combination improves your chances for recovering the file.

✔ If the file cannot be recovered — and this happens — you'll see the message No entries found or File cannot be recovered. Oh well. Be more careful when you delete next time.

✔ You cannot use the UNDELETE command on a network drive. Contact your network guru and explain the problem. Try not to refer to anything as *dumb* or *asinine*.

Oops! I Just Reformatted My Disk!

This Oops! is why you label disks — so that you don't accidentally format something that contains important files and other information. If you do pull this boo-boo, follow these steps immediately to recover:

1. **Press Ctrl-F1, 6.**

2. **At the DOS prompt, type**

```
UNFORMAT A:
```

That is, type **UNFORMAT**, a space, the letter **A**, and a colon (:).

3. **Press Enter.**

4. **Follow the directions on the screen.**

Insert the disk you just reformatted when you're told to. This operation takes some time to complete, so sit back and be patient.

✔ Unformatting a disk works best if you use the UNFORMAT command before putting any new files on the disk.

✔ After UNFORMAT recovers the disk, the documents may not have their original names. The UNFORMAT command may give them mechanical-sounding filenames. That's OK; the files' contents are unchanged. You can use the F5 key in WordPerfect to view the files and rename them. (Refer to Chapter 16 for details.)

✔ Chapter 21 covers disk formatting.

What's a Nonhyphenating Hyphen?

The hyphen key, which is also the minus key, works to hyphenate a long word at the end of a line. But sometimes you may not want the hyphen to split a word. For example, you may not want a phone number to split between two lines. Yet, when you use the hyphen key, that may be exactly what happens.

To create a nonhyphenating hyphen, press the Home key before you press the hyphen. The Home, hyphen key combination inserts a *hard hyphen* in the document — one that can't split a phone number, part number, figure number, or mathematical problem over two lines.

The Screen Looks Weird!

Let me qualify the title of this section: the screen looks *more weird* than it usually does. For example, you may not see a graphic that was there a second ago. Or maybe your text has disappeared or the formatting change you just made doesn't seem to affect the document. This stuff can really scare you if you don't know what's going on.

What's going on? I haven't a clue. Yet I do know that if you type the following key commands, the nonsense goes away:

Ctrl-F3, R

This key combination is the Rewrite command that redraws WordPerfect's screen. It eliminates any excess garbage, lines up paragraphs properly, and puts the screen in order.

The Darn Thing's Run Amok!

Ah, the eternal and mysterious Please wait message. I've seen it many times. After about one minute, you start looking for Godot. Will you ever get to *stop* waiting?

Press the Esc key to wrestle WordPerfect to the ground, knocking some sense into it. Who knows what happened? Pressing the Esc (Cancel) key makes the message go away and gives you control again.

Part VI
The Part of Tens

The 5th Wave — By Rich Tennant

"A STORY ABOUT A SOFTWARE COMPANY THAT SHIPS BUG-FREE PROGRAMS ON TIME, WITH TOLL-FREE SUPPORT, AND FREE UPGRADES? NAAAH — TOO WEIRD."

In this part . . .

Don't you just love trivia? And what's the best type of trivia? Lists! "Ten ways to ease stress" or "ten snappy come-backs for when your kids ask imponderable questions" or "ten good explanations why you won't crawl into bed and find hundreds of cockroaches under the sheets" or "five hundred million senseless things the government buys with your tax dollars."

This book deals with WordPerfect, so this part of the book is devoted to interesting lists about WordPerfect.

Most of the chapters in this section contain ten items. Some chapters contain more; others contain less. After all, if I was as thorough as I could be in Chapter 27, "Ten Features You Don't Use but Paid for Anyway," this book would be as fat as those other books on WordPerfect.

Chapter 25
The Ten Commandments of WordPerfect

In This Chapter

▶ Thou shalt not use spaces

▶ Thou shalt not press Enter at the end of each line

▶ Thou shalt not forget thy mouse

▶ Thou shalt not reset or turn off thy PC until thou quittest WordPerfect

▶ Thou shalt not manually number thy pages

▶ Thou shalt not use the Enter key to start a new page

▶ Thou shalt not quittest without saving first

▶ Thou shalt not press Y too quickly

▶ Thou shalt not forget to turn on thy printer

▶ Thou shalt not forget to back up thy work

*J*ust imagine Charlton Heston as Moses. He looks like a 36-year-old guy in a white wig with a ridiculous white beard. But he has the glow of the Lord on his face. Either that or it's a 1K leko light with an amber gel. And he's walking down the mountain with the Ten Commandments of WordPerfect carved in stone. Yes, God's printer can print on any surface.

And, lo, it came to pass that the tablet was transcribed. And over the course of time, it found its way to this book. *Ahem!* It's very hard for me to write stiffly, like the narrator in a Cecil B. deMille movie. Rather than drag this thing out, this chapter contains a bunch of dos and don'ts for working in WordPerfect. Most of these items are covered earlier in this book, particularly in Part I.

I: Thou Shalt Not Use Spaces

Generally speaking, you should never find more than two spaces in a row in any WordPerfect document. If you do, consider using the Tab key instead. Use the spacebar to separate words and sentences. If you're lining up lists of information or creating tables, use the Tab key.

II: Thou Shalt Not Press Enter at the End of Each Line

WordPerfect automatically wraps text down to the next line as you approach the right margin. You don't need to press Enter, except when you want to start a new paragraph. (Of course, if your paragraph is only a line long, pressing Enter at the end of that line is OK as well.)

III: Thou Shalt Not Forget Thy Mouse

You can do nearly anything in WordPerfect using the keyboard but don't forget Mr. Electric Bar of Soap over there. It's easy to use the mouse to select small bits of text, quickly pluck menu items, make the help screen useful, and play with the Button Bar and Ribbon. If you've made good use of the Button Bar, then you can do a lot of editing and formatting without ever touching the keyboard. (Refer to Chapter 19.) And if you become adept at using the mouse, you'll have a hand free for a beverage or to scratch.

IV: Thou Shalt Not Reset or Turn Off Thy PC Until Thou Quittest WordPerfect

Always exit properly from WordPerfect. Refer to the section on saving a document to disk and quitting in Chapter 14. Shut off or reset your computer only when you see the DOS prompt on the screen — never when you're running WordPerfect.

V: Thou Shalt Not Manually Number Thy Pages

WordPerfect has an automatic page numbering command. Refer to the section on where to stick page numbers in Chapter 11.

VI: Thou Shalt Not Use the Enter Key to Start a New Page

Sure, it works: press the Enter key a couple dozen times, and you're on a new page. But that's not the proper way, and you can mess up the new page if you go back and edit text. Instead, create a new page instantly by pressing Ctrl-Enter. This command inserts a hard-page break into the document. Refer to the description of starting a new page in Chapter 11.

VII: Thou Shalt Not Quittest without Saving First

Save documents to disk before you quit. Refer to the section on saving a document to disk and quitting in Chapter 14.

VIII: Thou Shalt Not Press Y Too Quickly

WordPerfect has many Yes/No prompts. If you press Y without thinking about it, you may delete text, delete files, or perform a bad replace operation without knowing it. Always read the screen before you press Y.

IX: Thou Shalt Not Forget to Turn On Thy Printer

The biggest printing problem anyone has is pressing Shift-F7, 1 when the printer isn't turned on. Ensure that the printer is turned on, healthy, and ready to print before you tell WordPerfect to print something.

X: Thou Shalt Not Forget to Back Up Thy Work

Keeping emergency copies of important documents is vital. Computers are shaky houses of cards that can collapse at any sneeze or hiccup. Always make a safety copy of your files at the end of the day or as you work. Refer to the discussion of backing up files in Chapter 21.

Chapter 26
Ten Cool Tricks

In This Chapter

▶ Using the autosave feature

▶ Using Ctrl-Home, Ctrl-Home to return to where you were

▶ Customizing your own Button Bar

▶ Inserting cool characters

▶ Inserting the date

▶ Sorting

▶ Using the unbreakable hyphen

▶ Using the Ctrl-R (Repeat) key combination

▶ Using Bookmark/QuickMark

▶ Using QuickList

I'm an old WordPerfect warrior. I have my receipt from 1985 when I first bought WordPerfect. Back in those rustic days, only *real men* could use WordPerfect. It was a cold and lonely life. Fortunately, so many long years of writing with the same software gains me some insight I'd be more than happy to share. After all, I wouldn't want anyone else using this product for that long without knowing the ten cool tricks in this chapter.

Using the Autosave Feature

WordPerfect has an autosave feature. When it's active, WordPerfect periodically saves your document to disk. Using this feature isn't the same as pressing Ctrl-F12 to save your document. Instead, WordPerfect makes a secret backup copy every so often. In the event of a crash, you can recover your work from the backup copy—even if you've never saved the document to disk.

To turn on the autosave feature, press Shift-F1, E, B. This command brings up the Backup dialog box. If there isn't an X in the Timed Document Backup check box, press T to activate the autosave feature. Then enter the backup interval by pressing M and typing the number of minutes you want between the times WordPerfect automatically saves your document.

I want WordPerfect to back up my documents every five minutes, for example, so I entered 5 in the box. If the power is unstable at your home or office, enter 5, 3, 2, or even 1 minute as the backup interval. Press Enter and then press F7 a few times to return to your document.

To specify a directory location for your autosave files, press Shift-F1, L, B. In the highlighted box, type the name of the directory where you want the backup files to be kept. If you face this prospect with a blank stare on your face, type the following:

```
C:\
```

Press Enter and then press F7 a few times to return to your document.

- ✔ When you activate the autosave feature, you won't recover all your document in case of a mishap, but you will get most of it back.

- ✔ I recommend that you back up your files to a temporary directory, such as C:\TEMP, or the root directory (C:\) on your hard drive. Never back up the files to a RAM drive because a power outage or reset cleans out the RAM drive.

- ✔ When you restart WordPerfect after a power outage or crash, you'll see a dialog box with something like the message *Backup files found*. To recover your document, choose the Rename button and rename the old file as OLD1. Then, when you start WordPerfect, use the Retrieve command to load OLD1 into memory. Press Shift-F10 and type **C:\OLD1** in the box.

Using Ctrl-Home, Ctrl-Home to Return to Where You Were

Press Ctrl-Home, Ctrl-Home to restore the screen and the cursor to its previous position. You can use Ctrl-Home, Ctrl-Home after you use the Search or Replace command, after a spell check, or when you're just plain lost.

Press Ctrl-Home to activate the Go To command — a handy way to zip right to a specific page in your document. Press Ctrl-Home, type the page number, press the Enter key, and you're there.

Customizing Your Own Button Bar

You can use WordPerfect's Button Bar and the mouse to edit your document quickly. Because you can select text with the mouse, when you put a few handy formatting commands or Cut, Copy, and Paste on the Button Bar, you can tinker with your document without having to use the keyboard. This cool trick works best if you create your own Button Bar considering that WordPerfect's native Button Bar was assembled by a random drawing. Refer to Chapter 19 for more information on building your own Button Bar.

Inserting Cool Characters

Use the Ctrl-W key — where the W stands for Weird — to stick odd and wonderful characters into a document. Appendix A lists several of the most fun characters.

To use the Ctrl-W WordPerfect Cool Characters command, press Tab, 2 when you first see the WordPerfect Characters dialog box. After you choose a character set from the list, press C and use the arrow keys or PgUp and PgDn to locate the character you want. Press Enter to insert the character in your document.

For more information on the Cool Characters command, refer to the section in Chapter 9 about inserting oddball characters.

Inserting the Date

WordPerfect's date command is Shift-F5, T. This command inserts the current date in a document just as though you typed it yourself.

If you press Shift-F5, C, a date *code* is inserted into your document. The date code always displays (or prints) the current date.

Sorting

To sort text that appears in a group of lines on the screen, first mark the lines as a block. Refer to Chapter 6 for details about marking a block. To sort the lines of text in the block, press Ctrl-F9, Enter.

Using the Unbreakable Hyphen

To insert a nonbreaking hyphen into a document, press the Home key and then press the hyphen. This feature prevents the phone number, for example, or word from being broken in two at the end of a line.

Using the Repeat Key

You use the Ctrl-R key combination to repeat a WordPerfect command a specific number of times. Ctrl-R, ↑ moves the cursor up eight lines, Ctrl-R, ← moves the cursor left eight characters. (Eight is the default number; you can enter any number of times for WordPerfect to repeat a command.) This feature can be really handy for speeding up your on-screen editing.

Using Bookmark/QuickMark

The Bookmark is a special placeholder that WordPerfect hides in a document. It works like putting a posty-note on a page, although WordPerfect simply "remembers" where you put the "note" and can instantly zap you back to that spot at any time.

A special type of bookmark is the QuickMark. You can instantly set a QuickMark in a document by pressing Ctrl-Q. To return to the QuickMark location, press Ctrl-F.

- ✔ Ctrl-Q is the QuickMark.
- ✔ Press Ctrl-F to find the QuickMark.

Each time you save and close a document, WordPerfect sets the QuickMark at the cursor's position when you close. To instantly beam to that spot when you open the document, press Ctrl-F.

Using QuickList

The QuickList is an English-language list describing various subdirectories or file storage locations on disk. You can use the QuickList to locate files (instead of typing subdirectory or pathnames) whenever you see the F6 key in a dialog box. Refer to Chapter 16 for more information on the QuickList command.

Chapter 27

Ten Features You Don't Use but Paid for Anyway

*W*ordPerfect comes with many more features than you'll ever use. There are definitely more than ten, and probably several dozen I've never heard of. Some people writing those massive "complete" WordPerfect tomes have been known to disappear into a room and not emerge for months — or years! Indeed, I seriously doubt that anyone who knows everything WordPerfect can do has kept his or her sanity.

This chapter lists nine of the more interesting features you bought when you paid for WordPerfect. (I'm not even bothering to mention the extra utility programs that come with WordPerfect.) I list only nine because I'm trying hard not to be cruel, and the Lists feature is really about a dozen things all lumped into one category. You probably didn't know that these goodies existed. That's OK; they're a bit technical to work with. This chapter covers each one briefly — so don't expect to learn how to use any of the paid-for-but-forgotten features.

Hyphenation

Hyphenation is an automatic feature that splits long words at the end of a line, making the text fit better on the page. Most people leave this option turned off because hyphenation tends to slow down the pace at which people read. If you want to activate hyphenation for a document — and see it work while you type — press Shift-F8, L, 6.

Hypertext

This is a doozie. Hypertext is something too grand and complex to explain in this book, but you paid for it. Indeed. Hypertext is like the ultimate cross-reference. You can use it to highlight specific words in your document and *link* them to other words or other parts of your document. WordPerfect's help system works in this way, allowing you to select highlighted (blue) words in the text to see related topics. WordPerfect lets you create such *hypertext links* in your document as well. This feature, however, is best left to the gods in swimming trunks to dive into.

Quick Finder

Here's a screwy one: in some dialog boxes where you can access files, you'll see a button labeled Quick Finder — usually with the F4 key assigned to it. I believe the function of Quick Finder is to provide long, descriptive names for files on disk — similar to what QuickList does with subdirectory and pathnames. However, I really can't tell. The manual uses the word *index* too much, and it hurts my brain. Maybe the WordPerfect Department of Describing Things should try harder if we're to get any mileage from this feature.

Lists

This feature is an interesting but cumbersome one to use. You use the Alt-F5 key to mark your text. You can press Alt-F5, for example, to mark a word and tag it for inclusion in an index, a table of contents, or a reference. Then, using other commands too complicated to mention here, you can have WordPerfect generate an automatic index or other page-reference list (including page numbers) based on the text you marked. This feature is a handy thing to have, but it takes time to learn and you often don't need a full index for a five-page letter to Mom.

Math

Did it ever dawn on the WordPerfect people that Math and English are two separate subjects for a reason? The Math and English parts of the SAT scores are separate. Math and English are always taught as separate courses. So who needs a math function in a word processor? I don't know. Even if you did need such a combination, it's still easier to calculate the numbers using your desk calculator and then type them in manually.

Complaining aside, the Math command in WordPerfect is Alt-F7, 3. But before you press those keys, you have to set the tabs to line up your rows and columns of numbers. Then you can press any of several keys that manipulate the numbers and calculate the results on the screen. Yech!

Spreadsheets

Isn't this stuff the same as Math? I guess we can't keep our word processor and spreadsheet separate, so welcome to an advanced case of featuritis. The Spreadsheet command is Alt-F7, S — yes, the same Math Alt-F7 key — where WordPerfect sticks its esoteric stuff (save for Tables, which are covered in Chapter 12 because readers of this book's other edition clamored for it).

Oh, right — spreadsheets. WordPerfect can read a spreadsheet and stick its values right into your document for convenient display. Do you need it? It doesn't matter! You paid for it!

Outlining

Outlining in WordPerfect is getting better. It's much improved over older versions of the program, where it was like Jason and kept coming back from the dead each time you killed it. Now outlining is almost useful — especially thanks to the handy Outline Bar Thingy and the mouse.

To switch on WordPerfect's outline feature — and really begin a long process of head pains — press Ctrl-F5, B. This command activates Outline mode, where the remaining paragraphs in your document are numbered according to an outline format you pick. (The long-awaited sequel to this book, *More WordPerfect For Dummies*, available soon, will provide outlining details as well as some of the other "I didn't know I had that" features in this chapter.)

Macros

Macros are automated processes — like little programs — that run in WordPerfect. For example, I have a Quick Print macro that prints my document without messing with Shift-F7, left-turn-signal, down-shift, nod right. To activate the macro, I press Alt-P. Then my document prints, nice and neat (to my surprise), saving me a few keystrokes and the need to remember that Shift-F7 is the Print command. After all, Alt-P makes much more sense.

Although macros can be really handy, they're a big hurdle to clear in the learning process. WordPerfect has a complete macro programming language that can get very complex but is very powerful. Heck, entire books are written just on using WordPerfect's macros. I hear Berkeley even offers a graduate program in them.

Comments

Comments are those rambling, pointless things people make on Sunday morning political talk shows — which immediately tells you how useful they are. In WordPerfect, you can stick comments into your text that act like little notes to yourself or others who may be working on the same document.

To "make a comment" in your text, press Ctrl-F7, C, C. Type the comment and then press the F7 key. You'll see your comment surrounded by a box on the screen; however, your comment will not print.

I admit that this feature is useful if you really want to type notes to yourself and others. But I prefer just to type stuff in all caps and pray that the editor will delete it before the book makes it to the final printing.

EDITOR: I CAN'T THINK OF ANOTHER USELESS FEATURE. QUITE FRANKLY, THEY'RE ALL PRETTY USELESS. DAN

AUTHOR: I LIKE ALL CAPS, TOO. HOPE <u>SOMEONE</u> CATCHES THIS BEFORE THE FINAL PRINTING! SANDY

Chapter 28
Ten Strange New Features of WordPerfect 6.0

*Y*ou can almost consider this chapter and Chapter 27 to cover similar topics. They do! The difference between them is that I've picked out these ten (OK, there are really only nine) near-useful features as being mildly interesting or amusing. I still question the usefulness of, say, inserting a Sound Clip of Mr. Spock's voice commenting on my text. "Fascinating," "Logical," and "I reach" make for great inspiration as I write, but it's just not the same thing as having him there with me. Also, the sound works only on the screen — not on the final printed document.

Sound Clips

The Sound Clip feature can be fun, and using it is an excellent way to waste a few hours — provided that you have on headphones so that no one is suspicious of your activities. I won't even bother to comment on what the heck this feature is doing in WordPerfect. But if you have a sound card in your computer, you can play — er — take advantage of it.

Figure 28-1:
A Sound
Clip in a
document.

♪ **Sound (Ctrl+S):** Clip #1

To insert a Sound Clip into a document, follow these steps:

1. Press Ctrl-F7, S, A.

2. Type the name of a sound file on disk.

WordPerfect can read the Windows WAV (wave form) sound files, as well as MID (MIDI score) files. Use the F5 key to locate sound files on your hard drive.

3. Press F7 a few times to return to the document.

The Sound Clip appears in the document, looking like Figure 28-1. To play the Sound Clip, position the cursor just before it and press Ctrl-S.

✔ No sound card in PC = no sound in document.

✔ The Sound Clip does not print.

✔ Sound Clips inhale memory. If memory is low on a PC, the Sound Clip does not play.

✔ Sound files are available from a number or sources. The most common sound files are stored on CompuServe, GEnie, or a number of other on-line services. You also can order sound files from software warehouses, local computer shops, and user groups.

✔ If you know your stuff, you can even record new sounds for inclusion in WordPerfect. The best time to do this is during an election, when the *sound bite* (or *byte*) proliferates. "Read my lips" makes for wonderful fun in documents — as does "I will not raise taxes on the middle class." Such fun!

Coaches

In its effort to make things easier to use, WordPerfect shot all its program designers. Seriously, the Coaches feature in WordPerfect's help system is designed to walk you through some of the hairier aspects of the program.

To see what Coaches can do for you, select the Coaches item from the Help menu or press Alt-H, O or F1, O.

The Coaches dialog box appears, looking similar to what you see in Figure 28-2. A scrolling list displays a number of topics. The Coaches feature can walk you through any topic, helping you perform the named task in a document. To use Coaches, just select the topic you want from the list.

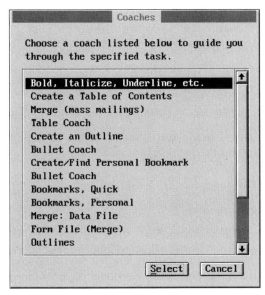

Coaches

Choose a coach listed below to guide you
through the specified task.

Bold, Italicize, Underline, etc.
Create a Table of Contents
Merge (mass mailings)
Table Coach
Create an Outline
Bullet Coach
Create/Find Personal Bookmark
Bullet Coach
Bookmarks, Quick
Bookmarks, Personal
Merge: Data File
Form File (Merge)
Outlines

Select   Cancel

Figure 28-2:
The
Coaches
dialog box.

✔ WordPerfect has too many Coaches for me to document all of them here.
My advice is to always read the screen carefully — the whole screen or
dialog box that is displayed — before you select an option.

✔ A good first step in using Coaches is to position the cursor in the document. For example, if you want to use the Tables Coach, position the
cursor at the spot in the document where you want a table.

✔ OK, everyone! Leg lifts! One, two, one, two. . . .

Colored Text

If you don't have a color printer, then the Colored Text feature is lost on you —
just like in the '60s when NBC used to forewarn viewers that a program was
broadcast "in living color." That information didn't do squat for you and your
19-inch black-and-white Zenith that shocked kids every time they put their feet
on its metal stand.

WordPerfect displays text in inky black letters on an ivory white background —
like you see on a printed page. *It's a revolutionary concept!* But the Colored Text
feature enables you to direct WordPerfect to display text in any of a spectrum
of colors, and you see the various colors right there on the screen — in living
color, no less. This feature can be fun for children. I use it sometimes to write
myself notes because the colored text stands out on the page, but my printer
prints everything in black.

To play with colored text, press Ctrl-F8, C. Select a color from the list. Some of the names are really corny — more like salad ingredients than color names. Keep in mind that unless you have a color printer, the text prints in black.

Bookmarks

Bookmarks are nifty things that you can stick into a document to help you find your place when you get lost. For example, suppose that you're editing along in the latter part of Chapter 8....

> Jeremy inched toward the door, keeping himself hidden in the shadows. He reached into his pocket and

And you forgot to put something interesting in his pocket earlier on in the chapter. Normally, you press the minus key a few times to page up and find a convenient spot for Jeremy to tuck something into his pocket. Then you have to lumber on down through the text and find the sentence that you were working on.

Nevermore! Thanks to the cool WordPerfect Bookmark feature.

To quickly keep your place, press Ctrl-Q. WordPerfect inserts the QuickMark bookmark. Then you can scan the text, find something, edit it a little bit, and press Ctrl-F to return to the QuickMark bookmark. This feature is ultimately handy.

You also can set numerous bookmarks in a document by using the handy Bookmark command, Alt-F5, B. Follow these steps:

1. **Position the cursor where you want to place the bookmark.**

2. **Press Alt-F5, B, C.**

   This action enables you to create a bookmark at a specific point in a document. The text next to the cursor appears highlighted in a Create Bookmark dialog box. This is great because the text will instantly remind you of the bookmark's location. If it doesn't (for example, if the text is rather generic, as in any government proposal), type a memorable name for the bookmark.

3. **Press Enter.**

   The bookmark is set.

To find a bookmark, follow these steps:

1. **Press Alt-F5, B.**

   In the Bookmark dialog box, you see a list of bookmarks that are set in the document — including the QuickMark if one was set earlier.

2. **Highlight the bookmark that you want to jump to.**

   Use the ↑ or ↓ key to highlight the bookmark name.

3. **Press Enter.**

   You're there!

   ✔ Bookmarks don't work unless you set them. Try to get into the habit of setting bookmarks for the parts of your text that you're working on or constantly reference.

   ✔ To delete a bookmark, highlight it in the Bookmark dialog box and press the Delete key.

   ✔ Press Alt-F5, B and see whether the check box by `Set QuickMark in Document on Save` at the bottom of the dialog box has an *X* in it. If you don't see an *X,* press S to put one there. This *X* tells WordPerfect to set the QuickMark to your last cursor position when you quit a document. To find that location when you open the document again, press Ctrl-F.

Faxing

The Shift-F7 key is really the Print/Fax key. For most of us, using it means that we're going to print something. However, if you have a fax card or modem/fax card installed in your PC, you can use Shift-F7 to send a fax instead of printing. In a way, faxing is like printing, but instead of sending a document to the printer, you send it to another fax machine. Need I say that this procedure is possible only if you have the proper hardware installed in your PC?

To send a fax, first prepare the document that you want to fax. It can include graphics, boxes, fancy characters — anything you would normally fax. Press Shift-F7, the Print command, but select option 9, Fax Services, to send a fax. Pick a phone number and send the document on its merry way.

In order to make this feature work, you need to have a fax or fax/modem card installed in your PC. A desktop fax machine doesn't count, nor does an ordinary modem.

How Do I?

In another vain attempt to make WordPerfect easier to use, the folks in Orem have endowed the Help system with a *How do I?* feature. You get at this feature by selecting How do I from the Help menu or in the Help dialog box (press F1).

You see a scrolling list of topics that WordPerfect can attempt to drag you through — and I agree that not enough topics are listed. Select a topic and pray that the information WordPerfect provides is of some help to you or continue to use this book to get the best possible help.

Watermarks

A watermark is an interesting graphic that appears when *the men* go outside in the snow. In WordPerfect, a *watermark* is an interesting graphic that appears in the background on each page that you print. For example, most fine paper has a watermark that you can see by raising the paper up to the light. The watermark is part of the paper (and proper printing etiquette requires that the watermark's writing has the same orientation as the text on the page).

WordPerfect's Watermark command enables you to create some fancy text that is printed in a light shade of gray — in the background — on every page or every other page that you print. This image isn't a true watermark. Instead, it's more like *subliminal writing*.

Follow these steps if you want to mess with a watermark on every page of a document:

1. **Press Shift-F8, H, W.**

2. **In the dialog box, select Watermark A or B.**

   The two options enable you to have two different watermarks that appear on every other page. I just pick A.

3. **Press Enter.**

4. **Highlight** All pages **and press Enter.**

   You see an editing screen where you can design the watermark. Be creative. Use big text or stick a graphic on the page. This stuff will appear as gray text over which WordPerfect will print the document in black text.

5. **When you're done editing, press F7.**

   ✔ If you really want to get into watermarks, consider having a printer (the human kind) make some paper that has your personal watermark embedded in it.

   ✔ Don't forget that you can include graphics in the watermark. A company logo or that all-important picture of a gorilla can really make or break an annual report. I prefer a half-moon-like coffee stain watermark.

Code Pages

Code pages are a massive pain, and only under extreme duress do I write about them here. Basically, a *code page* is a character set. Why they didn't call them character sets, I don't know. Probably for the same reason that we've never come up with a clever name for a TV remote control — something besides *twanger* or *flippa-flippa*.

When WordPerfect saves a document to disk, it uses a specific code page, normally the one that DOS and every other program uses. However, if you are dealing with someone in a foreign country (where most code pages are used, thanks to horrid U.S. foreign policy), then you may want to consider using a different code page when you save your document. To use a different code page, press F9 when you see the Save Document dialog box. Select a code page for, say, Norway so that Olaf and Gunter can enjoy the document without having to mess with American code pages.

✔ Yes, this is a new feature of WordPerfect.

✔ Yes, it's strange.

Labels

Printing mailing labels is a feature WordPerfect users have been clamoring for ever since WordPerfect first attempted to produce labels with Version 4.2. With Version 6.0, you can create them easily. Here's the low-down:

1. **Start over with a new document.**

   WordPerfect claims that you can insert labels at any spot in a document, but — ha! — you really don't want to. Refer to Chapter 14 for information on starting a new document.

2. **Press Shift-F8, P, L.**

   This action summons the Labels dialog box. Your task here is to select the type of labels that you want to use.

3. **Use the ↑ or ↓ cursor-control key to highlight and select a label type.**

   For example, if you have the handy Avery labels, then you select their product number from the list. My address labels come in a box with the number *5160,* so I select `Avery 5160 Address` from the list.

4. **Press the F7 key a few times until you return to the document.**

   The document looks weird. The reason for this weirdness is that WordPerfect has formatted everything to print labels rather than a regular page.

5. Type the label.

Do it! When you reach the end of the label, WordPerfect inserts a new page line of death. After that point, you're working on the next label.

You can press the Ctrl-Enter key combination when you're done with one label and want to start editing another one. Remember, you're working with labels and not with a true document. All the formatting codes and such are still available, however.

6. Whatever.

Save the labels to disk or print them. The labels work just like any other document, although they are specially formatted to print on the special label paper.

✔ Press Shift-F7, V to activate WordPerfect's Print Preview command and see how the labels are coming along. Refer to Chapter 8 for more information on Print Preview.

✔ If you just need to label one envelope, use the WordPerfect Envelope command instead. Refer to Chapter 8.

✔ Printing labels this way still isn't as elegant as using a true mailing label program. Avery makes a wonderful label program that uses the various Avery labels. I recommend it.

✔ You might also consider a specialized database mailing label program of sorts to do heavy-duty mailing lists.

Chapter 29
Ten Shortcut Keys Worth Knowing

In This Chapter

▶ Using general-purpose shortcut keys
▶ Using block and editing shortcut keys
▶ Using text-formatting shortcut keys

*S*hortcut keys are special Control key (Ctrl) combinations that can do things quickly in WordPerfect — things that would otherwise require twisting your fingers as if they were stuck in the Ronco Finger Vise or memorizing function-key combinations that turn your brain to putty. The sections in this chapter list a dozen or so handy shortcut keys — not all of them but the ones you use most often.

Using General-Purpose Shortcut Keys

The shortcut keys in this section save you time and make it easy to mark your position in a document and find it again, repeat a letter or editing command, use characters that you don't see on the keyboard, or switch from one document to another one.

Ctrl-Q, the Set QuickMark bookmark shortcut key

Pressing Ctrl-Q sets the QuickMark bookmark in a document — an on-the-fly bookmark that you use to mark your page and position. You can instantly zoom back to that bookmark by pressing the Ctrl-F key combination.

Ctrl-F, the Find QuickMark shortcut key

The Find QuickMark shortcut key, Ctrl-F, flies you back to the position in a document where you pressed Ctrl-Q. Also, if you direct WordPerfect to save a QuickMark at the cursor's last position whenever you close a document, you can instantly beam to that spot by pressing Ctrl-F when you open the document. Refer to Chapter 28 for more information on bookmarks.

Ctrl-R, the Repeat shortcut key

The Repeat shortcut key is Ctrl-R. Press Ctrl-R and then press a letter or WordPerfect editing command to have that letter or command repeated eight times. This shortcut key can come in really handy for editing or producing forms. Refer to Chapter 3 for more information on using the Repeat command, Ctrl-R.

Ctrl-W, the weird characters shortcut key

Weird characters are characters that you don't see on the keyboard — even though some of the keyboard characters have their fair share of weirdness. When you press Ctrl-W, WordPerfect displays an interesting dialog box from which you can pick and choose a funky character to insert in a document. Refer to Chapter 9 for more information on WordPerfect's Weird Characters.

Ctrl-Y, the cycle windows shortcut key

The Ctrl-Y shortcut key is used to switch to another document window in WordPerfect. If you're using only two documents, Ctrl-Y switches you back and forth (as the Shift-F3 command does). But if you're working on more than two documents, Ctrl-Y stops to visit each document window in sequence — much handier than fussing with the F3 (Switch) command.

Using Block and Editing Shortcut Keys

When you are editing documents, the Cut, Copy, and Paste shortcut keys speed those tasks and make them easier to do, and the Undo shortcut key can get you out of trouble fast.

The cut, copy, and paste shortcut keys

When you're working with blocks, these three shortcut keys are the most handy:

Ctrl-X, Cut

Ctrl-C, Copy

Ctrl-V, Paste

To use these shortcut keys, first highlight a block. Then press Ctrl-X to cut the block or Ctrl-C to copy it. Move the toothpick cursor to the spot where you want the block pasted and then press Ctrl-V. Refer to Chapter 6 for more information on playing with blocks.

Ctrl-Z, the Undo shortcut key

The Ctrl-Z shortcut key is WordPerfect's Undo key. It can undo just about anything WordPerfect can do: load a file, change a format, and delete text. The only limitation is that you must Undo immediately; it has a short memory.

Using Text-Formatting Shortcut Keys

You can use three shortcut keys — either as you type or on a marked block of text — to affect that text's character formatting:

Ctrl-B, Bold

Ctrl-I, Italics

Ctrl-N, Normal

Press Ctrl-B when you want to make text bold. Or, if the text is already bold and you mark it as a block, Ctrl-B removes the bold character formatting from the block. The same holds true for Ctrl-I and italics.

The Ctrl-N key returns text to normal. So if you mark a block of text that has all sorts of crazy, mixed-up formatting, press Ctrl-N to see a sea of sanity. Pressing Ctrl-N as you're entering text instantly switches off whatever formatting you're currently using.

Chapter 30
Ten Unpopular Error Messages and How to Fix Them

. . . .

In This Chapter

▶ Access denied

▶ Device not ready

▶ Invalid drive/path specification

▶ Invalid file name

▶ Not found

▶ Please wait

▶ Replace *filename*?

▶ WP disk full

▶ Write-protect error

. . . .

*W*hen the cat finally succeeds at capturing and eating little Molly's hamster, someone needs to sit down and explain things to Molly. And in spite of Molly's insistence, you just can't cut off kitty's head as punishment. The same kind of happy, friendly logic is behind a WordPerfect error message.

Error messages are a rude, but necessary, way to explain that something unexpected has happened. An error message indicates that a situation has arisen — like puffs of hamster fur floating all over the bedroom — that requires more attention than normal to correct. This chapter contains the ten (minus one) such messages you are most likely to see when you use WordPerfect.

Access denied

Don't plug your ears. Klaxons don't sound, and government agents don't sweep in to arrest you for illegally accessing a file. Instead, this message means that one of the following has occurred:

- ✔ You've tried to save to disk a document that won't fit on the disk.
- ✔ You've tried to save to disk a document that already exists and is protected against being overwritten.
- ✔ You've used the name of a directory that is already on disk.

The solution is to try to save the file again with a different filename. If the error persists, save the file in a subdirectory work area. Contact a WordPerfect guru to help you set up a subdirectory work area.

Device not ready

If you see this message, odds are pretty good that you tried to save a file to a floppy disk when the disk wasn't in the drive or when the drive's door latch was open. Stick the disk into the drive; if it's already in there, close the latch. Try the WordPerfect command again.

Invalid drive/path specification

The disk drive or subdirectory you're trying to use doesn't exist. Check your typing and try again.

Invalid file name

You used an illegal, forbidden, and terribly naughty letter in a filename. Try again, this time typing a proper filename. Remember that you can name a file by using only letters and numbers. Refer to Chapter 16 for more information on naming files.

Not found

The text you searched for was not found in the document. If you were using the Search Down command, F2, try using the Search Up command, Shift-F2, instead. Or press Home, Home, ↑ and try the Search command again.

To search for text in headers, footers, and note boxes, press the Home key before you press F2 to start the search.

Please wait

WordPerfect is busy. Sit and wait.

If this message hangs on the screen longer than, say, two minutes, press Esc to regain control. Sometimes, during some complex maneuvers or macros, WordPerfect may say `* Please wait *` for long periods of time. Have patience.

Replace filename?

You tried to save a document to disk with the name of a file that already exists. If you're updating a file on disk, press Y to replace the older version with the new copy. But if this message appears as a surprise, press N to keep the old file on disk. Think up a new name for the file you're saving.

WP disk full

WordPerfect has been stuffed to the gills. You see this message for every character you type because everything is full and WordPerfect just can't swallow another byte. (Ha, ha! Computer humor!)

The solution is to save the document to disk immediately. Then quit WordPerfect and start over.

If this problem persists, have a WordPerfect guru check the /D option that WordPerfect uses when it starts. The drive specified by /D is becoming full too quickly, and another drive should be used.

Write-protect error

You tried to save a document to a floppy disk, and WordPerfect won't let you. It's not being stubborn. Instead, WordPerfect is telling you that the disk has been *write-protected,* which means that it has been modified so that no information can be changed or added. Write-protecting is usually done for a reason, so my first suggestion is to try using another disk.

To unwrite-protect a disk, remove the sticky tape from the left edge of a 5¼-inch disk (the left edge as the disk is facing you, label up). Doing so uncovers a notch in the side of the disk, makes your fingers sticky, and enables you to write information to the disk (or change information on the disk).

For a 3½-inch disk, flip the disk over and slide the little tile doohickey over the little square hole. (If the disk has two holes, only one of them has the sliding-tile option.)

A disk is write-protected on purpose and for a reason. Be careful when you write new information to it — especially if you alter information that is already on the disk.

Chapter 31
The Ten Most Common Claw Patterns

*O*nly a WordPerfect user with a very twisted mind would memorize all 48 function-key commands. Truly, this type of dementia requires years of laborious psychiatric care. With a keyboard template, especially one as friendly as the one included with this book, you don't need to memorize WordPerfect commands. But if you feel compelled to memorize them, only a few common claw patterns are worth remembering. I've listed ten of them here for your convenience — or obsession, depending on how deep you're into this subject.

Block, Alt-F4

Move the cursor to where you want to start the block and press Alt-F4. This action turns on block-marking mode and the Block on indicator in the lower left corner of the screen. Use the cursor-control keys to highlight text to be included in the block. (Refer to Chapter 6 for more information on blocks.)

File Manager, F5

Press F5, Enter to bring up the File Manager window/menu/thing that enables you to manipulate files, copy them, rename or delete them, and peer into their contents. Using F5 is definitely more fun than using the DOS prompt. (Refer to Chapter 16 for additional information.)

Font, Ctrl-F8

Pressing Ctrl-F8 displays the character/font formatting menu.

Format, Shift-F8

Pressing Shift-F8 displays the main line/page/document formatting menu.

Open, Shift-F10

To load a document from disk into WordPerfect, press Shift-F10. WordPerfect prompts you to name a document file on disk. When you type its name and press Enter, that file appears on the screen. (Also refer to Chapter 14.)

Print, Shift-F7

Next to saving a document, the most common WordPerfect task is printing. Pressing Shift-F7 brings up the Print menu; pressing Shift-F7, 1 prints the document you're working on.

Replace, Alt-F2

You activate WordPerfect's Replace (or search-and-replace) command by pressing Alt-F2.

Save, F10 and Ctrl-F12

The task that you should perform most often in WordPerfect is saving the document. You use the Save key, F10, the first time you save a document. After that, you use the quick-save key combination, Ctrl-F12. You should program yourself to press Ctrl-F12 every so often as you work on a document. Frequently saving the document keeps the file on disk updated so that you have a safety copy in case something nasty happens to the copy on the screen. (Refer to Chapter 14 for more information on saving documents.)

Search, F2

You activate the basic Search command by pressing F2. Type the text that you want WordPerfect to find and press F2. WordPerfect goes looking for the text. (Refer to Chapter 5 for more information about the Search command.)

Spell Check, Ctrl-F2

Most people don't do a spell check because it takes too long. Yet a neatly spelled document — even if you have the grammar of a 10-year-old — is better than a poorly spelled document (with the grammar of a 10-year-old). Press Ctrl-F2, 3 to spell-check all the words in a document. And to get rid of the sixth-grade grammar problem, press Alt-F1, 3. (More information on both of these commands is in Chapter 7.)

The 5th Wave   By Rich Tennant

"...and to access the feature's "hot key," you just depress these eleven keys simultaneously. Herb over there has a knack for doing this - I think you'll enjoy this - Herb! Got a minute?"

Chapter 32
Ten Things Worth Remembering

● ●

In This Chapter

▶ Don't be afraid of the keyboard

▶ Have a supply of disks ready

▶ Keep printer paper, toner, and supplies handy

▶ Keep references handy

▶ Keep your files organized

▶ Remember the Escape and Undo keys

▶ Save documents often

▶ Start WordPerfect with a document name

▶ Use clever, memorable filenames

▶ Write first and then edit

● ●

*T*here's nothing like finishing a book with a few, heartening words of good advice. As a WordPerfect user, you need this kind of encouragement and motivation. WordPerfect can be unforgiving but not necessarily an evil thing to work with. This book tells you how to have fun with WordPerfect and still get your work done. To send you on your way, this chapter gives you a few suggestions that are worth remembering.

Don't Be Afraid of the Keyboard

Try to avoid pressing Enter repeatedly to start a new page, using the spacebar when the Tab key works better, or manually numbering pages. WordPerfect has a handy command to do just about anything. You'll never know that if you're afraid to try the commands.

Have a Supply of Disks Ready

You need floppy disks to use a computer — even if you have a hard drive. You need disks for backup purposes and for exchanging files with other PCs that run WordPerfect — between home and the office, for example.

Keep one or two boxes of disks available. Always buy disks that are the proper size for your PC: 5¼-inch or 3½-inch. And make sure that you buy the proper capacity as well — usually high-capacity or high-density disks. And format those disks! Refer to Chapter 21 for details.

Keep Printer Paper, Toner, and Supplies Handy

When you buy paper, buy a box. When you buy a toner cartridge or printer ribbon, buy two or three. Also keep a good stock of pens, paper, staples, paper clips, and all the other necessary office supplies (including disks) handy.

Keep References Handy

WordPerfect is a writing tool. Therefore, you are responsible for being familiar with and obeying the grammatical rules of your language. If that language happens to be English, then you have a big job ahead of you. Even though a dictionary and a thesaurus are an electronic part of WordPerfect, I recommend that you keep paper versions of these references handy. And I use Strunk and White's *The Elements of Style* for help with the complicated grammar of the English language. It's a great book for learning where apostrophes and commas go. If you lack these books, visit the reference section of your local bookstore and plan on paying about $50 to stock up on quality references.

Keep Your Files Organized

Store document files in subdirectories on the hard drive and keep related documents together in the same subdirectory. You may need someone else's help to set up subdirectories. Refer to Chapters 14, 16, and 21 for additional information.

Remember the Escape and Undo Keys!

Esc is the Undelete key; Ctrl-Z is the Undo key. If you're typing or editing away in WordPerfect, press Esc to undelete any text that you may have mistakenly deleted. This feature works for individual letters, sentences, paragraphs, pages, and large chunks of missing text. But be quick because the Undelete command remembers only the last three chunks of text that you deleted.

You can use the Undo key to reverse any formatting or changes that a WordPerfect command has just made to a document — but be quick or Undo will forget what you did. You also can use the Undo key to undelete text, but using Esc is much more reliable.

Esc is also the *cancel* key. Press Esc to cancel a menu selection or to back out of a series of dialog boxes. You also can use Esc to stop a Search command, a spell check, or another WordPerfect command that takes awhile to run.

Save Documents Often

Save a document to disk as soon as you put a few meaningful words on the screen. Then save every so often after that. Even if you use the autosave feature (discussed in Chapter 26), continue to manually save the document to disk: press Ctrl-F12.

Start WordPerfect with a Document Name

To quickly start WordPerfect and load a document on the screen for editing, type **WP** at the DOS prompt and follow it with a space and the name of the document file that you want to edit. For example, type the following at the DOS prompt:

```
C:\> WP CHAP32.WP
```

This command starts WordPerfect and loads Chapter 32 (CHAP32.WP) from disk for editing. Because you can load up to nine documents into WordPerfect, you can type up to nine different filenames to work on (although I recommend typing only one).

Use Clever, Memorable Filenames

A file named LETTER is certainly descriptive, but what does it tell you? A file named LTR2MOM is even more descriptive but still lacks some information. A file named MOM0023 may indicate the 23rd letter you've written to Mom. Even better is LTR2MOM.23. You get the idea here: use creative and informative filenames.

DOS gives you only eight characters to name a file. You can use letters and numbers in a filename, and you can add a period and up to three characters as an extension. This setup doesn't provide much room for being descriptive, but it opens wide the door to being creative.

Sadly, short filenames also make for extremely cryptic filenames. To hunt down a file, press the List Files key, F5. Refer to Chapter 16 for additional information.

Write First and Then Edit

The object of writing is to get information on paper — to communicate. It can be a lot of fun. Keep that in mind because WordPerfect tempts you with a lot of distractions — graphics on the screen, fancy fonts, open cash drawers, wanton she-vixens of Ft. Lauderdale, and so on. Playing with these features can get in the way of your writing, and it slows down WordPerfect.

As a suggestion, write the text first and then go back to edit it and apply formatting. Do like Dr. Frankenstein did: find a good brain and then build a body around it. Graphics should go in last because they tend to slow WordPerfect to a glacier's pace (and that's not being very nice to glaciers). But don't forget that the text is what's most important.

Appendix A
WordPerfect's Oddball Characters

*F*ollowing is a list of the weird characters you can insert into WordPerfect with the Ctrl-W command. Press Ctrl-W; then, in the first text box, type the two numbers listed in the Code column of the list that follows, making sure that the numbers are separated by a comma. The weird character is inserted into your document. (Also refer to the section on oddball characters in Chapter 9.)

Code	Character	Description
4,0	●	Dot
4,1	○	Hollow dot
4,2	■	Square
4,5	¶	Paragraph symbol
4,6	§	Section symbol
4,7	¡	Upside-down exclamation point
4,8	¿	Upside-down question mark
4,11	£	English Pound symbol
4,12	¥	Japanese Yen symbol
4,17	½	One-half
4,18	¼	One-quarter
4,19	¢	Cents
4,20	^{2}	Squared
4,22	®	Registered symbol
4,23	©	Copyright symbol
4,25	¾	Three-quarters
4,26	^{3}	Cubed
4,30	"	Start quotation mark
4,31	"	End quotation mark

Code	Character	Description
4,32	"	Inverted start quotation mark
4,33	–	En dash
4,34	—	Em dash
4,41	™	Trademark symbol
4,51	ff	FF ligature
4,54	fi	FI ligature
4,55	fl	FL ligature
4,64	⅓	One-third
4,65	⅔	Two-thirds
4,66	⅛	One-eighth
4,67	⅜	Three-eighths
4,68	⅝	Five-eighths
4,69	⅞	Seven-eighths
5,0	♥	Heart
5,1	♦	Diamond
5,2	♣	Club
5,3	♠	Spade
5,4	♂	Male
5,5	♀	Female
5,7	☺	Happy face

Code	Character	Description
5,9	♪	Eighth note
5,10	♫	Double eighth note
5,21	☞	Right-pointing hand
5,22	☜	Left-pointing hand
5,23	✓	Check mark
5,26	☹	Mr. Grumpy
5,30	☎	Phone
5,31	⊘	Watch
6,19	∞	Infinity (the concept, not the car)

Code	Character	Description
6,21	→	Right arrow
6,22	←	Left arrow
6,23	↑	Up arrow
6,24	↓	Down arrow
6,36	°	Degree symbol (temperatures)
6,184	★	Star

You may be able to find the complete list of oddball WordPerfect characters somewhere in the WordPerfect manual.

Special Bonus Section

The Old Hands Guide: Dragging Yourself Kicking and Screaming into WordPerfect 6.0

* * * *

by Dan Gookin,
Author of *WordPerfect 6 For Dummies*

Introduction

Greetings, fellow WordPerfect geezer! If you're like me, you've been using WordPerfect for ages — or even longer, if you've tried to print something recently. Welcome to the new version of WordPerfect, Version 6.0, which is pronounced *six-oh* (as in *Hawaii 5-0,* but with a six rather than a five). Some people will say that it's *six-point-oh,* but they're wrong.

Chances are that the newest version of WordPerfect will really shock you — maybe even rouse you from that catatonic state the older versions induced. By golly, it's graphics! You can see your text as bold, italics, or underline right there on the screen! This is criminal! It means that you wasted all that time memorizing "yellow equals italics" or "blue equals underline." Whether or not you'll miss the old, ugly gal is the subject of this guide, which attempts to drag you kicking and screaming into the latest and — dare I say it? — best version of the WordPerfect word processing program.

A lot can happen in 0.9 versions of a product. You have concerns about this new version of WordPerfect and want to know how easily you can sail the waters, whether just a small taste will kill you, or whether you'll fall all giggly in love with the savage beast you've before now only tolerated. This guide was written with those concerns in mind. There are three main sections to soothe your furrowed brow:

* ✷ "Should You Upgrade to WordPerfect 6.0?"
* ✷ "Using WordPerfect 6.0"
* ✷ "WordPerfect 6.0's Commands"

Should You Upgrade to WordPerfect 6.0?

You should question any software upgrade you make — including DOS. WordPerfect, your beloved word processor, is no exception.

In the olden days, software upgrades were must-have things. New versions offered more features, improved performance, and killed the bugs infesting older versions. Some old-timers bought software and tolerated it only in anticipation of a new release. And — get this — at one time it was Microsoft's policy to offer *free* upgrades to all registered owners. (Microsoft stopped that policy *real quick.*)

Today, the software industry introduces upgrades primarily to add features and, if the mood hits, to improve performance. Bugs are killed well in advance of shipment, although some may slip through. It's not like the old days when bugs, flaws, and glitches were heavily denied by the software giants, or they would timidly admit that the bugs were "features" and offer to improve them in the next version.

The WordPerfect 6.0 upgrade was designed to bring WordPerfect into the '90s with the rest of the popular DOS applications. Like them, WordPerfect now supports a *graphical user interface,* or GUI — which is pronounced as in the question to the Jeopardy answer "I stuck my finger in the mollusk, and it had this texture."

"What is *gooey,* Alex?" Correct for $150.

WordPerfect also added some handy features you'll be reading about in the main body of *WordPerfect 6 For Dummies.* In particular, refer to Chapter 28, "Ten Strange New Features of WordPerfect 6.0." It's not that you'll use any of these features, but I was coerced by IDG's marketing department to write about them.

As for yourself, you should consider several questions whenever you upgrade any piece of software — specifically, your word processor. Mull over the following sections and the explanations with patience and careful thought.

Will the WordPerfect 6.0 upgrade destroy all the files on my hard drive?

No.

Can my hardware support WordPerfect 6.0?

WordPerfect is a charming DOS product in that you can have any PC and still be able to run it. My sister has an old 8088 Leading Edge PC with only two floppy drives. She can run WordPerfect. It is that kind of loyalty to owners of older PCs that made fans of WordPerfect everywhere. With Version 6.0, WordPerfect HQ says, "Hey, who needs fans?"

You need massive PC hardware muscle to handle WordPerfect's new features. If you don't have it, WordPerfect is sloth on the screen. It can take days for some things to display — I grew a beard trying to scroll through a document one week.

To get the most from WordPerfect 6.0, you need the following:

* A PC with at least a 386 microprocessor — preferably a 486 or something you paid a lot for. If you have a 286 or an 8088 computer, then it's just too darn slow to make upgrading worth your while.

* VGA or SuperVGA graphics or anything of that ilk. WordPerfect will probably work on a monochrome monitor, but it will look like black-and-white photographs of food — hardly appetizing and definitely inedible.

* A mouse. You need a mouse to make the most of WordPerfect 6.0. Chances are that you probably need a mouse to use other programs on your PC as well. If you don't have one, buy one. Now.

If your system lacks any of these vital components, WordPerfect will be a slug on the screen. Glaciers will move faster. Einstein could perform space time experiments using the differential between WordPerfect-induced time and gravity-influenced real time. In other words, don't bother if your hardware is meek.

Do I need any of the new features?

No. The new features are designed primarily for titillation. This isn't like 1986 when word processors boasted of having an *integrated spell checker* or a *real live on-line thesaurus*. The things they stick in WordPerfect now are really quaint but questionably useful to enhance your writing. Here are the major hitters, in no particular batting order:

* WordPerfect displays character formatting right on the screen. You see bold. You see italics. You see small caps, boxes, lines, graphics, and all sorts of colorful bunting and festooning. This is truly a bend your knee and bow to Orem gift, long overdue. I tell you, if seeing colorful text on the screen and pretending it was beautiful formatting was frustration- and coma-inducing for you, then this feature alone makes the upgrade worth it (provided that you have the PC hardware to handle WordPerfect 6.0).

* The program has graphics — and lots of it. WordPerfect attempts to look like Windows here, with pull-down menus and a Button Bar and dialog boxes rather than text menus. This feature is the reason that you need a mouse. There are advantages to such an interface; just consider the millions of brainwashed Macintosh owners out there.

   Information on wrestling with the new graphical interface is offered in Part IV of this book, "WordPerfect's Bootiful Interface."

* The Grammatik grammar checker is included and can be accessed directly from within WordPerfect. Personally, I hate grammar checkers. But, if you loved the way your seventh-grade teacher picked apart your writing — and would have preferred that a warm, caring computer do it for you instead — then Grammatik will be a boon.

* You can work on more than two documents at once. I know, few people do. But I've always needed at least four documents loaded at once. WordPerfect now lets you do that — like almost every other word processor I can think of.

* WordPerfect can now painlessly do labels and envelopes and has a cool new *Bookmark* feature. Mail merge has been improved (although not much), and there are lots of shortcuts.

* The packaging has a pleasant, high-tech plastic smell to it.

These features are nice but maybe not worth the effort. To cite a personal example, I skipped upgrading from Version 4.2 to 5.0 because I didn't like the features and Version 5.0 was slow. Version 5.1 fixed that problem, so I upgraded to it later. However, a friend of mine needed some of the new features in Version 5.0, and she upgraded immediately. If any of these features strike you, then upgrade. For example, if you've been frustrated with WordPerfect's formerly lame method of doing mailing labels, then this upgrade is worth it now.

My friends are upgrading, so should I?

Something to be weighed heavily is whether the people you interact with are upgrading. WordPerfect 6.0 can read document files from older versions, and you can save documents to be read by older versions of WordPerfect. So file compatibility isn't the point here.

If your office guru decides to upgrade every machine at work to Version 6.0, then you should buy a WordPerfect upgrade for your home computer as well. If you're working with people who have upgraded, then you should upgrade, too. There is a benefit to compatibility here — call it *shared misery*. However, keep in mind that your upgrading need not be done simultaneously. Friends or coworkers who upgrade first are the guinea pigs. Give 'em about three months to see whether the complaints subside before you upgrade.

I know what I like, and I'm not upgrading!

You're used to what you know. The system works. Why mess with it? These are great arguments, but they also verge a bit on ignorance. (And if ignorance isn't bliss, then I don't know what is!) As an example, there are still people out there who use decrepit old CP/M computers and run WordStar software. Yeah, they get work done but not as fast as you do.

WordPerfect 6.0 is radically different but in a better way. Sure, they changed some keyboard commands. But the changes are logical and easy to get used to. So, if you have the hardware to handle WordPerfect 6.0, an upgrade should be in your future. Maybe not now. But I predict that you'll be a WordPerfect 6 convert someday.

Using WordPerfect 6.0

Although it's visually different, WordPerfect 6.0 remains true to form to its ancestors. The way you use the program is similar if not identical to the way you use your old version of WordPerfect. For this we should be thankful . . . but *naaa*.

The first major thing to note with Version 6.0 is that it's installed into a different subdirectory than your old version. For example, WordPerfect 5.1 stuck itself in a subdirectory named C:\WP51. WordPerfect 6.0 puts itself into another directory, named C:\WP60.

If you're using a batch file to run WordPerfect, you must edit it and enter the proper subdirectory for Version 6.0. This subdirectory will probably be C:\WP60 for everyone. Refer to Chapter 21 for batch file assistance.

You start WordPerfect just as you always did — by typing **WP** at the command prompt and pressing Enter:

```
C:\> WP
```

What you see next may induce coronary thrombosis. Parental advice is recommended. WordPerfect has gone graphical. (Pregnant women and people with back trouble may not be able to experience this high-speed thrill ride.)

Examining the visual differences

WordPerfect 6.0 comes at you with menus, buttons, windows, and dialog boxes that are functional and practical but not too visually creative — like former Eastern Bloc architecture but well painted. Here are some visual differences that will strike you in the chin when you first start working in WordPerfect 6.0:

* Clinging to the screen's ceiling is a menu bar. Also available are a Ribbon, an Outline Thingy Bar, and a Button Bar. These features can be switched off if you're a white-paper purist.

* The blank part of the screen (where you write) is still there. It's white and the text you write is black — a novel concept introduced by the ancient Egyptians.

* The bottom part of the screen looks the same as it did in your old copy of WordPerfect.

* The underline cursor is now a blinking vertical bar. The GUI-blind call it an insertion pointer. I call it the *toothpick cursor.*

* The line of hyphens that signaled the end of one page and the start of another now appears as a solid line — the black laser line of death. A hard page break, formerly a row of equal signs, appears as dual lines of death.

* The muse of confusion floats through the window, an oxygen bottle explodes, and Dr. John Carpenter stops his evil ways, vowing a life of chastity and reregistering as a liberal. In his pure burning heart is forged the white-hot sword of justice.

Working with multiple documents

WordPerfect marches into the '90s with the capacity to work on several documents at once. For most of us, using this feature is like watching more than one TV at a time. For the rest of us — those who do watch more than one TV at a time — it's a handy and long overdue feature. Here are some multiple-document tips:

* The documents are now numbered from Doc 1 through Doc 9. It's like they cloned one of the seven dwarfs. (Thank goodness they're not called Dopey 1 through Grumpy 9.)

* You use the F3 key to switch between documents: Press F3 and then press a number, 1 through 9, to beam to that document. (Yes, F3 used to be the Help key; refer to the last section of this guide for a list of new keys and replacement keys.)

* You can view your documents on the full screen or in tiny, graphical windows. The windows can overlap, appear side by side, or appear on top of each other, which helps when you're comparing documents.

Making it look comfortably familiar (sort of)

In addition to having a graphical mode, WordPerfect 6.0 also has a text-only mode. There are two reasons that you may want to use this mode. The first is that the graphics mode is just way too slow. That's understandable. The second is that you may want WordPerfect to look like your old version. If that's really true, the following notes will help you do it:

✱ To switch on the text mode, press Ctrl-F3, T. This action makes WordPerfect 6.0 look a lot like Version 5.1. Even so, you'll still notice some differences, such as dialog boxes (text panels) on the screen to display choices and options.

✱ To further customize the screen, press Alt-V, N. (If this action produces an error, press Alt-=, V, N instead.) In the Screen Setup dialog box, press 1 and then press the number key by any box with an X in it. Repeat this step until all the boxes lack Xs. Then press 2 and press the number key by any box with an X in it. Repeat this step until all the boxes in the number 2 area are X-less. Press the F7 key when you're done, and the screen will look very familiar.

✱ To use the old keyboard command keys, press Shift-F1, E, K, F7, F7.

Here's one final note: I don't recommend taking these steps. If it is your goal to make WordPerfect 6.0 look like Version 5.1, you can do it. However, instead of using Version 6.0, you should really continue using your older version of WordPerfect, which you'll no doubt be more happy with.

WordPerfect 6.0's Commands

They changed the look, but did they mess with the key commands? After all, you spent years memorizing your various claw patterns. They may be obtuse, but they're familiar. They may be uncomfortable, and yet . . . well, they are uncomfortable.

Out of all the dozens of keyboard commands you're familiar with, only three have been radically altered. They just happen to be three of the most important key commands, listed next:

Command	Old Key	New Key
Cancel	F1	Esc
Help	F3	F1
Repeat	Esc	Ctrl-R

These changes all make sense. The Help key has always been F1 in nearly every DOS program. The Cancel key is usually Esc in most DOS programs. Now WordPerfect follows suit. The old Esc key, the Repeat key, is now Ctrl-R. Aside from these three key changes, most of the other modifications are minor:

✱ The F3 key (the old Help key) is now the Switch command key. It lets you quickly switch to any one of the nine documents you can work on at once in WordPerfect 6.0.

✱ The Search command (F2 and Shift-F2) is no longer case sensitive, unless you tell it that you want it to be. So typing things in lowercase or uppercase makes no difference. To do a case-sensitive search, you must check on the Case Sensitive button in the Search or Search and Replace dialog box.

✱ You can no longer search for the secret codes in a document by typing them in the Search dialog box. You must use the new F5 key in that dialog box and insert the codes manually. On the up side, this means that you can now press the Enter key to start your search. The down side is that getting the codes into your search text is a big hassle (refer to Chapter 5).

✱ There is no longer a `Delete Block?` prompt when you delete a block of text.

✱ The spell checker no longer gives a word count. Use the Document information command, Alt-F1, 4, to find out those statistics.

✱ The Thesaurus command is no longer Alt-F1. Instead, that command brings up the Writing Tools dialog box. You can select the thesaurus by pressing the 2 key. So the new Thesaurus command is Alt-F1, 2.

✱ The Home, Backspace and the Home, Delete commands now only work if the cursor is in the middle of a word. Before, these commands deleted any word to the right or left.

✱ The Superscript and Subscript key commands have changed: Ctrl-F8, P, 2 is for Superscript, and Ctrl-F8, P, 3 is for Subscript. (The old command was Ctrl-F8, S.)

✱ Changing the font is now done through the Font dialog box, which still comes up when you press Ctrl-F8. But then you must press 1 to select your font from the drop-down list. You can also change fonts from the graphical Ribbon do-what, provided that you have it visible and can drive a mouse.

✱ Ctrl-V, the command prefix or Compose command, is gone, replaced by Ctrl-A. And the new, handy Ctrl-W command can be used to insert all sorts of weird characters into a document.

✱ The F5 key, List Files, has been overhauled into the File Manager — quite a complex place for file management and not intended for tourists.

✱ The Merge codes look different, and some of the functions have changed. The ugly tildes (~) are gone. Yeah!

Commands that you'll like and improved stuff

There is a lot of keen, good-to-get-used-to stuff you'll really like about WordPerfect 6.0. Here is a sampler of the commands and shortcuts you'll grow to admire:

* You can now get bold, underlined, or italicized text by pressing Ctrl-B, Ctrl-U, or Ctrl-I, respectively. The F6 key is still the Bold command, and F8 is still the Underline command. But having Ctrl-I and the other Ctrl keys available really helps speed up your text formatting.

* Cutting, copying, and pasting are all accomplished with the use of the handy Ctrl-X, Ctrl-C, and Ctrl-V keys. Although this command setup may not sound intuitive, it's certainly better than the oddball Ctrl-F4 commands used in WordPerfect 5.1.

* WordPerfect has an official Undo command, which is Ctrl-Z. In addition to undeleting text, this command also undoes formatting, search and replace operations, and a number of other previously un-undoable things.

* The Replace command now reports the total finds and replacements made.

* You can use wildcards in the Search command to find exact or near exact matches.

* A whole slew of *shortcut keys* have been added to WordPerfect, which makes some formerly complex operations a snap. (Refer to Chapter 29 for a list of the best.)

* The on-line help has been changed. Is it better? Maybe, but it certainly is different — and cross-referenced.

* After being ignored for seven years, F11 and F12 are finally put to use in WordPerfect. Most of the Shift, Alt, or Ctrl options aren't necessary, which is why they aren't on the keyboard template included with this book. However, the Ctrl-F12 combo for a quick save is very handy.

Conclusion

Even if you're intimate with WordPerfect, please look over the first part of this book very carefully. A lot of formerly basic stuff has been subtly altered, and there are many tips and how to's offered in Part I. Part IV is also worth looking at, especially if you're unfamiliar with using a graphical environment.

I won't beg you to enjoy WordPerfect because getting your job done is much more important than being enamored with a computer program. So, *please,* tolerate this new version of WordPerfect with the same vim and vile that you did the older version. And, remember, a journey of a thousand steps always begins with that strange feeling that you've forgotten something.

Index

Macworld Authorized Editions

Designed specifically for the Macintosh user, Macworld Books are written by leading *Macworld* magazine columnists, technology champions, and Mac gurus who provide expert advice and insightful tips and techniques not found anywhere else. Macworld Books are the only Macintosh books authorized by *Macworld*, the world's leading Macintosh magazine.

Macworld Guide To Microsoft System 7.1, 2nd Edition
by Lon Poole, Macworld magazine's "Quick Tips" columnist

The most recommended guide to System 7, updated and expanded!

$24.95 USA/$33.95 Canada/£22.92 UK & EIRE, ISBN: 1-878058-65-7

Macworld Networking Handbook
by David Kosiur, Ph.D.

The ultimate insider's guide to Mac network management.

$29.95 USA/$39.95 Canada/£27.45 UK & EIRE, ISBN: 1-878058-31-2

Macworld Guide To Microsoft Word 5
by Jim Heid, Macworld magazine's "Getting Started" columnist

Learn Word the easy way with this *Macworld* Authorized Edition. Now updated for Word 5.1.

$22.95 USA/$29.95 Canada/£20.95 UK & EIRE, ISBN: 1-878058-39-8

Macworld Guide To Microsoft Excel 4
by David Maguiness

Build powerful spreadsheets quickly with this *Macworld* Authorized Edition to Excel 4.

$22.95 USA/$29.95 Canada/£20.95 UK & EIRE, ISBN: 1-878058-40-1

Macworld Guide To Microsoft Works 3
by Barrie A. Sosinsky

Get inside the new Works so you can work more productively—the perfect blend of reference and tutorial.

$22.95 USA/$29.95 Canada/£20.95 UK & EIRE, ISBN: 1-878058-42-8

Macworld Music & Sound Bible
by Christopher Yavelow

Finally, the definitive guide to music, sound, and multimedia on the Mac.

$37.95 USA/$47.95 Canada/£34.95 UK & EIRE, ISBN: 1-878058-18-5

Macworld Complete Mac Handbook
by Jim Heid

The most complete guide to getting started, mastering, and expanding your Mac.

$26.95 USA/$35.95 Canada/£24.95 UK & EIRE, ISBN: 1-878058-17-7

Macworld QuarkXPress Designer Handbook
by Barbara Assadi and Galen Gruman

Macworld magazine's DTP experts help you master advanced features fast with this definitive tutorial, reference and designer tips resource on QuarkXPress.

$29.95 USA/$39.95 Canada/£27.45 UK & EIRE, ISBN: 1-878058-85-1 — Available July 1993

Macworld PageMaker Bible
by Jo Ann Villalobos

The ultimate insiders' guide to PageMaker 5, combining an authoritative and easy-to-use reference with tips and techniques. Includes 3 1/2" disk of templates.

$39.95 USA/$52.95 Canada/£37.60 UK & EIRE, ISBN: 1-878058-84-3 — Available July 1993

For More Information Call 1-800-762-2974

PC World Handbook

Expert information at your fingertips. Perfect for readers who need a complete tutorial of features as well as a reference to software applications and operating systems. All PC World Handbooks include bonus disks with software featuring useful templates, examples, and utilities that provide real value to the reader.

PC World DOS 6 Handbook, 2nd Edition
by John Socha, Clint Hicks, and Devra Hall

Completely revised and updated! Includes extended features of DOS and the 250 page command reference that Microsoft excludes. A complete tutorial and reference PLUS Special Edition of Norton Commander software.

$34.95 USA/$44.95 Canada/£32.95 UK & EIRE, ISBN: 1-878058-79-7

PC World Microsoft Access Bible
by Cary Prague and Michael Irwin

This authoritative tutorial and reference on Microsoft's new Windows database is the perfect companion for every Microsoft Access user.

$39.95 USA/$52.95 Canada/£37.60 UK & EIRE, ISBN: 1-878058-81-9

Official XTree MS-DOS, Windows, and Hard Disk Management Companion, 3rd Edition
by Beth Slick

The only authorized guide to all versions of XTree, the most popular PC hard disk utility.

$19.95 USA/$26.95 Canada/£18.45 UK & EIRE, ISBN: 1-878058-57-6

QuarkXPress for Windows Designer Handbook
by Barbara Assadi and Galen Gruman

Make the move to QuarkXPress for Windows, the new professional desktop publishing powerhouse, with this expert reference and tutorial.

$29.95 USA/$39.95 Canada/£27.45 UK & EIRE, ISBN: 1-878058-45-2

PC World You Can Do It With Windows
by Christopher Van Buren

The best way to learn Window 3.1!

$19.95 USA/$26.95 Canada/£18.45 VAT UK EIRE, ISBN: 1-878058-37-1

PC World Excel 4 for Windows Handbook
by John Walkenbach and David Maguiness

Complete tutorial and reference by PC World's spreadsheet experts, with a FREE 32-page Function Reference booklet.

$29.95 USA/$39.95 Canada/£27.45 UK & EIRE, ISBN: 1-878058-46-0

PC World WordPerfect 6 Handbook
by Greg Harvey

Bestselling author and WordPerfect guru Greg Harvey brings you the ultimate tutorial and reference – complete with valuable software containing document templates, macros, and other handy WordPerfect tools.

$34.95 USA/$44.95 Canada/£32.95 UK & EIRE, ISBN: 1-878058-80-0 — Available July 1993

PC World Q&A Bible, Version 4
by Thomas J. Marcellus, Technical Editor of The Quick Answer

The only thorough guide with a disk of databases for mastering Q&A Version 4.

$39.95 USA/$52.95 Canada/£37.60 UK & EIRE, ISBN: 1-878058-03-7

PC World You Can Do It With DOS
by Christopher Van Buren

The best way to learn DOS quickly and easily.

$19.95 USA/$26.95 Canada/£18.45 VAT UK EIRE, ISBN: 1-878058-38-X

For More Information Call 1-800-762-2974

Order Form

Order Center: (800) 762-2974 (8 a.m.-5 p.m., PST, weekdays) or (415) 312-0600

For Fastest Service: Photocopy This Order Form and FAX it to : (415) 358-1260

Quantity	ISBN	Title	Price	Total

Shipping & Handling Charges

Subtotal	U.S.	Canada & International	International Air Mail
Up to $20.00	Add $3.00	Add $4.00	Add $10.00
$20.01-40.00	$4.00	$5.00	$20.00
$40.01-60.00	$5.00	$6.00	$25.00
$60.01-80.00	$6.00	$8.00	$35.00
Over $80.00	$7.00	$10.00	$50.00

In U.S. and Canada, shipping is UPS ground or equivalent.
For Rush shipping call (800) 762-2974.

Subtotal _____

CA residents add applicable sales tax _____

IN residents add 5% sales tax _____

Canadian residents add 7% GST tax _____

Shipping _____

TOTAL _____

Ship to:

Name _____

Company _____

Address _____

City/State/Zip _____

Daytime Phone _____

Payment: ❏ Check to IDG Books (US Funds Only)   ❏ Visa   ❏ MasterCard   ❏ American Express

Card # _____   Exp. _____   Signature _____

Please send this order form to: IDG Books, 155 Bovet Road, San Mateo, CA 94402.
Allow up to 3 weeks for delivery. Thank you!

BOB4D

IDG BOOKS WORLDWIDE REGISTRATION CARD

RETURN THIS REGISTRATION CARD FOR FREE CATALOG

Title of this book: WordPerfect 6 For Dummies

My overall rating of this book: ❏ Very good [1] ❏ Good [2] ❏ Satisfactory [3] ❏ Fair [4] ❏ Poor [5]

How I first heard about this book:

❏ Found in bookstore; name: [6] ❏ Book review: [7]

❏ Advertisement: [8] ❏ Catalog: [9]

❏ Word of mouth; heard about book from friend, co-worker, etc.: [10] ❏ Other: [11]

What I liked most about this book:

What I would change, add, delete, etc., in future editions of this book:

Other comments:

Number of computer books I purchase in a year: ❏ 1 [12] ❏ 2-5 [13] ❏ 6-10 [14] ❏ More than 10 [15]

I would characterize my computer skills as: ❏ Beginner [16] ❏ Intermediate [17] ❏ Advanced [18] ❏ Professional [19]

I use ❏ DOS [20] ❏ Windows [21] ❏ OS/2 [22] ❏ Unix [23] ❏ Macintosh [24] ❏ Other: [25]_____
(please specify)

I would be interested in new books on the following subjects:
(please check all that apply, and use the spaces provided to identify specific software)

❏ Word processing: [26] ❏ Spreadsheets: [27]

❏ Data bases: [28] ❏ Desktop publishing: [29]

❏ File Utilities: [30] ❏ Money management: [31]

❏ Networking: [32] ❏ Programming languages: [33]

❏ Other: [34]

I use a PC at (please check all that apply): ❏ home [35] ❏ work [36] ❏ school [37] ❏ other: [38] _____

The disks I prefer to use are ❏ 5.25 [39] ❏ 3.5 [40] ❏ other: [41]_____

I have a CD ROM: ❏ yes [42] ❏ no [43]

I plan to buy or upgrade computer hardware this year: ❏ yes [44] ❏ no [45]

I plan to buy or upgrade computer software this year: ❏ yes [46] ❏ no [47]

Name: _____ Business title: [48] _____ Type of Business: [49] _____

Address (❏ home [50] ❏ work [51] /Company name: _____)

Street/Suite# _____

City [52] /State [53] /Zipcode [54]: _____ Country [55] _____

❏ **I liked this book!** You may quote me by name in future
IDG Books Worldwide promotional materials.

My daytime phone number is _____

IDG BOOKS

THE WORLD OF
COMPUTER
KNOWLEDGE